THE COMPLETE STAYMAN SYSTEM
OF
CONTRACT BIDDING

THE COMPLETE
STAYMAN
SYSTEM
OF CONTRACT
BIDDING

by

Samuel M. Stayman

RINEHART & COMPANY, INC.

New York

CONTENTS

CONTENTS

EDITOR'S NOTE

AT THE author's request, I not only edited this important contribution to the game of Contract Bridge, but reduced it from the original manuscript of 140,000 words to its present size of approximately 100,000 words.

To cut some books would be a service to mankind, but this one is so full of pearls that the task of pruning was both arduous and unnerving.

There was, however, the major compensation of reading and re-reading the system that carried Sam Stayman to his fourth World Championship contest.

EWART KEMPSON.

October, 1955.

AUTHOR'S FOREWORD

THE COMPLETE contract bridge bidding system described in this book is the end result of carefully balancing practical experience and theoretical science.

My debt for this experience at the bridge table is great—both to my opponents at home and abroad and to my regular partners for collaboration and experimentation in the development and practice of conventions. To all my thanks.

Contract bridge is essentially a human, not a scientific game. Yet science plays its lesser role. I have not hesitated to take those theories from all writers and directions which seemed best and capable of being integrated into one compatible system. I am, therefore, indebted to writers on contract bridge from the old masters to the current group who have produced so many stimulating ideas in the past few years. In this group may I especially mention A. H. Morehead, Terence Reese and Al Roth.

In the production of this work, I am thankful for the early help of Alfred Sheinwold and the editorial assistance of Ewart Kempson and Stephen White. Finally, to Lawrence Weiss my greatest thanks of all. Without his aid the final writing and editing of this book might not have been accomplished.

SAMUEL M. STAYMAN.

NEW YORK, N.Y.
September 1, 1955.

PROLOGUE

A MERE twenty years ago, the appearance of a new book on contract bridge would scarcely have required, as this one does, a preliminary explanation. Any player, then, was entitled to a system of his own—at times systems seemed to be as numerous as players. By the late 'thirties, bridge bidding had become fairly well standardized. Superficially certain differences remained—in hand valuation, for example—but they were not great enough to prevent two strangers from accommodating themselves to each other after a word or two of explanation.

The standard system was solid and dependable. It was intended to provide the bidder with a *modus operandi* whereby he could send out and receive messages that permitted the partnership to establish and engage for their best contract. The precision that bidding systems had reached was well exemplified by a pastime in which one of the country's greatest teams-of-four would frequently indulge. A hand would be dealt and bid; the opening lead would be made and the dummy exposed. At this point, the declarer was expected to name, card by card, the hands of the two defenders, and there were penalties when he failed by so much as a pip. The team was a good one and he rarely failed.

Since a bidding system was designed to do exactly this, it appeared that little progress remained to be made. It was, in fact, at this level that bidding methods became standardized, and stayed that way over more than a decade.

But recently, stirrings began to be felt among the more restless of the experts. The purpose of a bidding system is not alone to reveal the manner in which the fifty-two cards of the pack have been distributed. If this were once enough, it suffices no longer. A good system must encompass a studious inquiry into the facts of the deal, but it must also provide for great mobility, deception and constant harassment of the enemy. It must enable a player to fix his offensive and defensive positions firmly before the terrain has been occupied by the opponents; it must equip him to move confidently down a bidding road that is made treacherous by land-mines and booby traps. It must permit him to belabour his adversaries unremittingly so that they act always under pressure and with great tension. Bidding, in other words, must be more subtle than it has ever been.

This book is devoted to the assertion of this new method of bidding. It deals with Action, with Pre-emption, with Soundness. The bridge it counsels is more difficult and therefore more testing. It is winning bridge and must be mastered.

Like any bridge system, it is designed as a whole. There are few "ideas" here that can be engrafted on a standard system or adopted in isolation. This is not a book of suggestions, but a system as complete and self-contained as it is within our power to make it. We hope it will be read attentively, and we are convinced that the player who masters it will derive more enjoyment from the game than ever. And bridge— let us mention the fact here lest it may be forgotten in the pages of earnest text that follow—bridge is a game.

BIDDING: ITS GOALS

THE PURPOSE of this book is to produce a bidding system, but before we can plunge into the matter we must clear away underbrush. Specifically, we can scarcely discuss procedures until we have a clear idea where we plan to go, and why we wish to get there. Only when we have our objectives firmly fixed can we profitably discuss methods and routes.

Obvious as it may be, it is well to stress at the outset that bridge is entirely an artificial game, the creation of a set of arbitrary laws and rules. The whist family of card games has so long and so distinguished a history that its framework seems at first glance to be, somehow, a "natural" framework. But even so basic a matter as the relative value of the cards is a hierarchy imposed by the rules.

Similarly, the fact that nine tricks at no-trumps bring more reward than ten at clubs arises entirely from a few sentences in the rule-book. On still another level, the sheer power to take tricks is insufficient to dominate the course of the game:

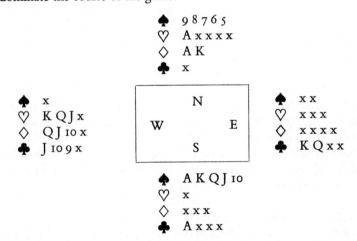

No power on earth can prevent the North and South pair from winning all thirteen tricks at a spade contract. But played by experts against experts, with North and South vulnerable, the final contract will be not 7S by North or South, but 7NT by East and West: they will take but four tricks, but by doing so will cut their losses appreciably. This is not a realistic hand; it is given merely to illustrate a point.

This example indicates clearly where we plan initially to fix our attention. Rewards at contract bridge are fixed not by hands played or tricks won, but by points, and it is to the scoring system that we must go in setting the foundations of our system.

In the laws of bridge, each suit is assigned a trick value, premiums are set for rubbers and slams, and penalties assigned for failure to fulfil a contract. But in two areas the scoring system does not state directly the cash value of a given result.

The first, and more important, area of obscurity arises from the fact that premiums are assigned by the laws in terms of rubbers, while the game itself is played one deal at a time. Consequently, each game that is won carries with it a hidden premium, in the form of increased likelihood of ultimately winning the rubber and gaining the rubber premium.

In more concrete terms: when two evenly matched pairs begin a rubber, each has the same chance of winning that rubber. But the moment one pair wins a game, the chances that they will go on to win the rubber climb from even money to 3—1. The first game carries with it a hidden premium in the form of a greater equity in the ultimate reward for the rubber.

As a consequence, a vulnerable pair considering a second game contract, which will give them a two-game rubber, must not value this second game in terms of all the points that will accrue if it is won. In the terms of probability, some of these points have already been won in capturing the first game (although they do not appear on the score sheet). The first game, in short, is worth more than immediately appears; a second game, while the opponents are still not vulnerable, is worth less.

The values of these games can be calculated by a simple mathematical process, the figures of which are corrected to allow for over-the-table psychological considerations.

A not-vulnerable game is worth 300 invisible points; a vulnerable game is worth 500. (In both cases, the trick-score of 100 points or more should, of course, be added to these figures.)

The second area in which the rules are silent is that of the part-score. Obviously, the pair that has a part-score is better off than the 60 or 90 points indicated, for its chances of winning the rubber premium has been improved. It is essential that some quantitative estimate be made of that advantage.

Here mathematics are of no aid; a computation would be insanely intricate. The value of a part-score is only to be measured by a combination of mathematical factors—how much does this improve my chances of winning the rubber?—joined with psychological considerations: in what foolish actions will this part-score involve my opponents? Valuation must be the fruit of experience, and the general experience of bridge players sets the value of the part-score at 50 points when not vulnerable, 100 points when vulnerable, in each case plus the trick-score.

Adding to these figures the premiums for slams, as set by the rules, produces the following table of values (*in each case add trick-score*):

	Not vulnerable	Vulnerable
Part-score . .	50	100
Game . .	300	500
Small slam . .	800	1,250
Grand slam .	1,300	2,000

This table sets a "par" for every deal, just as the measurement of distance sets par on a golf course. It makes it possible for a bridge player, after a deal has been bid and played, to scrutinize it in the light of all fifty-two cards and discover whether he has beaten par, matched par or lost points to par.

But unlike golf, there may be a different par for each pair on any given deal. Consider the hand given above. For the North-South pair, it is 2,000 points for the slam and rubber, 210 points for seven odd-tricks at spades, and 150 points for the honours, a total of 2,360 points. This is what they will collect if the opponents neither help nor hinder. If the opponents double, they can redouble and earn 680 points more; by that much they will have beaten par. But if the opponents bid 7NT, the penalty will be only 1,700 points, far below their par.

From the East-West point of view, however, par on the hand is minus 1,700 points. This is what they must expect to see on the score sheet if they are neither helped nor hindered by the opponents. If East and West permit the opponents to play the grand slam at spades, East and West thereby lose points to par. If, on the other hand, East and West manage to garner five tricks, instead of the four to which they are entitled, they have beaten par by going down only 1,500 points.

All this may seem simple to the point of being trite. Par, then, is to be established by an examination of all fifty-two cards, and the player must aim at meeting or at beating par, maximizing his gain on good hands, minimizing his loss on bad ones. A bidding system must provide a means of approximating the exact distribution of the fifty-two cards, beginning from the player's knowledge of his thirteen cards and proceeding by means of an informative bidding sequence.

But it is not enough that the bidder proceed toward meeting his own par; he must at the same time hamper the opponents in their own efforts to meet their par, and he must overcome their corresponding counter-efforts. For neither pair exists in isolation. In the deal we have given above, the North and South pair must not only reach a contract of seven spades; they must also do everything the rules allow to prevent East and West from learning that a sacrifice at 7NT will be profitable. East and West, meanwhile, are employing every means at their command to convince North and South that a grand slam will be an overbold contract. A bidding system that does not provide for this conflict of goals, and that does not encompass methods to serve all these ends, is only half a system.

And as if this were not enough, there remain still further considerations, more subtle by far than those we have already set forth. Let us take another deal (in which only East-West are vulnerable):

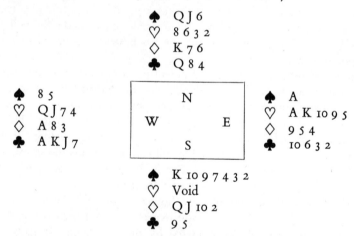

```
                  ♠  Q J 6
                  ♡  8 6 3 2
                  ◇  K 7 6
                  ♣  Q 8 4
    ♠  8 5                         ♠  A
    ♡  Q J 7 4          N          ♡  A K 10 9 5
    ◇  A 8 3      W          E     ◇  9 5 4
    ♣  A K J 7                     ♣  10 6 3 2
                       S
                  ♠  K 10 9 7 4 3 2
                  ♡  Void
                  ◇  Q J 10 2
                  ♣  9 5
```

East and West can win ten tricks at hearts, North and South can win nine tricks at spades. Par for East and West will thus be a contract of 4H, worth 620 points. Par for North and South will be a contract of 4S, worth minus 100 points if, as must be assumed on any sacrifice bid, the contract is doubled.

The goal of East and West will be to reach their contract, meanwhile deterring North and South from making the sacrifice bid or even attempting to goad North and South into doubling the impregnable contract of 4H. North and South must, meanwhile, seek to buy the hand at 3S, and failing that must bid 4S over a 4H contract. Every wile, every permissible device of chicanery and deceit, will be used by both pairs to reach their own goal.

But let us delve further and assume that the course of the early bidding has convinced West that the one crucial card in the hand, the club queen, is protected in the North hand. This means that East and West can take ten tricks and no more. And let us further suppose that the bidding has reached 3H, and that it is now West's turn to call. What might be going through the expert's mind?

West: "We can make 4H, and no more, which is worth 620 points. But they can bid 4S over 4H, and although we will double that contract, our gain will only be 100 points. Can't we do better than that?

"What will happen if I pass 3H? They may decide that since I have failed to bid game, they might just as well leave me undisturbed, rather than venture into sacrificial action. Then I will easily make 3H with an overtrick, worth 270 points.

"True, that's not as good as 620. But it's a lot better than 100.

"But then, they may bid 3S. But that can't harm me. I shall simply continue on to 4H, and I am no worse off than I was in the first place. I am better off, if anything, for they may take my failure to bid 4H at once to mean an indecision; they may be led to believe that I am not sure of making 4H, and they may decide to leave me there.

"Very well, then. I *know* I can make 4H. But nevertheless . . ."

And aloud, West says, "No bid."

So much for the hypothesis of perfect knowledge (which is not so rare as you might think). But what happens if we postulate for West a little less than perfect knowledge. Suppose, this time, that the bidding has reached 4S, and that again it is West's turn to bid.

West: "They've taken the save, and instead of the 620 points I was counting on they are threatening to let me down with a mere 100. If South holds the club queen, we can make 5H. But I don't know where the club queen is.

"Suppose I calculate the chances by assuming that I will be in this situation twice this evening. Once the finesse will lose, and once it will win, according to the laws of chance.

"If I double both times, I will collect two penalties of 100 points each, so I will end up plus 200 for the two hands.

"If I bid 5H both times, I will lose 100 points when the finesse is wrong, and win 650 points (500 plus 150) when it is right, so I will end up plus 550 on the two hands.

"Besides, they may decide to save again, at 5S, and then I am sure of 300 points on each hand.

"So here goes . . ."

And West says aloud, "Five hearts."

Now the paradox is manifest. Examination reveals that the par for East and West on this hand is 4H. Yet we have seen that perfect bidding, in the situations to which we have exposed West, will lead to a contract of 3H in one case, and 5H in another.

In terms of the specific deal, the first decision was right and the second one wrong. East and West would have been far better off if they could have found out, during the bidding, the location of the club queen. But to appreciate this, we must turn the statement around: North and South would have been much worse off if they had revealed the location of the club queen.

A bidding system, in short, must not only yield vital information; it must also conceal vital information. The two considerations are irreconcilable, and at some point or another a compromise must be made.

All these factors, then, must be kept in mind as we fix upon our definition of bidding objectives. We may sum them up as follows, keeping in mind the table of values with which we began:

(1) A bidding system must permit the partnership to establish in advance par on the hand, both for the partnership and the opposition.

(2) It must hamper the opposition in establishing the same pars.

(3) To achieve the first purpose, it must fix, with some precision, the content of all four hands.

(4) To achieve the second purpose it must conceal as far as possible the content of all four hands. A modern bidding system must provide a means of compromising, as profitably as possible for the bidder, the conflict of purpose. That is exactly what the system set forth in this book attempts to do.

2

ON HAND EVALUATION

SOME THOUGHTS ON POINT COUNT

A NUMBER of years have passed since those days in the 'forties when anyone who confessed that he used a point count to value his hand was denied the company of nice bridge players and was requested to take the first train home. Today, practically everyone uses this method of evaluation, and the area of disagreement on the subject is limited to the sole question of which point count renders the best service.

In the spring of 1949, we reached the conclusion that the most accurate point evaluation of high cards is:

Ace	.	.	$4\frac{1}{2}$
King	.	.	3
Queen	.	.	2
Jack	.	.	1
Ten	.	.	$\frac{1}{2}$

It is still our feeling today; nevertheless, we have abandoned this count in recognition of two practical considerations. First, the Milton Work Count:

Ace	.	.	4
King	.	.	3
Queen	.	.	2
Jack	.	.	1

is tremendously popular and it would be heartless to ask players to forsake it for a count that promises only slightly better results. Second, the Work Count has the great advantage of simplicity. No fractions are involved, the numbers are small and easily added. Each suit contains 10 points, the entire pack, 40.

Because the Ace is undervalued, and the ten not valued at all, we make some uncomplicated adjustments which will be discussed later on in this chapter.

It must be apparent that without a reasonably precise method of

7

evaluating high cards, it would be impossible for a player to estimate the trick-taking strength of his cards or to gauge the extent to which he could participate in any bidding sequence. The decision to open the bidding, for example, depends upon a calculation as to the trick-taking power of one's hand, its strength in relation to the other three hands, and its immunity to severe punishment.

So far, we have been talking only about the value of high cards. If every contract were played at no-trumps, and no player held a suit longer than four cards, a high-card point count would reflect quite accurately the trick-taking potential of hands. But the laws of contract bridge provide for suit contracts also, where long suits and short suits nullify the power of high cards; accordingly, we must give consideration to various elements of strength in addition to high cards.

When you have a long suit, the low cards may be promoted to winners and these cards must be taken into account when a hand is measured for strength. Short suits are likewise valuable when a contract is played at a suit and there are adequate trumps to provide ruffing tricks.

The point count is a common denominator which converts all the calculable elements of strength into a single unit of measurement, and thus permits the expression of power numerically. All offensive bidding depends on the acceptance of certain hypotheses, established from long observation and study, to the effect that a given number of points will produce a certain number of tricks. The science of bidding consists of devising a series of bids which, within the space of safe exploration, permits the partnership to engage for its best contract by ascertaining its combined point count and distributional patterns.

In addition to the points for high cards, the following are also given value:

LONG CARDS

For each card over four in length in a suit headed by two honour cards, 1 point.

For each card over four in length in a near solid or solid suit (A K Q x x, K Q J 10 x, etc.), 2 points.

SHORT SUITS

For each void suit, 3 points.
For each singleton, 2 points.
For each doubleton, 1 point.

It may be a good idea, at this point, to examine and count several hands illustrating the foregoing principles:

(1)	♠ A Q J 7 3	.	.	.	7	I	—	
	♡ K 8 4	.	.	.	.	3	—	—	
	◇ 9 5 .	.	.	.	.	—	—	I	
	♣ K 7 2	.	.	.	.	3	—	—	
					13	I	I	Total, 15

(2)	♠ 8	.	.	.	.	—	—	2	
	♡ J 9 6 3	.	.	.	.	I	—	—	
	◇ A 5 .	.	.	.	.	4	—	I	
	♣ A K J 8 5 2	.	.	.	8	2	—	
					13	2	3	Total, 18

(3)	♠ Void	.	.	.	.	—	—	3	
	♡ A K 6 3 2	.	.	.	7	I	—	
	◇ A Q 8 5 4	.	.	.	6	I	—	
	♣ A J 7	.	.	.	.	5	—	—	
					18	2	3	Total, 23

Very soon we shall make these figures more meaningful for you by letting you know what, in terms of tricks, they will produce, but for the time being it will be enough to recognize the fact that these hands differ in relative strength.

SOME FURTHER POINT ALLOCATIONS

As we stated at the beginning, the 4, 3, 2, 1 count slightly undervalues the Ace and thus overvalues the King, Queen and Jack. For the purpose of rectifying the count, 1 point is added if a hand contains all four Aces. Conversely, if a hand is Aceless, 1 point is deducted, but only when the bid under consideration requires a count of 14. Don't try to remember all of this now; we shall remind you about these adjustments later when we get into the business of bidding hands.

An average hand at bridge contains an A, K, Q, J, 10, 9, 8, 7, 6, 5, 4, 3, and 2. The top four cards are the only ones that are given point value, yet it is apparent that of the two hands below, hand (4) should be esteemed more highly:

(4)	♠ A 10 5	(5)	♠ A 5 3
	♡ K J 10 3		♡ K J 6 2
	◇ Q 9 4		◇ Q 8 5
	♣ A 10 9		♣ A 7 4

Where the bidding system provides for a choice between two bids—one a slight overbid and one a slight underbid—the presence of 10's and 9's warrants the overbid.

POINT COUNT ADJUSTMENTS FOR INSUFFICIENTLY GUARDED HONOURS

If a hand contains a singleton King, Queen or Jack, its value is diminished to a certain extent because the owner of the card must play it, perforce, when the suit is called for, and the card will, therefore, not infrequently fall victim to a higher honour in the opponent's hand. An unguarded honour has less chance to win a trick than a guarded one, and we reflect the lowered utility of the singleton King, Queen or Jack by deducting 1 point from the total of the hand.

To a lesser extent, certain doubletons headed by the King or Queen suffer a more than usual mortality in the play, and this susceptibility to premature death is recognized by valuing them as follows:

K Q alone	. .	4 points
K J alone	. .	3 points
Q J alone	. .	2 points
Q x	. .	1 point
J x	. .	0 points

To state this simply, deduct 1 point for each doubleton that includes the Queen or Jack, but not the Ace. Since the Ace is a powerful protector of any lesser card, no combination that contains the Ace loses point count by reason of being doubleton.

The tripleton Queen or Jack is not given full value because either three-card combination has to battle against tremendous odds to win a trick. For this reason, if a hand contains Q x x or J x x, 1 point is deducted. But only 1 point is deducted even if the same hand holds more than one of these three-card combinations.

So that you may take a breather and test your knowledge of what has so far been stated with regard to point count, we give you the following examples:

(6) ♠ A 9 5
    ♡ K J 8 2
    ◇ A Q 8 5
    ♣ K J

(7) ♠ A J 6
    ♡ A K 5 2
    ◇ A 8 3
    ♣ A 7 6

(8) ♠ Q x x
    ♡ A K Q 5 3
    ◇ 5 4
    ♣ A 9 6

(9) ♠ Void
    ♡ Q J 5 4 3 2
    ◇ J 3
    ♣ K Q J 10 5

(10) ♠ K Q
    ♡ A
    ◇ Q 9 5 4 2
    ♣ A 10 8 5 2

(11) ♠ Q 3 2
    ♡ J 7 4
    ◇ A Q J 7 5
    ♣ K 3

The counts for each hand:

	High Cards	Long Cards	Short Suits	Unguarded Honours	Total
(6)	18	0	1	−1	18
(7)	21	0	0	0	21
(8)	15	2	1	−1	17
(9)	10	4	4	−1	17
(10)	15	1	3	−1	18
(11)	13	1	1	−1	14

Note that the four Aces in hand (7) increase the value of the hand by I point; that the fifth diamond in hand (10) is given no value because the suit is not headed by two honours; and that in hand (11) only I point is deducted although it contains both Q x x and J x x.

ADJUSTMENTS FOLLOWING BIDDING DISCLOSURES

When a player evaluates his hand before any bidding action by the other three players indicates the location of the unseen high cards, he must necessarily rely on the law of averages when he calculates the point value of his high cards and distribution. Once, however, a bidding sequence develops, certain factors hitherto unknown stand revealed and, accordingly, as they indicate that the hand has been overvalued or under-valued, the point count must be adjusted downwards or upwards to reflect the more exact definition of the outstanding hands that is now available as evidence.

HONOURS IN PARTNER'S SUIT

If a hand contains the King or Queen of partner's bid suit, or the King *and* Queen, add I point to the count of the hand. If the King or Queen is singleton, remember that the hand loses a point because the high card stands unguarded. In such cases, the singleton factor is offset by the factor of promoted value, and the result is that the King or Queen keeps its normal count: 3 or 2 points. The reason for promoting the King or Queen of partner's bid suit a point is based on experience which proves that the solidification rendered by these key cards gives them trick-taking power in excess of that which the cards normally possess.

CORRECTING SHORT-SUIT POINT AWARDS

When the opening bidder examines his hand at the moment of initiating a bidding offensive, he assigns value to voids, singletons and doubletons on the basis that frequently he will strike a distributional pattern in his partner's hand that will combine well with his own. If partner responds in a suit which is short in the opener's hand, the opener must now adjust his sights downward in anticipation of a possible misfit. All points counted for shortness in a suit by partner must be eliminated when the opener next values his hand. In the following example, South places a value of 18 on his hand when he opens the bidding with 1H:

(12) ♠ 5   ♡ A K J 5 3   ◇ K 10 5 4   ♣ A 7 3

If, however, partner's response is 1S, the 2 points assigned to the spade shortage must now be deducted, and the opener will take his next action on the basis of holding a 16 count.

CORRECTING THE COUNT FOR LENGTH

After a raise from partner, it is fair to assume that consolidating cards in partner's hand will greatly increase the probabilities that long cards in that suit will win tricks. Thus if Q J x x x is raised, it is not unreasonable to credit partner with A x x or K x x or x x x x, in which case the fifth card will almost certainly be a winner. We reflect the enhanced value of the long card in a raised suit by increasing it 1 point. A long card may not, however, be given a point count in excess of 2 points. If, therefore, we have already valued the long cards at 2 points —as in the case of a solid or near-solid suit—a raise does not increase its point count. A K Q 5 4 is 11 points before a raise or after it.

TRUMP RAISE ADJUSTMENTS

When you raise your partner's suit, he is likely to count on you for four trumps and some distributional advantages. To offset this not-unwarranted assumption, you should deduct 1 point if you are valuing your hand for a raise and it contains only three-card trump support. A downward adjustment of 1 point is also demanded when a raise is in contemplation and the distribution is flat: 4-3-3-3. The value of the following hand in support of hearts

(13) ♠ K 8 5 3   ♡ Q 6 4   ◇ A 9 3   ♣ K 7 2

is 11 points. In high cards, the hand contains 12. The Queen of hearts gains a point in value because it is in the trump suit. But the hand loses 2 points by virtue of the three-card trump holding and the 4-3-3-3 distribution.

4-4-4-1 HAND PATTERN ADJUSTMENT

Nowhere in the principles previously set forth do we call for additional value by reason of an increased likelihood that the opener will find a well-matching hand across the table. With a 4-4-4-1 distribution, the opener has a hand of great flexibility for there are three different suits in which trump support may be found. This unusual attacking feature is recognized in *rebidding* or *responding* only, and 1 point is then added to the hand.

The foregoing material is meaty, and some preliminary hardship may be involved in learning these point counts and adjustments so that they will come quickly to mind when a hand is inspected for strength. But there are great compensations which attend the investment of study in the initial stages, and we urge the reader to examine a great number of hands carefully until the principles illustrated are completely understood.

For easy reference purposes, the following tables are presented:

TABLE OF HAND VALUATION

Basic Valuation of High Cards:

Ace	4
King	3
Queen	2
Jack	1

Plus Values: Short Suits:

Void Suit	+3 (unless in partner's bid suit)
Singleton	+2 (unless in partner's bid suit)
Doubleton	+1 (unless in partner's bid suit)

Plus Values: Long Suits:

Fifth and longer cards in suit headed by two honours	+1
Fifth and longer cards in solid or near-solid suit, of supported suit	+2

Plus Values: Miscellaneous:

All Four Aces	+1
King, Queen, or King, Queen of partner's bid suit	+1
4-4-4-1 Distribution (to be valued by Responder or Rebidder only)	+1

Deductions:

Aceless Hand (opening bidder only)	−1
Singleton King, Queen or Jack	−1
Doubleton containing Queen or Jack, but not Ace	−1
Q x x and/or J x x	−1
4-3-3-3 Distribution (for trump raise)	−1
Three-card trump raise	−1

TABLE OF PRODUCTION

Total partnership count			will generally produce
20—22	.	.	. 1NT or 2 of a suit
23—24	.	.	. 2NT or 3 of a suit
25—26	.	.	. close game
27—32	.	.	. easy game
33—36	.	.	. Small slam
37—	.	.	. Grand slam

NOTE: When the combined count is divided more or less evenly between the partnership hands, contracts may be made with the minima indicated above. When, however, the strength is mainly in one hand the maxima indicated above will frequently prove inadequate because play will be inflexible, being constantly out of one hand.

3

THE OPENING BID

A BRIDGE PLAYER is called upon to make many decisions in the course of a bidding sequence, but the one whose consequences are most extensive involves the opening bid. The first bid in a bidding structure is a foundation upon which an entire series may be erected, and it must be sound enough to stand the tests to which the opponents may subject it. Equally as important to the partnership is the selection of the suit in which the bid will be made. Merely to begin an offensive is not enough, for force applied in the wrong direction may be completely dissipated.

We speak in this chapter mainly of opening bids that signify a desire to undertake the offensive. There are other opening bids: pre-empts, lead-directing bids, etc., about which we shall have a great deal to say later on.

By referring to our Table of Production in Chapter 2, we find that 3NT, 4H or 4S, the usual game contracts, will be made with satisfactory frequency when the combined partnership point count totals 25—26. Hence it may be stated tentatively that a hand that counts 13 holds at least one-half of what is needed to engage for game, and should be opened. We say "tentatively" because the count of 13 is just barely on the right side of the border line, and we shall soon see that where the decision is close, other factors may turn us away from the opening bid. We may, for example, have adequate playing strength and yet decline to open the bidding because the structure of the hand, or the problems involved in defining it, are prejudicial to a smooth sequence.

BIDDABLE AND REBIDDABLE SUITS

Since most opening bids are made in a suit, we must next consider the kind of suit that may be held by the opener. It is advisable that the opening bid be selected with a view to informing one's partner that the first suit announced will, with adequate support, make a satisfactory partnership contract. We call such a suit a "biddable" suit, by which we mean that if partner contributes his proportionate part of the outstanding high cards and number of the suit, the partnership can expect to dominate the trump suit.

A player with three cards in a suit cannot reasonably expect that his partnership will dominate that suit, but when a suit is four cards long, the chances favour superior trump length in the combined hands. Three cards in the suit from partner will mean an advantage in length; four cards will create one of the choicest types of partnership trump patterns.

This leads us to the minimum requirement for a biddable suit: it must contain four cards.*

So that the partnership will also have more top-card control than the opponents, a four-card suit to be biddable must contain at least the Jack and a higher card; or the Ace and 10.

A five-card suit is always biddable, regardless of its top cards, the reason being that the suit, if raised, will practically guarantee an 8 to 5 numerical superiority and this is enough to offset any advantage in high cards that may favour the opponents. The following are minimum biddable suits:

6 5 4 3 2   Q J 8 4   A 10 5 2

REBIDDABLE SUITS

A biddable suit should be bid only once and abandoned if partner cannot raise it. A "rebiddable" suit is one that may be bid a second time even though it has not been supported. In general, a rebiddable suit is a biddable suit with a card added. Hence *any* six-card suit is rebiddable. A five-card suit should contain the Jack and a higher card, or the Ace and 10. The following are minimum rebiddable suits:

7 6 5 4 3 2   Q J 8 6 5   A 10 6 4 2

While the five-card rebiddable suit is, by definition, one that contains at least the Queen and Jack, there will be times when a player will rebid such a suit as Q 10 9 8 6. The reader will discover that not infrequently he has a choice between two or more bidding actions, neither of which conforms perfectly to the prescribed characteristics. In such cases he selects that bid which comes closest to conveying an accurate picture. Once in a great while, accordingly, an opening bid may turn out to be such a suit as Q 10 7 2, or a rebid, K 9 5 4 3. But for the purposes of visualizing the opener's hand, a partner may assume that he will find at least the minimum as defined.

* *NOTE:* There are occasions when a three-card minor will be bid by the opening bidder for particular reasons which we shall later touch upon. Remember, however, that this is quite exceptional, and although the suit is bid, it is not "biddable" within the generally accepted definition.

SELECTION OF THE OPENING BID

Now that we have considered the purpose of the opening bid, its point requirements and the strength of the suit, it remains for us to speak of the manner in which the opening bid is chosen. We shall treat, herein, only those hands that qualify for opening bids of one in a suit. In everything we say, the reader must assume that the one-over-one principle is operative in this bidding system as it is in practically all other systems today; by which we mean that the opener promises to rebid if partner responds in a new suit at the lowest level available to him. The selection of the opening bid is, therefore, a very important matter. The opener generates a series of bids by which he hopes to direct the partnership to that contract which will be the most rewarding.

In selecting his first bid, the opener must prepare himself for any response that he may normally be called upon to handle when he rebids. In general, he has two important tasks to perform: he must without undue risk define the strength of his hand and its distributional pattern; and he must so arrange his bidding that the elements that must remain undisclosed do not seriously impair the partnership's ability to reach makable games.

When the declarer has a one-suited hand, the suit being a rebiddable one, no rebidding problem is involved:

(1)	♠	5 2	(2)	♠	6 5 3
	♡	A K J 7 5		♡	A 2
	◇	A 5 3		◇	K Q J 5 4
	♣	Q J 4		♣	A 10 8
		Bid 1H			Bid 1D

With two adjacent five-card suits, the selection of the opening bid is just as easy:

(3)   ♠ K J 10 9 5   ♡ A Q J 6 3   ◇ Q 3   ♣ 8

Bid 1S

On this hand, the opener will wish to show both major suits while still keeping the bidding within the most economical limits. By bidding 1S, he may next bid 2H, thus giving his partner the option of selecting the suit he prefers without moving out of the two level. Observe that had the opening bid been 1H, a response of 1NT, 2C or 2D would embarrass the opener; a rebid of 2S would force responder into the three level if he preferred the heart suit, a contract higher by one level than the opener's minimum hand warrants. And to rebid hearts without disclosing the excellent spade suit would be a worse expedient.

The general rule governing the choice of suits when the opener has two or more biddable suits from which to select is:

(1) *With suits of unequal length, bid the longer suit first.*

(2) *With suits of equal length, bid the suit of higher rank first.*

In the foregoing example hand, ♣ K J 10 9 5 ♡ A Q J 6 3 ◇ Q 3 ♣ 8 we saw the application of part (2) of the rule which dictates the opening bid of 1S. Under this rule, if we change heart and diamond suits, the opening bid would still be 1S:

(4) ♠ K J 10 9 5   ♡ Q 3   ◇ A Q J 6 3   ♣ 8
Bid *1S*

Similarly, the opening bid in the following hand is 1H:

(5) ♠ Q 3   ♡ K J 10 9 5   ◇ 8   ♣ A K J 7 5
Bid *1H*

When, however, the two five-card suits are spades and clubs, an exception to part (2) calls for the opening bid of 1C:

(6) ♠ K J 10 8 6   ♡ Q 3   ◇ 6   ♣ A K J 7 5
Bid *1C*

Anticipating that the response will frequently be 1D or 1H, the opening bid of 1C paves the way for the economical rebid of 1S and makes for a smoother bidding sequence.

With a 6-5 two-suiter, the longer suit should be bid first under the general rule, part (1). Thus 1S is bid on the following hand:

(7) ♠ Q J 7 6 3 2   ♡ 4   ◇ 5   ♣ A K 9 8 4
Bid *1S*

We make an exception, however, when the suits are touching and the higher-ranking is the five-carder. The problem of *touching suits* is illustrated in the following two bidding sequences:

(A)   1S   1NT
      2H   ?

(B)   1H   1NT
      2S   ?

In both sequences, South has bid a suit and has rebid a touching suit. In Example (A), he has started with the higher-ranking suit, spades; in Example (B), with the lower suit, hearts. There is an important difference to the partnership which becomes clearly apparent if we observe North's situation when the bidding reaches him for his second response. In Example (A), if North prefers hearts to spades, he may pass. If he prefers spades he bids 2S. The partnership need not move beyond the two level. In Example (B), if North prefers hearts, he must bid at the three level. The difference between the two levels is so important that we depart from part (1) of the general rule (which provides for the bid of the longer suit first) whenever a hand is minimum or near-minimum and consists of two touching suits, the higher-ranking being five cards in length, the lower-ranking six. Thus

(8) ♠ A Q J 5 4   ♡ Q 10 8 6 4 3   ◊ K 5   ♣ Void
Bid 1S

If with *touching* suits distributed 6-5, there are 10 high-card points in the two suits, the longer should be bid first for the reason that there is no economical necessity to depart from the general rule. To state it another way, even if the partnership is forced to enter the three level, the strength massed in the two suits is ample protection against penalties and fair assurance that the contract will make.

(9) ♠ A Q J 5 4   ♡ A 10 9 8 6 2   ◊ 7   ♣ 5
Bid 1H

1H	1NT, 2C or 2D
2S	

When the opening bidder starts the auction with 1H and over a response of 1NT, 2C or 2D he bids 2S.

(1) We can state positively that the heart suit is longer than the spade suit.

(2) The opener has a good hand, because he is willing to reach the level of three if responder prefers hearts. Had opener wished to be economical (and thereby show a near-minimum hand) he could have bid 1S first.

We further illustrate the treatment of 6-5 hands with the following examples:

(10) ♠ A 2   ♡ A J 9 8 2   ◊ Q 10 8 5 3 2   ♣ Void
Bid 1H

You have only 7 high-card points in your long suits and you must therefore start the bidding in the higher-ranking suit even though the diamonds have greater length.

(11) ♠ 7 2   ♡ A J 9 8 2   ◊ A Q 10 8 5 3   ♣ Void
Bid 1D

You have 11 high-card points in your long suits and can bid your long suit first in accordance with the general rule.

(12) ♠ A J 9 8 2 ♡ A 2 ◇ Q 10 8 5 3 2 ♣ Void
Bid 1D

Compare this hand with Example (10). Notice that it is only when suits are *touching* in a minimum hand that we bid the five-card higher-ranking suit before the six-card lower-ranking suit. With non-touching suits, as above, six-carder is bid first.

5-4 DISTRIBUTION

In general, with a 5-4 two-suited hand, bid the longer suit first. But for reasons of economy, if the hand contains less than 17 points, bid the higher of the two touching suits, even though it is the shorter of the two suits.

(13) ♠ A Q J 4 ♡ 7 3 ◇ K Q 9 3 2 ♣ 8 5
Bid 1D

You have a count of 15. This is a minimum hand. Since the two suits are not touching, the longer is bid first.

(14) ♠ A K J 10 ♡ A K J 4 2 ◇ 7 3 ♣ 8 5
Bid 1H

You have a count of 19. With a hand of such strength there is no reason to be economical. Show the long suit first.

(15) ♠ 7 3 ♡ 8 4 ◇ A Q J 5 ♣ K Q 9 3 2
Bid 1D

You have a count of 15. Since the hand is weak and *the suits are touching* you must begin with the higher-ranking.

4-4-4-1 DISTRIBUTION

When all three suits are biddable, the general rule calls for the bid of the minor suit first below the singleton.

(16) ♠ 5 ♡ A Q 7 3 ◇ K J 9 4 ♣ K Q 5 2
Bid 1D

(17) ♠ A J 7 3 ♡ 5 ◇ Q J 8 5 ♣ K Q J 3
Bid 1D

The choice of the biddable minor suit first below the singleton is for reasons of convenience. If partner responds in your singleton suit, your rebid will be economical. If partner responds in one of your four-card suits, you will be able to raise.

1D		1H
1S	or	
1D		1S
2S		

Observe that when the diamond suit is not biddable, the club opening bid is made as on the following hand:

(18)   ♠ A Q 4 3   ♡ J   ◇ J 9 8 2   ♣ K Q J 10
Bid 1C

the general rule calling for the *biddable* minor suit first below the singleton.

4-4-3-2 DISTRIBUTION

If the two suits are biddable and touching, bid the higher-ranking first. If the suits are not adjacent, bid the lower first:

(19)		(20)	
♠	7 3	♠	7 3
♡	8 3 2	♡	A Q 7 5
◇	A Q 7 5	◇	8 3 2
♣	A Q J 3	♣	A Q J 3
	Bid 1D		Bid 1C

Regardless of the strength of the hand, if the proper opening bid is a suit bid of one, the lower-ranking of the two non-touching biddable suits is opened.

(21)   ♠ A Q 2   ♡ 7 3   ◇ J 7 5 3   ♣ A K J 9
Bid 1C

In the hand above, there is only one biddable suit.

PRINCIPLE OF ANTICIPATION. THE PREPARED BID

The one-over-one principle of bidding, which we previously pointed out as being implicit in all offensive bidding methods, imposes on the opener the obligation to bid again (unless an intervening bid assures responder another chance to bid) over a response in a new suit. This requirement makes it indispensable for the opener to prepare the bidding in such a way that he will be able to rebid without grossly distorting the hand's appearance as to high-card strength or distribution.

The opening bidder has not properly selected his first bid until he has mentally determined what his rebid will be over any normal response. To borrow again from the game of golf, a good golfer does not automatically drive down the centre of the fairway; he looks to see what approach to the green will be easiest for his next shot and then plays the first one to permit the approach he has selected. The bridge player must do exactly the same thing. By looking ahead for traps and obstacles, he lays out a pre-pared series of bids that will bring him safely past the hazards.

There is no rebid problem when the opener's hand is a rebiddable one-suiter.

(22) ♠ A 5 3   ♡ 9 8   ◇ A Q J 5 2   ♣ Q 3 2
　　　　1D　　　　　　　　　2C
　　　　2D

Likewise, there is no difficulty when you have two or three biddable suits. If your first bid is properly selected, your rebid will permit you to bid a second suit or raise partner:

(23) ♠ A Q 5 3   (24) ♠ K Q 9 5 4
　　♡ 8 5 2　　　　　♡ A 9 7 3 2
　　◇ K 5　　　　　　◇ K 9
　　♣ A J 10 7　　　　♣ 8
　　1C　　1H　　　　1S　　2C
　　1S　　　　　　　2H

Holding a very good hand, the prime reason for preparing the bidding —economy—is not present. So, if you have only one biddable suit, and a raise for partner is lacking, the rebid in no-trumps is always available:

(25) ♠ A 5 3   ♡ K 9 2   ◇ A Q J 5 2   ♣ J 3
　　　　1D　　　　　　　　2C
　　　　2NT

There is need for thought when the opener holds a minimum hand containing only one biddable suit:

(26) ♠ A K 9 2   ♡ 7 3 2   ◇ 8 5 4   ♣ A K 2

This hand must be opened, since it contains 14 points. If the bidding is opened with 1S, the opener will be in trouble if partner responds 2D, 2H or even 2C.

The solution is to open such hands with a bid in a three-card minor suit. If the hand is opened with 1C, the rebid of 1S presents itself as economical over a response of 1D or 1H. If the response is 1NT, opener may pass. If the response is 1S, opener may raise to 2S. And if partner bids 2C, you may pass.

The opening bid in a minor suit, particularly 1C, solves many bidding problems. But the bid should not be made on two-card suits or worthless three-card suits. It should be used only when no other bid serves as well to anticipate partner's response.

THE OPENING SUIT BID OF ONE

As a rule, if a hand is worth some opening bid, a bid of one of a suit will be the best way to start a sequence. Sometimes, to be sure, you will bid more than one, and at other times a bid in no-trumps will more properly describe your hand. But at least two-thirds of the time the strength and distributional pattern will call for an opening bid of one in a suit. The principal reason for this is that practically every other opening bid tells a precise story and the usual run of hands does not fit the prescription. The opening bid of one in a suit has a wide range. You may hold as few as 13 points or as many as 23. You may have flat distribution (no very long suit and no very short suit) or you may have a freak.

THE OPENING BID OF 1NT

When a hand is in balance (no voids or singletons and not more than one doubleton) it may qualify for an opening bid of 1NT. In the chapters on no-trump bidding which follow, we shall see that a high-card count is required, and since the bid of 1NT tells a precise story, it is seldom advisable to depart from its requirements.

FORCING TWO BIDS

When the opener's hand counts 24, he may be in a position to force to game by making a bid that commits the partnership to reach a game contract. There are other factors involved, however, and a discussion of them now would be out of place.

OPENING BIDS OF THREE OR FOUR OF A SUIT

An opening bid of three or four in a suit describes a one-suited hand with little strength in high cards outside the long suit. The bid should never be made on a suit less than six cards in length.

We restate the general rule as to the requirements of an opening bid: With a count of 14, an opening bid should be made unless there are high-card deficiencies. With a count of 13, an opening bid is optional and may be passed if the hand is short of high cards or lacks a rebid. Bear in mind that in the point count calculated to measure an opening bid, points for high cards, long cards and short suits are totalled.

SOME ADDITIONAL EXAMPLES OF OPENING BIDS OF ONE

(27) ♠ A Q 7 3 2   ♡ K Q 4   ◇ 9 2   ♣ 9 6 3
No Bid

You have 13 points, but no sound rebid. The spade suit is too shabby for enthusiasm; a pass is therefore preferable on this borderline hand.

(28) ♠ A Q 10 9 2   ♡ K Q 4   ◇ 9 2   ♣ 8 5 2
Bid *1S*

You have the same count of 13 as in hand (27) but the 10 and 9 of spades give you a comfortable spade rebid.

(29) ♠ A Q 3   ♡ K Q 9 8 5 3 2   ◇ A 4   ♣ 2
Bid *1H*

The hand has too much side strength for an opening pre-empt. Moreover, the hearts do not have the solidity which should be sought in high opening bids.

FOURTH HAND OPENING BIDS

If the auction has reached a player fourth hand after three passes, he may assume that the cards missing from his hand are well divided. He may shade the requirements for opening down to 12, but before doing so he should give considerable thought to what he hopes to gain by stirring up the lions. In a rubber bridge or duplicate game governed by aggregate points, only a part-score can be counted upon as the maximum return on such a hand, and unless there are special reasons for seeking 40 or 60 points, the hand should be thrown in. At duplicate match-point bridge, however, a successful part-score contract may be as rewarding as a grand slam, and any hand should be opened that has an odds-on chance of returning a plus-score.

(30) ♠ A 7 4   ♡ A Q 9 6 5   ◇ 7 6 3   ♣ J 8
Bid *1H*

You have a count of 12. (Doubleton Jack of clubs is given no value.) You will probably pass any non-forcing response.

In deciding whether to pass or bid fourth hand, the location of your strength is of controlling importance. If the power of a hand is almost evenly divided between two pairs, the side that has possession of biddable major suits will be able to outbid its opponents at any level by virtue of holding suits of ranking denomination. All other considerations being equal, the player who has a good spade suit has a critical advantage on a close hand.

(31) ♠ K Q 10 9 4 ♥ A 10 9 3 ♦ 7 2 ♣ 6 5
Bid *1S*

The hand counts 12 points and the good spade suit makes it a sound fourth hand opening. Compare

(32) ♠ 7 2 ♥ K 9 5 ♦ A K 10 9 2 ♣ 9 8 4
No bid

You have the same count of 12, but if the opponents compete in hearts or spades, you may only have succeeded in opening the hand for them.

THIRD HAND OPENING BIDS

When the bidding reaches you third hand following two passes, you may shade your requirements down to 11 points provided you have a strong suit. There is a reason for bidding light in third position entirely additional to that which motivates a thin fourth hand bid. With one player still to be heard from and the weakness of first and second hands manifest, third hand's objective in bidding may be to establish a good line of defence for partner should fourth hand become the declarer. There is, of course, no point to a third hand bid which may attract a bad lead and only marks a few key cards for the opponents.

(33) ♠ 7 2 ♥ K Q J 8 3 ♦ 6 5 ♣ Q 10 6 2
No bid No bid 1H

You have a count of 11. The hand will almost surely go to your adversaries and you must take advantage of this opportunity to indicate a sound opening lead.

(34) ♠ 6 5 ♥ 7 3 2 ♦ A Q J 4 ♣ K J 7 5
No bid No bid 1D

With a count of 12, the bid of 1D permits you to establish the line of attack against the adverse declaration that can be foreseen.

(35) ♠ A 4 ♥ Q 7 6 3 2 ♦ K 5 ♣ Q 8 5 3
No bid No bid 1H

You have a count of 13 and no rebid problem since your partner's original pass relieves you of the obligation to bid again.

(36) ♠ A 5 ♥ 9 8 6 3 2 ♦ A 7 5 ♣ Q 9 5
No bid No bid No bid

The effect of a 1H bid may be to draw a lead that costs you a trick and will merely mark the position of your high cards, simplifying the play for the enemy.

OPENING BIDS WITH FEW HIGH CARDS

Although a count of 14 points generally warrants an opening bid, advanced players will pass these minimum hands when they contain fewer than 9 points in high cards. With only 8 points or less, there is a risk that your partner will count on you for key cards that you do not hold, and once you have opened the bidding it will be difficult to erase this misimpression.

(37)   ♠ A J 10 8 6 3   ♡ K 7 6 4 2   ◇ 8   ♣ 6
No bid

You have 14 points, only 8 of which are represented by high cards. It is wiser to defer action.

(38)   ♠ Q J 10 9 7 6 2   ♡ K J 10 9 6 4   ◇ Void   ♣ Void
No bid

The hand counts 18 points, but is so lacking in high cards that it will certainly be opened by another player. You may later bid quite vigorously, thus defining your hand for partner.

With a long suit, a pre-emptive bid, later to be treated at length, will probably be your best action:

(39)   ♠ A Q J 9 7 6 3   ♡ 4   ◇ Q 6 3 2   ♣ 5
Bid 3S vulnerable
Bid 4S not vulnerable

There is really no compulsion on you to bid 13 point hands. This is a matter of bidding style and you may open or pass as you prefer.

(40)   ♠ 7 3   ♡ K Q 10 9 4   ◇ K Q 8 5   ♣ 8 4
Bid 1H or No bid

The reader may not, perhaps, have observed that in the foregoing forty hands, we did not once present an opening bid of one in a four-card major. This was not mere coincidence. The opening bids of 1H and 1S are avoided with suits of less than five-card length. But rather than weave this principle into the fabric of this long and important chapter, we have given it prominence in a chapter of its own which follows.

4

MAJOR-SUIT OPENING BIDS OF ONE

THE OPENING bids of 1H and 1S differ in certain important respects from 1C and 1D. In Chapter 3 we defined a biddable suit as a four-card suit with a high-card point count of four or more; and we implied that an auction could be begun with any biddable suit provided the opener anticipated the various normal responses and prepared himself to handle them intelligently. We must now inform the reader that where the opening bids of 1H and 1S are involved, the opener is subject to certain prohibitions that require another departure from a general rule of bidding.

The opening suit bid of one functions primarily to get the bidding under way. In this respect the opening bids of 1C and 1D are indistinguishable from 1H and 1S. But in another particular, there is a vast difference. The bid of 1C gives the responder practically the entire one level from which to select a bid and the opening bid of 1D also leaves room for economical exploration. On the other hand, the opening bid of 1S takes the entire one in a suit level from the responder and the opening bid of 1H, although it enables the partnership to test both major suits, denies the flexibility that comes with a 1C bid.

Another hardship imposed by the opening major-suit bid of one, when it may be of four cards, is the problem presented to a responder who holds three-card support. He may find it impossible to determine within the limits of available space and time, whether three cards will combine with the opener's suit to give the partnership a dominant trump. This situation confronts a responder in its most dramatic form when an intervening pre-emptive bid, or even a simple overcall, forces him to guess at the level of four, when the wrong decision may cost his side enough points to swing an entire match.

Before contract bridge had emerged from its swaddling clothes, a small group of players, conscious of the difficulties involved in handling major-suit opening bids, came forward with the idea that only five-card major suits should be considered adequate length for an opening bid of 1H or 1S. The arguments advanced in support of this departure from the then standard practices were both logical and persuasive. If a responder could count on the opener for five cards in the major, a great deal of guesswork in shaping his own bidding action could be eliminated. He could raise with three cards, and in many common sequences his refusal to raise would convey important negative inferences to the opener.

The simplest explanation for its almost universal rejection was the failure of the petitioners to integrate the idea into the one-over-one system. True, it was advantageous to be immediately assured that partner had a rebiddable heart or spade suit, but it was hardly worth revising an entire bidding system to get at a piece of information that would ultimately be revealed in a leisurely bidding sequence.

But with the passage of years, leisurely bidding sequences have become harder to come by. Opponents dedicated to harassment and skilled in the principles of action and pre-emption are not inclined to sit amiably by while bidders meander toward the proper contract. Correspondingly, a modern bidding system demands the stability that is provided by the requirement of five cards for a major-suit bid, and that requirement has been integrated into the Stayman System. But note, please, that we say "integrated", not "added". There is a difference.

There is of course no method short of assassination to make all pre-emptive action ineffective. But in view of the primacy of the major-suit contract as a game-producing vehicle, a great deal is accomplished when the opener establishes by his bid of 1S or 1H that he has a five-card suit or a near-solid four-carder which, with three-card support will provide a fortress to the partnership and not a mausoleum, if, as and when responder signs a quick lease for the premises at the four level.

Accordingly, we set forth here the requirements for the major-suit opening bid of one:

(A) A five-card suit, rebiddable in type, or occasionally.

(B) A four-card suit so rich in high cards that a minimum raise provides the partnership with an adequate trump suit.

The following are minimum holdings for the opening bids of 1S or 1H:

A J 8 5 2   A K J 3

We have already discussed at great length the methods by which we select our opening bids so as to prepare for a simple rebid. In the application of the principle of anticipation, we found that many hands containing four-card majors could not be opened with 1S or 1H, not because of any limitation imposed by the "five-card major" doctrine, but for the very good reason that the opener, at the point of rebidding, would find himself in a hole of his own digging. Thus, the following hands are opening bids of 1C, not because the spade suits are only four cards long, but because if the bidding starts with 1S, the responses of 2D or 2H are unanswerable:

(1)	♠ A Q 5 3	(2)	♠ A K 9 2
	♡ 8 5 2		♡ 7 3 2
	◇ K 5		◇ 8 5 4
	♣ A J 10 7		♣ A K 2
	Bid 1C		Bid 1C

To this group of hands which cannot initiate the bidding with the four-card major for reasons of preparedness, we thus add hands of the following type which would have qualified for the opening spade or heart bid but for the introduction of this new principle:

(3)	♠ A Q 9 2	(4)	♠ A J 9 5	(5)	♠ 8
	♡ K 10 5		♡ K J 8 4		♡ K J 8 7
	◇ A K 3		◇ 8 2		◇ Q J 10 5
	♣ K 8 4		♣ K Q 2		♣ A Q 8 2
	Bid 1C		Bid 1C		Bid 1D

The principle of anticipation would have been served in hand (3) with an opening bid of 1S, for over the responses of 2C, 2D or 2H, the rebid of 2NT is perfectly tailored for the job. In hand (4) a 2H rebid would handle perfectly the expected responses of 2C or 2D. In hand (5) the opening bid of 1H leaves available the rebid of 2C or a raise in diamonds. Yet in all these cases, it will be observed, the major-suit opening bid is abandoned.

It must not be imagined that, in fixing the requirement of five cards (or a strong four) for the major-suit opening, we turn our backs upon these four-card trump holdings and treat them with disdain. The very opposite is true, as will be seen when we get into the subjects of responses and rebids. A responder who holds four hearts or four spades must always be alert to the possibility that the opener has four cards in a major, and he will prepare his responses so as to permit a low-level investigation of this possibility.

There is much more to the five-card major principle than the mere rejection of the four-card suit as a basis for the opening bids of 1S or 1H, as we shall discover in the chapter on rebids.

THIRD AND FOURTH HAND BIDS OF 1H AND 1S

The fact that one's partner has already passed, and that one or both opponents have shown inability to open the bidding change substantially the considerations which govern the handling of four-card majors in the third and fourth seats. If the opener has less than the requirements of an opening bid himself, his object in opening must certainly be a modest part-score at the most. It may be that his purpose in opening the bidding is merely to establish lines of defence in the not-unlikely event that fourth hand becomes the declarer. Thus, if we imposed on a third hand bidder the prohibition against four-card majors, we might be defeating the very purpose for which third hand action is frequently intended: the direction of a lead. Holding the following hand, for example, a third hand bidder, bound by the five-card major principle, would have the choice between a no bid and the bid of 1C, and the chance to indicate the heart lead that might defeat a 3NT or 4S contract would have to be forgone.

(6) ♠ 8 2 ♥ K Q J 10 ♦ Q 3 2 ♣ A 7 6 4

Further, the player in third or fourth position may open a hand either with a part-score as his sole objective, or with the intention of proceeding to game only if particular responses are forthcoming. We remind the reader that when the opener's partner has himself failed to open the bidding, the opener is not bound to rebid. The responder, aware that opener may look to the first response for evidence as to game possibilities, will often conceal the four-card major he holds in order to make a strength-showing declaration. Consider, for example, the problem a responder faces with the following hand:

(7) ♠ A 9 8 5 ♥ K 8 2 ♦ A J 5 ♣ 6 4 3

The bidding has proceeded:

No bid   *No bid*   *1D*   *No bid*

If he bids 1S, he risks the possibility that he will be passed at that contract by an opener who has less than adequate spade support and who had opened the bidding with no intention to rebid over a spade response. If he bids 2NT, he risks the chance that the partnership holds an excellent 4-4 spade fit which will not be revealed if the opener, holding such a hand as the following, passes his response:

(8) ♠ K Q 10 4 ♥ 7 3 ♦ K 9 8 3 ♣ K J 10

Relying on the opener not to conceal a biddable four-card major (unless opener intends to rebid over any response) the responder may bid 2NT with hand (7) with confidence that hand (8) does not stand opposite him in the opener's hand. With hand (8), the opener would have initiated the bidding with 1S since that bid accomplishes all his possible objectives: the most rewarding part-score or an effective opening lead.

Finally, the failure of one or both opponents to take pre-emptive action at their first bidding opportunity diminishes the likelihood that crowding action will be visited on the offensive team. For all the foregoing reasons, five-card major principle is not applicable to third and fourth hand opening bids. After two passes, therefore, problems, concerning the selection of the opening bids are resolved according to rules set forth in Chapter 3.

This being so, it becomes necessary to qualify a rule stated in Chapter 3 in connection with bidding 4-4-4-1 hands. The reader will recall that we stated the opener should bid the *minor* biddable suit first below the singleton, and among the examples given was the following hand, there numbered (16):

(9) ♠ 5   ♡ A Q 7 3   ◇ K J 9 4   ♣ K Q 5 2

for which we advocated the opening bid of 1D. In all systems that do not forbid opening four-card majors, the generally accepted rule governing 4-4-4-1 hands is: Bid the biddable suit first below the singleton. The introduction of the word *minor* in our rule was made necessary, of course, by the application of the five-card major principle to opening bids. Since that doctrine has no application to third and fourth hand bids, we revert to standard practice with 4-4-4-1 hands following an initial pass by partner.

5

RESPONDING TO SUIT BIDS OF ONE

LIKE THE opening bidder, the player who sits opposite an opening bid must first decide whether to take action of any kind; if action seems appropriate, he must then determine the manner in which he will express the shape and strength of his hand. Just as the opener must look ahead and prepare himself with a sound rebid, so the responder has a responsibility to plan his subsequent responses. Where the system permits only one response with a particular hand, a choice does not exist; but generally, the responder must choose between two or more responses. In this situation, he will govern himself in accordance with principles that have already been touched upon, but that may, with profit, be restated.

There are three distinct ways of scoring game (aside from piecing together part-scores). The security afforded to a partnership by a dominant trump suit makes trump contracts more desirable than no-trump declarations. At a trump declaration, only high cards held by the opponents win tricks, and many of those can be nullified by ruffing. The play at no-trumps imposes on the declarer the necessity of fighting against the high-card strength in all four suits. In addition, at no-trumps, he fights always against the time element, and if his adversaries establish long cards in a suit before declarer has gained control or possession of nine tricks, he is powerless to stem the flow of the long suit.

But the advantage of suit play does not compensate for the two-trick differential in favour of the no-trump as against the minor-suit game. Faced with the task of winning all but two tricks, in order to engage successfully for 5C or 5D, the declarer must be so impregnable at all points of siege that the twenty-six cards he controls must be extraordinarily rich in Aces and Kings (in which case nine tricks at no-trumps will be a surer and quicker harvest) or voids and singletons must stand sentinel where high cards are lacking. So the minor-suit play for game is generally accorded the last place in the order of desirability of game contracts.

The hierarchy of game probabilities governs the responder in his selection of bids. Opposite an opening bid he must first decide on the quantum of his bidding. He must then so arrange the order of his responses that, within the limits of permissible exploration, the partnership will be able to estimate its chances of playing at a major suit; failing that, at no-trumps; and finally in a minor suit. The whole science of responding is, accordingly, concerned with the two elements of power and direction. The responder helps to direct the partnership along its best course by selecting those responses that will enable his partner and himself to probe the possibilities of the deal within their joint resources.

WHY RESPOND AT ALL?

The opening bid, you will remember, may run from 13 points all the way to 23. We shall learn that many of the hands that count 20 or better are described in ways other than opening suit bids of one. As a practical matter, therefore, the responder generally bases his bidding decisions on the assumption that the opener's hand does not exceed 20 points. The reader will recall that a combined count of 26 points will frequently produce a game, and for that reason the opener's partner, when he holds 6 or more points, must make some response to cover the possibility that the opener holds a maximum.

Another reason for responding with few high cards is in order to place the partnership in its best denomination. The opening bid is very often purely probative, and this is particularly so when the first bid is 1C or 1D.

Even when no game contract is possible and when there is no better trump suit than the one suggested by the opener's initial declaration, there are sound reasons for engaging in an offensive that stops at a partial. In rubber bridge, a part-score of 20 or 30 has almost no practical value, since it must be complemented by so large a partial that only rarely will the 20 or 30 points be the margin of making game. On the other hand, 40 or 60 point part-scores are tremendously useful. A partnership with only a slight preponderance of strength may engage successfully for another small score and take game or rubber. Equally important, the severest penalties are given away by players who cannot stand the thought of letting their opponents take a game with a part-score; and 40 or 60 below the line seems always to be an irresistible lure.

Finally, a bid by responder may create just enough interference or threat to keep the opponents from entering the auction with a call that will lead to a makable contract.

What about the danger of getting too high with a weak responding hand when the opener himself holds a minimum? It is true that on occasion the bidders may incur a penalty—even a bad one—but in the long run it will be found that the penalties suffered in small part-score contracts are not appreciably greater than the value of contracts that could have been produced by the defenders had they entered the bidding.

The idea of responding with a weak hand can, of course, be carried too far. If you respond with a worthless hand, you may suffer substantial losses disproportionate to the small part-scores that were available to your adversaries.

We may state our first general rule governing the action of the responder as follows:

(1) RESPONDER IS REQUIRED TO BID WHEN HE HAS 6 POINTS

It is sometimes permissible to shade the requirements to 5 points when responder has good support for the opener's suit. But our first yardstick is 6 points for any responsive action.

Returning for a moment to our Table of Production, we recall that with a combined count of 26 there is a reasonably sound play for game at the partnership's most desirable declaration. Since the opening bid indicates the presence of 13 points, we may by simple arithmetic establish our second general rule controlling the responder:

(2) RESPONDER IS REQUIRED TO BID UNTIL GAME IS REACHED WHEN HE HOLDS 13 POINTS OR MORE

Only where the partnership's game lies in clubs or diamonds will 26 points prove inadequate to produce the game-going tricks. If no-trump and major-suit possibilities have been properly investigated and rejected, it is perfectly proper to stop at a minor-suit partial when the partnership possesses less than 28 or 29 points.

Responding hands that fall between the extremes of 6 points and 13 points will often stand opposite sufficient strength to produce game, and the responder must be equipped to convey the information that will enable the opener to distinguish the intermediate from the minimum and the maximum.

When responder holds 6—11 points, the partnership will be able to engage for game if the opener possesses 20—16 points. Experience teaches us that whereas game will generally result from a combined ownership of 26 points, 27 or 28 may be needed if the high cards are largely in one hand. Accordingly, when responder has no more than 11 points, game is beyond the capacity of the partnership unless the opener has 16 or better. With a King better than a minimum opening bid, the opener has several ways of informing the responder that 11 points or less will be sufficient for game. For example, he will often be able to open the bidding with 1NT (which indicates 16—18 when vulnerable).

Since the burden of moving aggressively will be undertaken by the opener when he holds 16 points, the responder with 6—11 points should make but one voluntary bid, after which he takes no further action in the bidding except (1) to indicate a preference if a choice of denominations is presented, or (2) when further bidding is demanded or requested by a strength-showing rebid.

The inability to bid by a responder who holds less than 6 points we may call the action of Refusal. The response with hands counting 6—11 points, we designate the action of Co-operation, by which is implied no positive enthusiasm about game prospects.

In the next higher category of responder's hands, we find those that count 12—13. Here the production of game is more than likely for it depends upon opener holding a *good* minimum rather than a *bad* minimum. But the opener with 15 or 16 points is hardly in a position to make an aggressive move towards game after he has started the auction, and he need not do so by virtue of the third rule governing responsive action:

(3) RESPONDER IS REQUIRED TO BID *TWICE* (UNLESS GAME IS BID BY PARTNER) WHEN HE HOLDS 12—13 POINTS

We call the second response chance-giving when it is made at a level one trick under game for the purpose of demanding that opener go on to game if he has 15 or 16, a good minimum.

Since there will generally be a good play for a slam when the combined partnership count is 33 or more, a responder who holds 19 points is required to announce slam possibilities in his first response. He does this by making a jump-shift response (or a jump response in no-trumps). Thus,

1D—2H   or 1S—3C   or 1D—2NT

So, our fourth rule:

(4) RESPONDER IS REQUIRED TO MAKE A JUMP-SHIFT (OR JUMP IN NO-TRUMPS) WHEN HE HOLDS 19 POINTS OR MORE.

Let us condense these principles into a simple table:

RESPONDER'S ACTION

Point strength	Obligation	Category
0—5	None	Refusal
6—11	Respond once	Co-operation
12—13	Respond twice	Chance-giving
14—18	Reach game	Insistence
19—	Game force	Slam-probing

SELECTION OF THE RESPONSE

What we have already considered may tell you *when* or *how much* to bid, but it does not tell you *what* to bid. The selection of the first response depends on the pattern of your hand, but there are several basic principles that are controlling. In trying to reach a game, your search must first be for a dominant major suit. It is generally as easy to make 4H or 4S as it is to make 3NT—and it may be far safer.

When a fitting major cannot be found, the partnership must next consider game at no-trumps. Are all suits adequately stopped? Can the onslaught in the partnership's weakest suit be stemmed long enough to bring in nine tricks? Sometimes the selection of 3NT as a final contract is not so much a choice of no-trumps as it is a rejection of the minor-suit game.

When you have adequate trump support for partner's major suit, your first responsibility is the communication of this information to him. If your partner opens the bidding in a minor, you respond in a major if you have one. When neither partner can trot out a major, the partnership probes the possibilities of no-trumps, resorting to a minor suit with great reluctance only after no-trumps have been investigated and found to be inappropriate.

In a general way, therefore, responder shows the strength of his hand by the number of times he bids, and the distribution of his hand by the denominations he selects to describe the pattern. One more general comment about responding before we go into details. The whole vocabulary of the responder is the bid or series of bids wherein he informs the opener about the salient characteristics of his thirteen cards. As with the opener's first bid, the responder's initial action is of wide implications. But every time he speaks thereafter, he must sharpen the focus so that the fine details are revealed as the advance towards game increases the importance of precision.

TRUMP SUPPORT

The definition of trump support becomes necessary when one partner weighs the desirability of raising a suit bid by the other. A voluntary raise should generally be avoided regardless of the quality of a hand unless adequate support for the suit is one of its components. A better bid can usually be found to describe the features of the thirteen cards to be portrayed. The aim of the partnership is a combined holding of eight or more cards in a suit well controlled (although seven cards containing three of the four honours will do). The raise is appraised on the basis that partner holds only the weakest suit permitted by his bidding. Thus, if the opening bid is 1D, the raise to 2D shows at least four-card support, since the responder asserts that the partnership has a combined length of eight cards of which the opener has undertaken to produce only four.

When the opening bid is 1H or 1S, a five-card suit (or near-solid four-carder) is promised, and three cards in support of the major suit become adequate trump support, for the partnership is again assured of an eight-card combination.

Since the requirements for a biddable suit are four cards containing the Jack and a higher card (except for the opening bids of 1H or 1S), the contribution of three-card support containing the Ace, King or Queen will give the partnership a small measure of suit dominance and for that reason such a holding is deemed adequate.

TRUMP SUPPORT TABLE

Opposite	Your raise promises
Biddable suit	x x x x
Q J x x	A x x
	K x x
	Q x x
Rebiddable suit	x x x
Q J x x x	A x
	K x
	Q x
A suit that has been	x x
bid three times (or	A
a jump rebid)	K
K Q J x x x	Q

When partner opens the bidding with 1H or 1S, your inclinations must be to raise if your hand contains adequate trump support; and the strength of your raise must be based on the point count of your hand. We have already stated what constitutes trump support, and it remains only to present in terms of point count the requirements for single or multiple raises. This we do in the following table:

Strength of your hand	Raise suit to
9—11	Two level directly
12—13	Three level indirectly
14—18	Four level indirectly
Special hand	Four level directly

The single raise of a suit, 1S—2S, needs no discussion. It represents a hand of sound strength—one that will produce game opposite opening bids ranging from 15—17. The raise to three with hands counting 12—13 demands explanation. The reader will recall that when the responder holds 12—13 points, he is bound to bid twice, for his hand lies in the chance-giving category where games hinge on opener holding merely a good minimum (15). If in our bidding system, 1S—3S meant that the responder held sufficient strength to guarantee a good play for nine tricks only, there would be no reason not to jump directly to three with such a hand. But the immediate double raise is reserved for responder's hands that are good enough to demand game (14 or better) and we must, therefore, not confuse partner by jumping to three with a chance-giving hand. It may seem odd that the immediate raise to game is not made by the responder whose hand requires game insistence. The underbid is made so that the opener may probe for slam before the partnership reaches game. We shall see that the triple raise 1S—4S is not a sign of great strength but is pre-emptive in nature. Thus 1S—3S says: "Partner, we have game in spades. If you have a good hand, let me know by cue-bidding; otherwise, merely go on to 4S."

To indicate a hand that has the values for two raises, but cannot quite guarantee game, responder first bids a side suit and on his second response bids three of opener's. The first response is just the tail of the dog and it is really a matter of indifference which suit responder selects for his first bid so long as he reveals the chance-giving character of his hand in his second response. So:

1S	2C
2S	3S

or

1S	2D
2H	3S

Observe, in the second bidding sequence, that the responder's second response is 3S, notwithstanding that the two level is open for the spade raise. The second response with hands of chance-giving strength is always at the level of one trick under game in the denomination bid.

For reasons already expressed, responder does not raise directly to game when he holds 14 or more, but makes the double raise which is game-forcing. Finally, with no more than 8 points *in high cards*, five cards of opener's major, and a singleton or void, the triple raise is made:

1H	4H

This crowding action is warranted by the defensive weakness of a hand that is unsuited for anything but play at opener's suit, and is not good enough to suggest the possibility of slam. The jump to game is designed to keep the opponents out of the lower levels of bidding where they might, with impunity, investigate their own capacity to seize the initiative.

Do not make the mistake of thinking that your raise to game will shut out your partner. You have defined your hand as one that lacks 9 points in high cards, but a hand rich in distribution and long in trumps.

Let us test our familiarity with the foregoing material:

The bidding has proceeded

North	South
1H	?

You are South. What is your response?

(1) ♠ A 8 3   ♡ K 10 7 4   ◇ J 2   ♣ 8 5 4 2

Bid *2H*. With a count of 9, your hand qualifies for a constructive raise. Your action is "co-operative" only and you do not intend to bid again unless compelled to do so.

(2) ♠ K 9 5 2   ♡ Q 6 5   ◇ A J 3 2   ♣ 9 4

Bid *2H*. Here you have 11 points, which is the best hand you may hold in the single raise bracket. Since the opening bid of 1H guarantees a five-card suit, Q 6 5 will provide adequate trump support. Observe that hand (2) is a Queen stronger than hand (1). Not infrequently this difference will mean game, and when we come to the chapter on rebids we shall see how the opener extracts this information from responder when it is important to the partnership.

(3) ♠ A Q 3 2   ♡ J 9 7 4   ◇ 6 2   ♣ K J 2

Bid *1S*. Since you have strong support for hearts, the only question you must answer is: How many raises does your hand merit? With 12 points, our table informs us that we may bid up to 3H. We cannot make the immediate response of 3H because that would be forcing to game. Accordingly, we temporize with 1S, intending next to bid 3H over opener's rebid.

(4) ♠ 6 2   ♡ J 9 7 4   ◇ A Q 3 2   ♣ A Q 2

Bid *3H*. With adequate heart support and a count of 14, you force to game.

(5) ♠ 6 2   ♡ J 9 5 4   ◇ A K J 3 2   ♣ K 2

Bid *3H*. Note that your first obligation is to indicate that there is a game at hearts. If opener can now see slam possibilities, he will make a slam move and responder will uncover the excellent diamond suit. But observe that if opener merely goes on to 4H (thus ruling out the slam), the opponents have not had the advantage of previewing the dummy. In duplicate bridge particularly, where the extra trick is tremendously remunerative, the concealment of distributional information, when concealment cannot damage the declarant pair, is of major importance.

(6) ♠ 6   ♡ J 9 7 4 2   ◇ K Q J 3 2   ♣ 8 5

Bid *4H*. If North has only 13 points, the contract may be defeated, but the penalty cannot be severe and the shut-out may well make it impossible for either opponent to enter the auction.

(7) ♠ 6 2   ♡ J 9 7 4 2   ◇ K Q J 3   ♣ 8 6

Bid *2H*. The distribution of the hand does not bring it within the requirements for pre-emptive action. The hand counts 10 and qualifies for a single raise.

(8) ♠ 6   ♡ J 9 7 4 2   ◇ K Q J 3 2   ♣ K 3

Bid *3H*. With 11 in high cards, this hand is too good for a pre-emptive raise to 4H. Such action might result in failure to reach a slam, for opener would underestimate the strength of your hand. Having 15 points, your response is 3H, a game force.

THE ONE-OVER-ONE RESPONSE

When your partner has opened the bidding with one of a suit, he has pledged the partnership to win seven tricks. He has suggested his own suit as a possible trump, but he may be quite willing—even delighted—to consider a different trump—*your* suit, for example.

If your response is at the level of one, you do not increase the contract; you have merely introduced another possible trump. If your partner, the opening bidder, likes the suit you have offered, he will raise. (We shall discover that he will raise only when he is really enamoured of your suit, because he will make allowances for the possibility of your having a weak four-carder.)

If the opener has no great affection for responder's suit, he may bid a second suit; or his first suit may be a stout one, in which case he will rebid it. Lacking a second suit, a rebiddable suit or support for responder's suit, the opener may seek the shelter of 1NT.

For these reasons, it is safe and proper to respond in a suit when you have 6 points and a biddable suit that is higher ranking than the opener's. The bid at the one level does not, of course, deny a good hand. You will recall that the range of the initial response is extremely broad: 6—18, and the response of 1D to an opening bid of 1C may be based on the weakest or the strongest kind of one-over-one response. The opener will patiently await clarification.

The responder is in no danger of being denied a second call. Under one-over-one principles, a new suit by responder charges the opening bidder to rebid (in the absence of contention); and since a second response is thus assured to the responder, he is certain to have an opportunity to define his hand more precisely.

The bidding has proceeded as follows:

North	South
1H	?

You are South. What is your call?

(9) ♠ K J 7 4   ♡ 5 3 2   ◇ 6 4 3   ♣ 9 8 7

No bid. You have 4 points. You are not required to bid with less than 6 points, and to do so might lead to trouble.

(10) ♠ K J 7 4   ♡ 5 3 2   ◇ K 4 3   ♣ 9 7 3

Bid *1S.* You have 7 points and a biddable suit higher ranking than the opener's.

(11) ♠ J 4 3 2   ♡ 5 3 2   ◇ K J 7   ♣ K 7 3

Bid *1NT.* You have a count of 8 and must respond. Your spade suit is not biddable.

(12) ♠ K J 7 4   ♡ Q 4 3 2   ◇ K 3   ♣ 9 7 3
Bid *2H.*

The hand qualifies for a single raise or for the bid of 1S. Limited to one voluntary action, you must make the most telling bid—the raise. However, when the opening bid is 1C or 1D, a four-card biddable major takes precedence over a single raise in accordance with the policy of investigating majors before committing the partnership to minor-suit play.

(13) ♠ K J 7 3   ♡ 5 4   ◇ A 9 5 3 2   ♣ 8 2

Bid *1S.* With a count of 9 points, you may respond at the one level only. You have the higher-ranking suit available and must therefore bid it.

(14) ♠ K 8 3   ♡ 9 5   ◇ A Q 8 4 2   ♣ 7 6 5

Bid *1NT.* You have a good diamond suit, but your hand counts 10 for suit bidding and confines you to the one level. No higher-ranking suit being available and a response being obligatory, 1NT is, by elimination, your response.

(15) ♠ K J 7 3   ♡ 5 4   ◇ A Q J 5 3   ♣ 8 6

Bid *2D*. If your hand qualifies for more than one response—and this one counting 13 does—bid your suits in order of length in accordance with the general rule.

When the opening bid is 1C or 1D, the responder when he is limited to one voluntary action, should announce the lower of two four-card majors; further one-over-one exploration of the spade suit is thus preserved.

(16) ♠ Q J 9 5   ♡ K J 4 2   ◇ 8 5   ♣ 9 6 2

Bid *1H*. If the opener holds four spades, he will bid the suit and still be at the one level.

THE TWO-OVER-ONE RESPONSE

When opener starts the bidding with one of a suit, responder's possession of a lower-ranking suit presents the question of when it is permissible for him to enter the two level. In most systems, the requirements for this bid are 10—11, about a Queen short of the range of chance-giving action.

In the Stayman System, we impose on responder who enters the two level on his first response the obligation to make a second bid. Since by bidding at the two level the responder not only guarantees sufficient capital for that venture but signs, at the same time, a promissory note for an additional undertaking, it is only sensible that he have something in reserve beyond what is ordinarily required for the two-over-one response. And this is so. The immediate entry into the two level in a new suit indicates a point count of 12 at the minimum. The responder's promised second action may take the partnership as high as 2NT or three of a suit. A count of 25 will produce these eight or nine tricks.

The ability to defer action with the sure knowledge that partner will protect him, gives the opener great flexibility and permits him to make single rebids on hands that require gradual delineation. Equally important is the opportunity it affords the opener to stay out of the auction when his right-hand opponent enters with a bid he cannot himself punish, but which may be severely mauled because of responder's concealed strength. One of the remarks heard most frequently at the bridge table, and usually in a most plaintive voice, is: "Partner, why didn't you just let that bid come around to me?" Many opponents have been rescued from catastrophe by an opening bidder who could not take penalty action himself, but dared not pass for fear that his silence would be misconstrued as weakness.

In many respects the two-over-one response resembles the one-over-one which we have just examined. The maximum remains at 18 points; with 19 or more, a jump-shift is obligatory. The minimum for this response is 12 instead of 6. This does not mean, of course, that you pass hands that contain 6—11 points. Any hand with 6 points is worth *some* response; it just doesn't qualify for a response in a new suit at the two level.

What should you do with hands counting 6—11? We have already gone into that question pretty thoroughly. This is the area of courtesy responses, where you announce a higher ranking biddable suit if you own one, raise your partner or bid 1NT.

Test yourself on the following examples; the opener bids one heart.

(17)   ♠ 6 2   ♡ 5 3 2   ◊ A K 9 7 5   ♣ K 6 3

Bid *2D*. You have a biddable suit and a count of 12—10 in high cards, 1 for the doubleton spade and 1 for the fifth diamond. You can just pay your way into the two level.

(18)   ♠ 6   ♡ J 3 2   ◊ A K 10 9 5   ♣ 9 6 3 2

Bid *2H*, not 2D. You have a count of 11 points—8 in high cards, 2 for the singleton and 1 for the long diamond. This hand is 1 point shy of the requirement for a two-over-one response.

(19)   ♠ 6   ♡ 5 4   ◊ A K J 7 5   ♣ A J 9 3 2

Bid *2D*. Since the two suits are five cards in length, you bid the higher-ranking first. You will make a second response of 3C, thus defining your hand as a two-suiter.

(20)   ♠ 6 2   ♡ 5 4   ◊ A K J 7   ♣ A J 9 3 2

Bid *2C*. With suits of unequal length, the longer suit is bid first.

(21)   ♠ A Q 4   ♡ J 4 3 2   ◊ A 9 7 5   ♣ 7 2

Bid *2D*. You have good support for partner's heart suit, but your hand is too good for a single raise and not good enough for a jump to 3H. When the bid of a suit is used merely as a temporizing measure—an indirect double raise—any suit is biddable.

(22)   ♠ A J 7 4   ♡ 5 3   ◊ Q 9 7 4 2   ♣ 3 2

Bid *1S*. The hand is not strong enough for 2D, so you must find a bid at the one level. Had partner opened with 1C, you would have responded with 1D, showing your longer suit in accordance with the general rule.

THE JUMP-SHIFT RESPONSE

When your partner has opened the bidding with one of a suit and you have a count of 19 or more, your first response must be a jump in a new suit. (*NOTE:* The jump response in no-trumps also is employed to show hands of great strength, as will appear when we discuss the immediate no-trump responses.) This immediate strength-showing bid informs the opener that you intend to make a strong move towards slam and asks partner to rebid thereafter so as to reveal those characteristics of his cards that will enable the partnership to proceed to slam or stop at game as the combined strength warrants.

If the opener has a minimum hand—13 to 14—his rebid will indicate that he has no reason for optimism. With 15 points (and the partnership thus assured of 34) he will be moderately responsive to his partner's slam move. With more than 15 points, opener will immediately engage in positive slam action because he knows that at the partnership's best de-nomination, the twenty-six cards will yield twelve tricks or perhaps thirteen.

The jump-shift does not guarantee a fit in the opener's suit. The re-sponder may have any one of the following types of hands:

(1) A fine suit of his own.
(2) A fine fit for opener's suit.
(3) A good fit for opener's suit and a good suit of his own.
(4) Great all-round strength.

Over partner's opening bid of 1H, what call do you make?

(23) ♠ A Q J 7 4   ♡ A J 6 3   ◇ 5   ♣ A 8 5

Bid 2S. You have a count of 19 points—16 in high cards, 2 for the single-ton and 1 for the long card in spades. By making the jump-shift response, you place your partner on notice about slam possibilities at once. You will, of course, disclose strong support for hearts in your subsequent bidding.

(24) ♠ K 5 2   ♡ 6 3 2   ◇ A K Q 7   ♣ A K 9

Bid 3D. You have a count of 19 points in high cards. You will indicate the balanced pattern of your hand by making a second response at no-trumps.

(25) ♠ 7 3 2   ♡ A 5 3   ◇ A K Q J 6   ♣ 5 2

Bid 2D. The hand does not count 19 and therefore does not qualify for a jump-shift.

RESPONSES IN NO-TRUMPS

THE FIRST RESPONSE OF 1NT

The response of 1NT is a catch-all or utility bid and in general is not so much a positive selection as it is a rejection of other responses. With the exception of the response of 1NT to an opening bid of 1C, the bid indicates merely that the responder lacks sufficient strength to enter the two level in a lower-ranking suit, has no higher-ranking biddable suit, but does have a point count ranging from 6 to 11 points.

When the opening bid is 1H or 1S, the Stayman System treats the response of 1NT as forcing. The reasons for this are various and require some explanation. In general, there are three types of hand with which, in the typical bidding system, a responder will bid 1NT over an opening bid of 1H or 1S. Let us present an example of each. The opening bid is 1H.

(26)		(27)		(28)	
♠	A 5	♠	A 5 2	♠	K 5 2
♡	9 4	♡	9 6	♡	A 9 8
◇	K J 8 7 6 2	◇	K 10 8 6	◇	6 4 3
♣	9 5 3	♣	J 9 5 4	♣	10 6 5 2

Hand (26) is the type with which responder must bid 1NT because he lacks sufficient strength to enter the two level. If partner bids again, in the standard systems, he will probably rebid hearts, in which case his partner must choose between a pass and a bid of 3D and he will never know when to stay and when to move. With hand (27) the response of 1NT is routine and painless. No problem is involved and responder will have no regrets whatever opener does on his rebid. With hand (28) responder is urged to bid 1NT in most systems because the immediate raise to 2H may have an unduly encouraging effect on partner.

The reader will observe that on hands (26) and (28) other contracts are superior to 1NT; yet 1NT may be the last bid if the bidding system does not make it forcing. There ought to be some way to permit responder to play hand (26) at 2D and hand (28) at 2H. This is accomplished in the Stayman System by imposing on opener the obligation to bid a three-card minor suit at the two level if he has no available second suit that may be shown and does not have a six-card major. The second-round minor-suit bid cannot seriously mislead responder, since he knows that the opener's initial major-suit bid reflects a five-card suit. We shall discuss opener's rebid in the next chapter. Suffice it to say, for the time being, that 1NT cannot be passed by the opener when the auction has started in a major suit (unless, of course, the opener has a four-card major in third or fourth position, in which case he may pass).

When we treated the trump raise earlier in this chapter, we defined it as a hand counting 9—11 and containing adequate support for partner's suit. Our readers might have wondered, at that time, what a responder would do with the following hand after partner's opening bid of 1S:

(29)   ♠ 7 6 4 2   ♡ A 9   ◇ K 8 5 3   ♣ 6 5 2

The proper response is 1NT. Inasmuch as the response of 1NT is forcing, the responder may reject the immediate raise in favour of the unencouraging response of 1NT, knowing that he will be able to return to 2S on his next call. The delayed major-suit raise makes it possible for opener to identify the weak raise just as the immediate raise permits him to count on 9—11 points in responder's hand.

THE RESPONSE OF 1NT TO 1C

The responder who holds a minimum hand and who bids at the one level may have strength ranging from 6—11 points. If the responder has no four-card major suit and a balanced hand, there is little reason to pass information back and forth about suit distribution when frequently the hand will play in no-trumps—at least as far as responder is concerned. Recognizing this, the Stayman System provides that the response of 1NT to 1C represents a specific type of hand: a count of 9—11 and no four-card major. Two results are thus achieved:

(1) Opener may now move towards game when he holds 15 or more points, and he does so by bidding 2NT with 15 or 16 and 3NT with 17 or more. The rebid of 2NT is chance-giving and will be carried to 3NT by the responder when he has 10—11.

(2) Opener need not reveal four-card majors, and simplify the defence of the hand for the adversaries, because the denial of a four-card major by responder leaves little point to exploring them.

So the following hands are bid as indicated, the opening bid being 1C:

(30)   ♠ A 9 5   ♡ K 4 3   ◇ Q 8 3 2   ♣ 9 5 4
                    1C   1NT

(31)   ♠ A 9 5 4   ♡ Q 4 3   ◇ K J 5 2   ♣ 6 4
                    1C   1D

The presence of the four-card spade suit in hand (31) demands a response that will permit opener to show a spade suit secondarily if he has one, in which case the partnership will play in that suit.

Over an opening bid of 1H, what call do you make with the following?

(32)   ♠ K J 7   ♡ 5 3   ◇ Q 9 8 3   ♣ 8 6 4 2

Bid *1NT*. You have a count of 6 points which is just enough for a response. You cannot raise and have no higher-ranking biddable suit to offer.

(33) ♠ K J 7 3   ♡ 5 3 2   ◇ Q 9 8   ♣ 8 6 4

Bid *1S*. Remember always that your first thought must be to ascertain whether the partnership has a dominant major suit. Although you only have four spades, it is quite possible that partner has the same number and that, between you, you have one of the finest trump combinations: 4-4.

(34) ♠ K J 7   ♡ 5   ◇ Q 9 8 3   ♣ 10 8 6 4 3

Bid *1NT*. It hurts to have to respond in no-trumps with an unbalanced hand, but partner is bound to bid again, and if his rebid is 2C or 2D—which we shall find is his second bid the greater part of the time—we may drop him in that contract.

(35) ♠ 9 8 7   ♡ 5 3   ◇ K 9 7 6   ♣ A K 6 5

Bid *1NT*. Your count of 10 gives you a very fine hand for 1NT, but it does not qualify for a bid at the two level.

(36) ♠ K Q J   ♡ J 3   ◇ Q 9 8 3   ♣ K J 4 2

Bid *2C* (not 1NT). With a count of 12 points, you must indicate the chance-giving strength of your hand. You will probably make a second response of 2NT.

JUMP RESPONSES OF 2NT AND 3NT

As in many other systems, the responder who has so-called no-trump distribution initially bids 2NT to show 13—15 and 3NT to show 16—17 points; the response of 2NT, so used, is forcing to game if the bidder has not passed initially.

The responder promises a stopper in each of the unbid suits *and that he has neither more nor less than the point count promised.*

THE RESPONSE OVER AN INTERVENING BID

Let us suppose that your partner opens the bidding with one of a suit and that the next player bids. You have a hand with which you would have bid had there been no contention. How does the intervening over-call affect your choice of action?

The fact that the opponent has bid and has thus discharged you from the obligation to respond gives significance to your action. Since you need not bid out of courtesy, your partner may assume that you are able to make a man-sized contribution when you voluntarily enter the bidding

contest. In general, you should stay out of the auction with only 6 or
7 points. With 8 or more points, you may respond freely if your response
is at the same level as it would have been had there been no interference.

The bidding has proceeded:

North	East	South
1D	1S	?

You are South. What action do you take with the following?

(39)   ♠ 9 6   ♡ K Q 7   ◇ 9 8 2   ♣ K Q J 7 4

Bid *2C.* You were ready to make the response before East spoke, and his
bid does not alter your decision. With 13 points, you are optimistic about
the chances of game and will respond twice.

(40)   ♠ 9 6   ♡ K J 7 6 3   ◇ 9 8 2   ♣ K 7 4

No Bid. Had there been no intervening overcall, you would have bid 1H,
but you may not enter the two level with a hand of this limited strength.

(41)   ♠ K J 6   ♡ J 7 6 3   ◇ 9 8 2   ♣ K J 4

Bid *1NT.* Your response shows 9—11 points, at least one stopper in the
enemy's suit and balanced distribution.

TRUMP RAISES OVER CONTENTION

THE SINGLE RAISE

When, after partner has opened, your right-hand opponent enters the
bidding, he announces a certain amount of high-card and distributional
strength and invites his partner to put up a contest for the final declaration.

Contrary to the mandates of almost all the popular systems, the Stayman
method meets the overt threat of the adversaries with action and not with
immobility. The requirements for the direct single raise, instead of being
9—11 as ordinarily they would be if no overcall intervened, now become
6—11, thereby permitting the responder to cast some impediment in the
way of his left-hand opponent while he informs his partner that trump
consolidation is available in a hand that may be of very modest strength.
The reduced requirements for the single raise serve a dual purpose. The
single raise not infrequently presents a hindrance that inhibits further
interference; and when the raise does not silence the adversaries, the information conveyed may make it possible for the opener to outbid the
opponents either at a makable contract or at a cheap sacrifice. It must be
emphasized that the requirements for free bidding are relaxed for the suit
raise only and not for other responses. It is the security of a consolidated

trump suit that protects the weak raise against penalties, and other responses would not share that impunity. On the following hand, the bidding having been 1H—1S, responder makes a single raise:

(42)   ♠ 9   ♡ K 8 6 3   ◇ Q 9 5 4 3   ♣ 8 6 2

whereas had there been no intervening bid, he would have responded 1NT and then returned to hearts on his next call, as in this sequence:

| 1H | No Bid | 1NT | No Bid |
| 2D | No Bid | 2H | |

So, the apparent inconsistency of raising freely with a weak hand and disdaining the immediate raise when no opposition has appeared, is explained. Action and pre-emption require the quick thrust before the opponents have been permitted to marshal their strength and establish their lines of communication.

THE DOUBLE RAISE

For reasons identical to those stated above, the requirements for the immediate double raise are reduced, when contention intervenes, to enable the responder to bid the full limit of his cards at once and get the benefit of the tremendous barrier that the jump raise presents to the opponents. The raise from 1S to 3S in a typical auction:

| | 1S | 2D | 3S |

must, of course, be backed up by enough power to warrant an engagement for nine tricks; and it will ordinarily be characterized by substantial trump support and a point count of 11—12. The following two hands are typical double raises over intervention:

(43)   ♠ K J 8 5   ♡ 9   ◇ A 10 5 4 2   ♣ 9 5 4
                1S   2H   3S

(44)   ♠ Q J 8 5   ♡ 9 2   ◇ Q 10 5 4 3   ♣ A 2
                1S   2H   3S

It will be noted that the raise to three over contention is made with a hand on which, had there been no enemy action, the responder would have given a single raise or might first have bid a side suit and then followed up with a second response in opener's suit. For example, with hand (43) if the adversaries did not enter the bidding, the following sequence might take place:

| 1S | No Bid | 2D | No Bid |
| 2S | No Bid | 3S | |

The double raise in a competitive auction is a limited bid—a bid that exhausts every ounce of strength in the responder's hand. It is, if anything, a slight stretch. If the opener goes on it is because he feels that the information conveyed by the double raise is sufficient to warrant bidding game.

POINT COUNT ADJUSTMENTS BY RESPONDER

When the responder holds a hand distributed 4-4-4-1, he adds a point to the count of his hand to reflect the great partnership value of this distribution. If partner has opened the bidding in the suit held singleton by the responder, no points are counted for the shortage, but the additional point is nevertheless added for distribution. Thus, in the following hand, the responder counts 9 points, his partner having opened 1D.

(45) ♠ K J 4 2   ♡ 8 5 4 3   ◇ 6   ♣ A 10 6 2

The hand contains 8 points in high cards and 1 point for its distribution.

6

THE REBID

SINCE THE opening bid of one in a suit imposes on opener's partner the obligation to keep the bidding alive with 6 or more points, the opener will generally be called upon to bid again. If he has prepared his second bid before announcing his first, he will find no difficulty in handling any normal response. There will be occasions when his hand qualifies perfectly for one and only one bid, but much more often than not the rebid will involve him in a choice between two or more actions none of which conveys the perfect description of his hand.

The function of the rebid is to bring into sharp focus the picture of the opener's hand that is only vaguely defined in the opening bid.

REBID OVER RESPONSES AT THE ONE LEVEL

The opening bidder must rebid on the basis that he will find his partner with a minimum. Thus, if the response of 1H is made to an opening bid of 1C the opener rebids on the basis that he will find the responder with a count of 6 points and a four-card biddable heart suit. When, in turn, the responder makes a second bid, he will presume—and properly so—that if he holds strength substantially in excess of 6 points, this increment may be employed for additional progressive action. This is good common sense and good bridge: the burden of carrying the ball forward must always rest on the player whose strength has perhaps not yet been entirely consumed in the bidding sequence. So, if the bidding has proceeded—

North	East	South	West
1D	No Bid	1H	No Bid
4H	No Bid		

we can say with certainty, as to North's rebid of 4H, that the opener has a fine hand. If we translate North's bidding action into point count—a process, incidentally, that is indispensable to the expert—we may conclude that he holds at least four hearts and a point count of 20. We arrive at this result by simple subtraction:

Game at hearts requires . . . 8 hearts with 26 points
Responder's bid promised . . . *4 hearts with 6 points*
Opener promises to provide . . 4 hearts with 20 points

If responder has 13 points, for example, instead of the 6 which North has counted upon, he may now proceed to investigate slam possibilities on the basis of his knowledge that the partnership has a combined count of 33 at least. In this fashion do expert partners proceed from level to level, computing their trick-taking capacity with reliance on what previous bidding has committed to the joint stock-pile.

At the point of rebidding over a response of unspecified strength, the opening bidder will possess a hand that can be classified, as to strength, in one of the following three categories:

(1) Minimum.
(2) Chance-giving.
(3) Game-forcing.

A minimum hand is one that has the requirements of an opening bid and little to spare. Its range is 13—16. A chance-giving hand is one that will combine with partner's to produce game if partner has 9—10 points. Its range is 17—19. A game-forcing hand is one that will combine with 6 points to produce game. Its range is 20—21.

We must now address ourselves to the task of learning those rebids that reflect the strength of each classification. It will then be an easy matter to determine what choice is available to the opening bidder.

THE MINIMUM REBID OVER A RESPONSE AT THE ONE LEVEL

To a response of a new suit at the one level, the opening bidder shows a minimum hand and thereby warns that his first bid has used up all (or almost all) his point count when he makes any one of the following rebids:

(1) 1NT.
(2) Single Raise of Responder's Suit.
(3) New Suit at the One Level.
(4) Rebid of His Own Suit.
(5) New Lower-ranking Suit at the Two Level.

As we have stated before, the opener may hold a hand that is clearly a minimum and yet may have an apparent choice between two or more rebids, each of which adds further definition to his distribution and point count. Following are five hands with ready-made rebids:

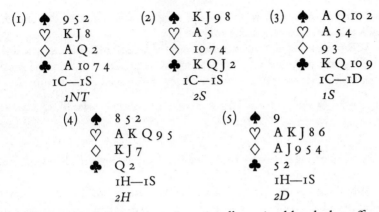

(1) ♠ 9 5 2
♡ K J 8
♢ A Q 2
♣ A 10 7 4
1C—1S
1NT

(2) ♠ K J 9 8
♡ A 5
♢ 10 7 4
♣ K Q J 2
1C—1S
2S

(3) ♠ A Q 10 2
♡ A 5 4
♢ 9 3
♣ K Q 10 9
1C—1D
1S

(4) ♠ 8 5 2
♡ A K Q 9 5
♢ K J 7
♣ Q 2
1H—1S
2H

(5) ♠ 9
♡ A K J 8 6
♢ A J 9 5 4
♣ 5 2
1H—1S
2D

In this group of examples, we intentionally omitted hands that offered a rebidding problem.

In general, it may be stated that, among the minimum rebids, such action should be selected as to permit the partnership to investigate the more desirable high-roads to game. Take the following hand:

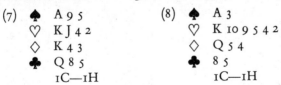

(6) ♠ 8 4 2   ♡ A Q 3   ♢ A 7 6   ♣ A 10 9 2

North opens with a bid of 1C. The point count at initial valuation is 14, a minimum. If the response is 1D, the rebid of 1NT not only defines North's hand as a minimum, but states that no four-card major is offerable. Here we have North setting the stage for a purchase at the economical contract of 1NT if South lacks sufficient strength to move towards game thereafter.

If the first response is 1H, North has a choice of rebids. He may bid 1NT or 2H. Since the most desirable high-road to game is the major suit, the rebid of 2H is preferred; this does not impose obstacles to the investigation of game at no-trumps. If South has a count of 12 or more and a balanced hand, he will select no-trumps as his second response whether the opener's rebid is 1NT or 2H. But with less than 12 points, and an unbalanced hand, the heart raise may enable the partnership to reach game. Consider the following two hands as those that might be held opposite hand (6):

(7) ♠ A 9 5
♡ K J 4 2
♢ K 4 3
♣ Q 8 5
1C—1H

(8) ♠ A 3
♡ K 10 9 5 4 2
♢ Q 5 4
♣ 8 5
1C—1H

Whether the rebid is 1NT or 2H, responder will bid 3NT with hand (7) But observe that if the rebid is 1NT, the responder who holds hand (8) will find it impossible to estimate the value of his heart length and the opportunity to reach a game may be lost.

When the opening bidder has a choice between 1NT and a new lower-ranking suit at the two level, 1NT should be preferred as the rebid, since it unequivocally marks the opener's hand as balanced and a minimum.

(9) ♠ A 5   ♥ 8 3 2   ♦ A J 10 7   ♣ K Q 5 4
1D   1S
1NT

The rebid of 1NT may be made even though the opener's hand contains a worthless three-card suit.

When the opener has an unbalanced two-suited hand or a semi-two-suiter, the bid of the second suit ordinarily does the job of describing his hand with most fidelity:

(10) ♠ 3 2   ♥ 9 5 4   ♦ A K 7 5   ♣ A Q J 2
1D   1H
2C

(11) ♠ 5   ♥ A Q 9 5 4   ♦ 10 3 2   ♣ K Q J 7
1H   1S
2C

With hand (10), opener cannot rebid 1NT because his spade suit is a worthless doubleton. With hand (11), the rebid in clubs may enable responder to visualize game; and at worst a choice of suits is offered.

MINIMUM REBID OVER RESPONSE OF 1NT

When the response of 1NT is made to the opening bid of 1C, the opener who holds 16 may bid 2NT and thus give responder the chance to bid game with 10 or 11 points. Any other minimum rebid by the opener demands a pass or a preference since the opener knows the strength and distribution of the response and denies the possession of sufficient strength to yield game. When the opener has a balanced hand, there is, of course, no particular point to moving out of no-trumps. Thus, the opener takes the action indicated below in the example hands:

(12) ♠ A 5 4 2 ♥ K 7 6 ♦ Q 3 ♣ A J 10 5   1C—1NT   No Bid

(13) ♠ A J 7 5 ♥ K 7 6 ♦ 2 ♣ K Q 5 4 3   1C—1NT   2C

(14) ♠ K Q J ♥ A 7 6 ♦ 8 5 ♣ A J 10 8 2   1C—1NT   2NT

The opener moves into 2C with hand (13) because his hand is obviously unsuited for no-trumps. Since the response of 1NT denied possession of a four-card major, opener knows that the spade suit needs no further investigation. Hand (14) is the best minimum hand—a count of 16—and South accordingly makes a chance-giving rebid of 2NT.

The response of 1NT to an opening bid of 1D may range from 6—11 points. The rebid in the sequence 1D—1NT is handled almost exactly as when the bidding has proceeded 1C—1NT, except that with only 16 points, particularly in duplicate bridge, it is unwise to move beyond 1NT. Of the six possible counts that responder may hold, only two afford a play for game, and if responder holds 6, 7, 8 or even 9 points, 2NT may go down. Furthermore, when responder holds 10 or 11 points, he will generally create a suit response rather than sound a pessimistic note with 1NT. Thus, with the following hand, the expert bids 1H as responder:

(15) ♠ K 5 4   ♡ A K 9   ◇ 7 5 4   ♣ 6 5 4 2
          1D   1H

knowing that he will be raised to 2H only when the opener has four hearts.

The response of 1NT to an opening bid of 1H or 1S is, we recall, a forcing bid, and since it would be pointless to rebid a five-card suit—rebiddability already having been communicated in the opening bid—the opening bidder rebids his suit only when it is six cards in length or a near-solid five-carder. In this way he informs the responder that his suit will make a dominant trump if partner can contribute two small cards or a singleton honour.

When the opener's hand is a balanced 5-3-3-2 distribution, the rebid is made in a three-card minor. This bid of a short minor gives space to the responder at the two level wherein he may bid a suit of his own—one that is at least five cards in length—and thus frequently place the partnership into its only sound contract. If the responder has three cards of the opener's major, he will generally return to it, but he is not forced to bid over the rebid.

This is a good time to review the principles set forth in the foregoing material. You are South, the opening bidder, in the following example hands. Select your rebid.

(16) ♠ A 5 4   ♡ K 9   ◇ A J 9 5 2   ♣ K 7 5
          1D   1NT
                    ?

(17) ♠ 9 5 4 2   ♡ A 5   ◇ K 3 2   ♣ A Q J 4
       1C   1S
       ?

(18) ♠ K 7   ♡ 8 5 4   ◇ A Q 3 2   ♣ K Q J 5
       1D   1H
       ?

(19) ♠ 9 5   ♡ A K J 6 4   ◇ 9 7 6   ♣ K Q 2
       1H   1NT
       ?

(20) ♠ 9 5   ♡ A K J 5 4   ◇ 9 7 6   ♣ K Q 2
       1H   1S
       ?

(21) ♠ A 7 6 5   ♡ K Q J 10 2   ◇ A 7   ♣ 3 2
       1H   1NT
       ?

(22) ♠ A Q 5 4   ♡ Q 9 6 2   ◇ 8   ♣ K Q J 8
       1C   1H
       ?

ANSWERS TO ILLUSTRATIVE HANDS

(16) Since responder shows a hand ranging from 6 to 11 points and would probably have made an artificial one-over-one suit bid if he held 10 or 11, game is not worth seeking, and we merely pass.

(17) Bid 2S. A typical single raise based on a minimum opening bid and four-card trump support.

(18) Bid 1NT. There is no point to entering the two level with your balanced hand. Remember that hands distributed 4-3-3-3, 4-4-3-2 and 5-3-3-2 are considered no-trump patterns.

(19) Bid 2C. The response of 1NT is forcing. The rebid is made in the better three-card minor. Responder has already been informed concerning the five-card length of North's heart suit.

(20) Bid 1NT. This 5-3-3-2 hand is well-balanced for no-trumps. If North sees any advantage to heart play, he may be counted on to return to a heart contract. He now knows your hand is distributed 5-3-3-2.

(21) Bid 2H. You have a near-solid heart suit and no three-card minor.

(22) Bid 2H. With one dominant major suit already discovered, do not bother to investigate the other. You have one bid coming to you on this minimum hand. Select the rebid that may strike pay dirt.

MINIMUM REBID OVER A RESPONSE AT THE TWO LEVEL

The response at the two level will never embarrass the opening bidder who has selected his first bid in anticipation of that possibility. If the opener wishes to make certain that he will have a rebid at the one level, the opening bid of 1C is always available to him. Depending on the distribution of his hand, the opener will make one of the following bids:

     (1) Rebid of the Suit Initially Bid.
     (2) Single Raise.
     (3) New Lower-ranking Suit at the Two Level.

(23) ♠ K 3   ♡ A Q J 5 4   ◇ 9 5 2   ♣ K 10 7
         1H   2D
         2H

With a choice between rebidding his own suit and raising partner's suit, two questions must be considered in making an election. Will a raise improperly suggest that opener has better than a minimum hand? Does the raise do the best job of indicating where game possibilities are most likely to be found? In the Stayman System, the response at the two level promises a second response. Since the opener may count on an opportunity to make another rebid, he need not fear that if he does not immediately raise responder's suit, he will never have a chance to do so. With no need to rush into a raise, an inference of strength may be drawn from the fact that opener is willing to enter the three level on his first rebid:

(24) ♠ A 9 5   ♡ A Q 8 6 3   ◇ K J 10   ♣ 3 2
         1H   2D
         3D

(25) ♠ A 10 5 4 2   ♡ K Q 3   ◇ K 5 4   ♣ 7 6
         1S   2H
         2S

Hand (24) counts 16, and is therefore the best of the minimum hands (13—16). The opener knows he can count on 12 points in responder's hand. The opening heart bid makes it unnecessary to bid the suit a second time to show five-card length; the system assures this. With a willingness to commit the partnership to game, opener shows diamond consolidation, hopeful that this information may assist responder in determining the denomination that gives the greatest promise of producing game.

With hand (25) we have an example of a rebid that temporarily conceals the fact that adequate trump support is held for partner's suit. By first bidding 2S and then showing heart support at his next rebid, the opener is able to communicate the fact of weakness without losing the opportunity to support hearts. In other systems where the responder is not obliged to respond twice, opener has to make an unhappy choice between rebidding spades—in which case he may never get a chance to support hearts—or raising hearts, in which event the responder may go on to an impossible contract because he counts on the opener for a better hand.

The new suit at the two level qualifies as a minimum rebid just as when the response is at the one level. Thus, with the following hand, the rebid of 2D is made over a response of 1S or 2C:

(26)   ♠ 5 3 2   ♡ A Q 10 5 4   ◇ A K 9 5   ♣ 6

THE STRENGTH-SHOWING REBID

When the opener's hand contains 17 points or more, he has sufficient strength to warrant bidding action that is more aggressive than he may take with hands counting 13—16. With a balanced hand and a count of 17 or 18, the initial bid of 1NT (vulnerable) will perfectly define his strength and balanced distribution in a single call, and leave to the responder the simple task of selecting a final partnership contract. But if the pattern of opener's hand (or the state of vulnerability) is not such as to permit the initial bid of 1NT, a suit bid of one must be employed to launch the bidding, preparing the stage for a rebid that will distinguish opener's hand from a minimum.

Depending on the strength and distribution of his hand, the opener shows better than a minimum hand by making one of the following rebids:

STRENGTH-SHOWING REBIDS

(1) 2NT.
(2) 3NT.
(3) Jump-raise.
(4) Jump Rebid.
(5) Jump-shift.
(6) Reverse.
(7) New Suit at the Three Level.

(1) *The Rebid of 2NT over a Suit Response at the One Level.* Since the opener may only count on responder for a count of 6 points when the response is a suit at the one level, we can calculate the point count that is required for the jump rebid of 2NT. From our Table of Production, we

learn that eight tricks at no-trumps will generally be produced by 24—25 points.

Part score of 2NT requires	.	.	24—25 points
Responder's one-over-one promises	.	.	*6 points*
Opener promises to provide	.	.	18—19 points

The hand with which opener rebids 2NT over a response at the one level may seemingly contain other possible actions:

(27) ♠ 5 2   ♡ A 10 7   ◇ A Q J 5   ♣ A K J 4
          1D   1S

The opener has a second biddable suit, but he must not bid 2C, because that rebid is one of the group that indicates a minimum opening bid. Nor can 3C be bid, for this jump-shift is forcing to game and there is no assurance that responder holds more than 6 points, in which case game should not be bid and must not be forced on responder. The rebid of 2NT emphasizes the factor of strength and does it in a precise way so that responder's decision becomes a very simple one. In general, hands that count 19—20 and are balanced distributionally are best described by a re-bid of 2NT over a response at the one level.

THE REBID OF 3NT OVER A SUIT RESPONSE AT THE ONE LEVEL

A typical 3NT rebid is: ♠ Q 2; ♡ A 10 7; ◇ A Q J 5; ♣ A K J 4. It contains a count of 22 and is balanced. Opener knows he can count on responder for a count of 6 and a four-card spade suit containing two honours. The bid of 3NT should never be made when the opener's hand contains a singleton, although it may be the ultimate selection of the partnership.

THE REBID OF 2NT OVER A SUIT RESPONSE AT THE TWO LEVEL

The responder shows 12—13 when he enters the two level in a new suit. If we apply our subtraction method to determine how much the opener would require to rebid 2NT, we should come out with 12—13 points. But we know that the opener will always have at least 13 by virtue of his opening bid. The rebid of 2NT, being a strength rebid, should not be employed to show a minimum hand by the opener. In the Stayman System, accordingly, *the rebid of 2NT is forcing to game* when made over a suit response at the two level. The bid shows 15—17 points.

THE REBID OF 2NT OVER A RESPONSE OF 1NT

Since the response of 1NT to 1C shows 9—11 points, the rebid of 2NT indicates 16—17. Inasmuch as the response of 1NT to other opening bids indicates 6—11 points, the rebid of 2NT, again based on finding a minimum, requires 19 (25—6).

REBID OF 2NT OVER A SINGLE RAISE

The single raise ranges from 9—11 points. The rebid of 2NT over the raise shows 16—17 points and a balanced hand. When the opening bid is a major, the opener's hand is almost certainly patterned 5-3-3-2. The following are typical rebids of 2NT over a single raise:

(28) ♠ A J 9 5 4   ♡ A 10 2   ◇ K J 5   ♣ K 7
     1S   2S
     2NT

(29) ♠ K 8 5 3   ♡ A Q 5   ◇ K Q J 2   ♣ K 10
     1D   2D
     2NT

The reader will observe that we frequently require a point more for the rebid than our table of production would seem to indicate. Since 24—25 will produce 2NT, it might appear that 15—16 would be enough for the rebid of 2NT. The increased requirement recognizes the likelihood that 1 or 2 points in the responder's hand may be based on suit shortages which are valueless at no-trumps.

THE JUMP-RAISE

The double raise of a major-suit bid by the responder at the one level shares the strength characteristic of its sister: the 2NT rebid. Both are rebids one trick short of game; both require 19—20 points:

(30) ♠ A 10 5 4   ♡ 7 2   ◇ A K J 9   ♣ A Q 5
     1D   1S
     3S

The jump-raise is rarely made without four trumps, for without eight trumps assured in the combined hands, it would be unsound to urge a major-suit game on the responder.

The jump-raise in a minor suit is usually made to induce the second response of 3NT. Inferentially, the opener lacks a stopper in a side suit, for he would rebid 2NT if he had all-round strength. Thus:

(31)   ♠ A 5   ♡ K J 3   ◇ K 9 5 2   ♣ A K J 10
              1C   1D
              2NT

(32)   ♠ A K   ♡ 10 2   ◇ K 8 6 3   ♣ A K J 7 4
              1C   1D
              3D

THE JUMP REBID

When the opener rebids his first suit at a level one higher than necessary, he indicates that he has a suit that requires the contribution of a doubleton or a singleton honour card to make it a dominant trump. Since the bid is one less than game, it is chance-giving and shows 19—20 points. The following is typical:

(33)   ♠ A K 2   ♡ A K J 10 8 2   ◇ Q 5   ♣ 7 4
              1H   1NT
              3H

The jump rebid in a minor is generally based on a solid six-card minor with about an Ace and a King on the side, and urges responder to engage for 3NT if plastic valuation reveals that nine tricks are likely. Thus:

(34)   ♠ K 10 3   ♡ 7 5   ◇ A K Q 8 5 4   ♣ A 8
              1D   1S
              3D

THE JUMP-SHIFT

The jump-shift is forcing to game and therefore guarantees the possession of the difference between what is needed for game and the 6 points already promised by the response at the one level. The jump may be made into the two or three level; it is a bid of one more than necessary in a new suit. The requirements for the jump-shift are 21 or more:

(35)   ♠ A K Q 2   ♡ 7 5   ◇ A K 5 4   ♣ A J 2
              1D   1H
              2S

THE REVERSE

A reverse is a series of two bids that requires responder to bid at the three level if he prefers the suit bid initially. Since nine tricks may be the ultimate engagement of the partnership, the opener must have 19—20 points opposite a response at the one level:

(36) ♠ 7   ♡ A K 10 2   ◊ A J 10 5 4   ♣ A Q 2
           1D   1S
           2H

Observe that the first suit bid is longer than the second. In a reverse consisting of the opener's bid of adjacent suits, this is *invariably* true.

NEW SUIT AT THE THREE LEVEL

When the opener bids a new suit at the three level, not as a jump-shift, but at the most economical level, he indicates a hand that counts 17—18:

(37) ♠ A K 10 8 3   ♡ 9   ◊ K 7 6   ♣ A 10 3 2
           1S   2D
           3C

The bid of a new suit at the three level is often employed as a "pre-game cue bid" to show a side-suit control before backing in with a trump raise:

(38) ♠ A K 10 7 3   ♡ K J 6 2   ◊ 9   ♣ A 10 2
           1S   2H
           3C

When North subsequently supports hearts strongly, it will be clear to South that the club bid was designed to show the Ace.

New Suit at Three Level After a Single Raise. The bid of a side suit after a single raise is the equivalent of bidding three of the suit agreed upon. It is, accordingly, chance-giving because its function is to ask responder to advance to game with a full single raise and to return to three of the first suit if the raise is a minimum. Since the major-suit raise shows 9—11, the bid of a new suit promises about 17:

(39) ♠ A 10 2   ♡ A K J 5 4   ◊ 9   ♣ Q 10 9 6
           1H   2H
           3C

The rebid of the side suit is made in preference to 3H in order to indicate to responder that consolidating high cards in the side suit, or a singleton or void, will be of particular value to the opener. The rebid of clubs, in the hand above, makes it easier for responder to appraise his few elements of strength.

Since one of the functions of expert bidding is often tactical, it is good bidding practice to use a forcing side-suit bid as a smoke screen when the opener intends to go on to game regardless of responder's second action. Thus, he may employ the bid to inhibit an opening lead, as in the following hand:

(40) ♠ K Q 10 9 5 4   ♡ A Q 3   ◇ K 5   ♣ 3 2
             1S   2S
         3C

REVALUATION BY THE REBIDDER

In the light of information revealed by the response, the opener re-assesses the point count of his hand by giving effect to the adjustments set forth in the chapter on point count and valuation. We illustrate these adjustments in the following example hands:

(41) ♠ A Q 10 4 3   ♡ K 9 5 2   ◇ A 7   ♣ 8 6
             1S   2H

The original count of the hand was 16, but on revaluation 1 point is added because the heart King increases in value through promotion.

If a point count has been taken for a shortage, the bid of that short suit by responder eliminates it as an element of strength:

(42) ♠ K   ♡ A K 5 4 3   ◇ K 7 4 2   ♣ A 9 5

The original count of 19 consists of 16 in high cards (the singleton King is worth 2 points only), 2 points for the singleton spade and 1 point for heart length. On revaluation the hand counts 18: 17 points in high cards (the promotion of the spade King offsets the deduction for being singleton) and 1 point for the fifth heart.

The opener adds 1 point to the count of his hand *on revaluation* if its distribution is 4-4-4-1:

(43) ♠ A Q 10 4   ♡ 5   ◇ A K Q 2   ♣ A J 10 7
             1D   1H

The original count was 22. The adjusted value of the hand is 21. The 2 points initially attributable to the heart shortage must be eliminated, and 1 point is added for distribution.

If your suit has been raised, adjust the value originally placed upon its long cards. Thus:

(44) ♠ K 10 5 4 3   ♡ 7   ◇ A Q 2   ♣ A J 10 5
             1S   2S

The original count was 16, no value having been given to the fifth spade. On revaluation, the hand is worth 17, the raise having increased by 1 point, the value of each spade in excess of four.

(45) ♠ Q J 9 7 6 2   ♡ A K J   ◇ 9   ♣ Q 10 3
             1S   2S

The original count was 16. The adjusted count is 18. The fifth and sixth spades were initially valued at 1 point each. The promised consolidation enhances their value 2 points.

(46) ♠ A Q   ♡ A Q J 10 5   ◇ 9 8 7   ♣ 6 4 2
         1H   2H

The original count was 16. The adjusted count is still 16. The fifth heart has already been valued at 2 points and cannot be increased.

THE EFFECT OF CONTENTION ON THE REBID

When a bid by the player on his right intervenes and thereby relieves the opener of the necessity to honour his partner's forcing response, or when opposite a pass or a non-forcing response, opener chooses to bid freely over contention, responder may assume that the opener has a message to convey additional to that communicated by his opening bid. Ordinarily, the free bid over a response at the one level marks a hand that may reasonably expect (in combination with the hand indicated by responder) to produce the announced declaration despite the fact that the opponents will have the advantage of a proven lead. To produce 1NT against a marked opening lead into a suit that is known to be held in strength by an opponent, the opener should be able to count on 22 points, and must, therefore, hold at least 16 points in a no-trump count. Since the entry into the two level often meets with penalty action, a free rebid of two, either in a new suit or in the suit opened, should be backed by a combined count of 23 or 24. Thus, with less than 17 points, opener should stay out of the bidding. For example:

(47) ♠ K J 5   ♡ 7 6   ◇ A Q 10 3 2   ♣ A 7 6
         1D   No Bid   1H   1S
         1NT

(48) ♠ A 9 3   ♡ A 6   ◇ A Q 10 3 2   ♣ Q 5 4
         1D   No Bid   1H   2C
         No Bid

THE SINGLE RAISE OVER CONTENTION

When vulnerability favours the offensive pair, the single raise over an intervening bid or double is intended to pave the way for a possible sacrifice. The opponents being vulnerable, the opener, not vulnerable, raises with the following hands:

(49) ♠ 9 5   ♡ K J 4   ◇ K Q 10 8 6   ♣ A 7 3
         1D   No Bid   1H   1S
         2H

(50) ♠ A 7 6   ♡ K 5   ◇ 9 8 4 2   ♣ A Q 7 6
         1C   1H   1S   2D
      2S

With hand (50), the raise to 2S may suffice to deter opponents from rebidding hearts which, because of the 2S bid, would now require him to
enter the three level.

We thus complete our treatment of the rebid. It is at the rebid stage
that the bidding structure of the attacking pair gets most of its definitive
lines, to which only a few last finishing touches are needed to complete
the perfect edifice of a fine bidding sequence.

7

THE SECOND RESPONSE

WHEN RESPONDER HOLDS 6—11 POINTS

IF THE opener's rebid is one that indicates a minimum hand, the responder's second action will be practically automatic within the areas of permissible bidding as set forth in our Table of Responsive Action. Thus, with a minimum hand, responder having made a co-operative response, will perhaps pass at his next bidding opportunity in the absence of a strong rebid:

(1) ♠ K J 7 6   ♡ 8 4 2   ◇ K 5   ♣ 9 6 4 2

1H	1S
1NT	No Bid

or

1H	1S
2D	*2H*

When the response of 1NT is made to an opening bid of 1H or 1S, the responder's second action may be other than a mere preference or pass, even though his first call indicated a minimum. The reader will recall that the player who opens the bidding with 1H or 1S does not customarily rebid his major if of five-card length, but may, of course, rebid a major when it is six cards in length or is a near-solid five-carder. In every other case, the opener is required to bid the better of his two minor suits (provided one of them is at least three cards long). This artificial rebid has tremendous utility. To begin with, it tells responder that he may pass if he prefers opener's three-card second suit to the revealed five-card major. So, with the following hand, the partnership reaches its best contract only by virtue of the unusual rebid:

(2) ♠ A Q 10 5 4   ♠ 9
    ♡ 7 6   ♡ J 5 4 2
    ◇ A J 10   ◇ Q 8 7 6 5
    ♣ K 10 9   ♣ A 7 6
    1S   1NT
    2D   No Bid

66

In the second place, it affords the responder bidding space within which he may offer a suit of his own which, but for the artificial rebid, might never see the light of day. For example:

	(3)		
	♠ A Q 10 5 4	♠ 9	
	♡ 7 6	♡ Q J 9 8 5 2	
	◇ A J 10	◇ K 7 5	
	♣ K 10 9	♣ 8 6 2	
	1S	1NT	
	2D	2H	

In the deal above, an excellent 2H contract is reached, but in standard systems the pair would normally play the deal in 1NT or 2S, inferior contracts both.

The artificial rebid also has the advantage of permitting the responder to distinguish between a good trump raise and a minimum one. Since responder is assured of a second response when his initial call is 1NT, he may defer his raise and thus convey the fact of its weakness. Thus:

(4)	♠ Q 9 8 5	♡ K 3	◇ Q 8 4 2	♣ 9 5 4
	1S	1NT		
	2D	2S		

Needless to say, many major-suit games may be pursued successfully by reason of opener's confidence in the strength of the immediate single raise; and conversely, the chase after hopeless games may be abandoned through the precise knowledge conveyed by the indirect single raise which frequently indicates that chance-giving action on the part of the opener would be superfluous.

ACTION OF RESPONDER WITH 12—13 OVER A MINIMUM REBID

When the responder holds 12—13 and general all-round strength, his second response will ordinarily be 2NT. With the same count and dominant support for partner's major suit, the second response will be a raise to three. In the following examples, responder indicates that game may be engaged for successfully if the opener has 15 or 16:

(5)	♠ A 10 2	♡ K J 5	◇ Q J 10 9 2	♣ 7 5
	1C	1D		
	1S	2NT		
(6)	♠ 9 8 3 2	♡ A 5	◇ K Q J 3 2	♣ 10 7
	1S	2D		
	2H	3S		

Observe that on both hands the second response at the chance-giving level is made although a lower level is available for the bid of the denomination selected. A second response of 1NT with hand (5) would erroneously suggest that responder had made a co-operative response initially and was bidding a second time under compulsion.

When the responder has initially bid at the one level, he should select for his second response a bid that unequivocally shows the strength of his hand, if such a bid is available to him. For example:

(7) ♠ K 7   ♡ Q J 10 5 4   ◊ A 7 6   ♣ J 10 2
           1C   1H
           2C   2NT

The second response of 2H would be misleading, because it would conceal the chance-giving strength of responder's hand. The rebid of hearts by the responder, being a voluntary action, would reveal 10—11 and a good suit; but with 12—13, responder should try to urge game. Thus:

(8) ♠ A 9 5   ♡ K Q J 9 8 2   ◊ 7 4   ♣ 6 3
           1C   1H
           2C   3H

When it appears from the bidding that the partnership has a dominant trump suit, the responder indicates game possibilities in the following manner:

(9) ♠ K 10 5 4   ♡ 9 7 2   ◊ A Q 7 6 2   ♣ 9
           1C   1D
           1S   3S

Observe that a second response of 2S would merely honour the one-over-one forcing rebid of 1S and would fail to reflect the strength of South's cards.

The jump rebid of a minor suit, as in the following sequence, ordinarily suggests a solid six-card minor:

(10) ♠ 10 2   ♡ Q 5   ◊ A K Q J 7 6   ♣ 9 8 2
            1C   1D
            1S   3D

and asks opener to bid 3NT with stoppers in unbid suits.

There are times when, no better bid being available, responder bids a second suit and thus understates the strength of his hand by a point or two:

(11) ♠ Q J 10 5 4   ♡ A K J 7   ◊ 5 4   ♣ 3 2
             1D   1S
             2D   2H

With no chance-giving bid that he can call upon to portray his count of 13, South does the next best thing and bids voluntarily a second time, indicating at least a count of 10 or 11.

ACTION OF RESPONDER WITH 9—11 OVER A MINIMUM REBID

We have previously stated as a general rule that the responder who holds a hand ranging in strength from 6—11 points is obliged to make one response and thereafter should bid only under compulsion or to show a preference. This principle, while ordinarily sound, is subject to a few exceptions and they occur when the responder has hands in the upper limit of the co-operative category: 9—11.

When the responder evaluates his cards at his initial call, it is, of course, with reference to a particular opening suit bid by partner. If the opener makes a minimum rebid that does nothing to enhance the value of responder's cards, the responder is governed by the general rule and either passes or shows a preference. In one case, however, where the responder is indifferent about the opener's offerings and has a good suit of his own, he may rebid the suit if he feels that it makes the best denomination for the partnership. There is a risk to this rebid by responder inasmuch as the opener will construe the second voluntary action to be mildly game-encouraging and may go on to game with 15 points. The responder should, accordingly, forgo a second bid except with hands counting 9—11. It would be nice if responder could bid twice with a weak six-carder and on a subsequent deal bid twice to indicate a very good minimum, and convey the desired message on both hands. But the responder's suit rebid cannot represent both types of hands without serious confusion. Accordingly, the responder's rebid of a suit is assigned the function of indicating a hand containing a good suit and a count of 9—11. For example:

(12) ♠ Q J 9 8 4 2 ♡ 5 ◇ A 7 6 4 ♣ 3 2
           1H   1S
           2C   2S

When the opener's rebid is 1NT, there is very little likelihood that opener will be disposed to bid again over a suit rebid by the responder. With this safeguard working for him, the responder may bid his suit a second time if it appears that suit play will make a better contract than no-trumps. He may do this with rather weak hands. Thus:

(13) ♠ Q J 9 8 4 2 ♡ Q 8 4 ◇ 9 3 2 ♣ 5
           1C   1S
           1NT   2S

In rare cases, the responder may take chance-giving action holding a count of 11 when the opener's bid and rebid are such as to suggest that the opener may hold more than a minimum, but has no strong rebid available to him. So, with the following hand, the responder makes a slight overbid:

(14)   ♠   K 10 8 3   ♡   K Q 7 6   ◇   Q 10   ♣   7 6 5

         1D   1H
         2C   2NT

When Responder's Hand Gains Strength through Revaluation. Not infrequently, the opener's rebid, though of the minimum variety, may add value to the responder's hand:

         1D   1S
         2C   ?

You hold:

(15)   ♠   K 10 9 5 4   ♡   A 3 2   ◇   5   ♣   Q 5 4 3

Opposite the opening bid of 1D, you gave no count to your singleton diamond and valued your hand at 9 points. Your partner's bid, 2C, adds quite a bit of strength to your cards. With good club consolidation, the diamond singleton is worth 2 points, and the club Queen moves up a point through promotion. On revaluation, your hand counts 12. The second response is, therefore, 3C. Take another hand. You hold:

(16)   ♠   K 10 8 5   ♡   A J 10 3 2   ◇   5 4 3   ♣   9

         1C   1H
         1S   ?

Your hand, initially valued at 9 points, has, by virtue of the rebid, gone up to 12 points, and you reflect this strength in a second response of *3S*, a chance-giving bid that, you recall, asks opener to proceed to game if he has a good minimum or better.

When Opener Rebids a Major Over the Response of 1NT. The rebid of a major suit over the response of 1NT shows a six-card suit. With the knowledge that only a doubleton is required in support of opener's suit, responder may raise the rebid with a good minimum. So:

(17)   ♠   Q 9   ♡   A 7 6 5 4   ◇   K 10 8 2   ♣   9 3

         1S   1NT
         2S   3S

When Opener Raises Responder's Major Suit. An unusual situation occurs when the opener's rebid is a single raise in that the responder is unable to estimate closely the strength of the opener's hand which may range from 14—18 points. If the opener has 17 or 18 points, a responder with 10 or

11 may have enough to produce game and must, therefore, guard against missing game by taking chance-giving action with a little less than is ordinarily required for a bid of a trick under game. Consider the following:

(18)
♠ K 10 5 4	♠ A 9 8 3 2
♡ A 9 5	♡ 3 2
◇ 2	◇ A 7 6 3
♣ A Q 8 5 2	♣ 9 7
1C	1S
2S	3S

Although he holds a good hand, the opener is not quite strong enough for the jump-raise (which would show 19—20). Since the opener's range, *when the rebid is a single raise*, is 14—18, South asks that the game try be accepted if North has 17—18 and that it be rejected if North has 14—15. With 16, at rubber bridge, he would probably bid 4S and at duplicate he would pass.

ACTION OF RESPONDER WITH 12—13 OVER MINIMUM REBIDS (CONTINUED)

With 12—13 points in hands of all-round strength, 2NT will be found to be the best second response. Some 12—13 unbalanced hands are set out below.

(19)
♠ A Q 5 4 2	♡ 9 5	◇ 8 3 2	♣ K Q 7
1D	1S		
2C	3C		

Without a heart stopper, South makes the advancing bid of 3C to give North an opportunity to contract for a no-trump game if North guards the heart suit. It is quite possible that North may be able to give a deferred raise to South's spade suit, in which case the major may prove to be the ultimate game contract.

(20)
♠ K 3 2	♡ K Q 8 4 3	◇ 9 5	♣ A 5 4
1D	1H		
1S	2NT		

Observe that the second response of 2NT is made even though the level of one is open. Only by bidding one under game is the count of 12—13 evidenced.

(21)
♠ Q 5	♡ A Q 7 6	◇ 9 7 5	♣ K J 5 4
1C	1H		
1S	3C		

Here again the strength of responder's hand is shown by a jump-raise of opener's first suit. Inferentially, South says that 3NT will make a good contract if North can stop the unbid diamond suit. The jump-raise of a minor is a chance-giving bid even when it is two tricks below the minor-suit game. In effect, the bid of 3C in the sequence above says that South has the values for 2NT, but lacks diamond protection. Since South's response looks to a no-trump game, it is treated as being equivalent to a bid of one less than game in terms of point count.

(22) ♠ A 10 7 5   ♡ K 2 ◇ K Q 8 4   ♣ 10 5 2
         1C   1D
         1H   1S

The responder properly defers his second response of 2NT in order to show a four-card major at the one level. Since the bid of 1S is forcing, responder is sure to get another opportunity to show the full strength of his hand. Major suits should be thoroughly investigated before directing the partnership into no-trump channels.

(23) ♠ A J 10 5 2   ♡ 9   ◇ A 8 4   ♣ K 9 5 2
         1H   1S
         2S   4S

North's spade raise has increased South's hand by a point, and with 14 there is no reason to place the onus of going forward to game on the opener. South should bid the game at once.

(24) ♠ A 9 5   ♡ A K 10 3 2   ◇ 9 5   ♣ 6 4 2
         1D   1H
         2D   2H

(25) ♠ 8 3   ♡ 9 5 2   ◇ A K Q J 8 4   ♣ Q J
         1S   2D
         2S   3D

With no better second response to call upon, responder may have to rebid his suit and hope that opener may carry on.

ACTION OF RESPONDER WITH 14 OR MORE OVER MINIMUM REBID

With 14 or more points, game is assured at the partnership's most favourable contract. Since every new suit by responder is forcing for at least for one round, he need not jump quickly into game. The reader will recall that major suits must be explored before no-trumps are resorted to, and, accordingly, holding a balanced hand containing a major, the first response will be a simple bid of spades or hearts. In the absence of a raise, the second response will frequently be 3NT, as with the following:

(26) ♠ A J 3 2   ♡ K Q 5   ◇ A 10 8   ♣ 9 5 3
       1C   1S
       1NT   3NT

Similarly, where the first response has been in a minor, the second response of 3NT is a logical continuation:

(27) ♠ K 3 2   ♡ 8 5   ◇ A Q J 3 2   ♣ K 10 9
       1H   2D
       2H   3NT

Since all new suits bid by responder are forcing, the responder may show the distribution of his hand at the economical one level:

(28) ♠ A Q 9 7   ♡ 3 2   ◇ K Q J 8 6   ♣ K 5
       1C   1D
       1H   1S

With a strong two-suiter, a jump response in the second suit is ordinarily the best vehicle for defining responder's hand while forcing to game:

(29) ♠ A Q 9 5 4   ♡ A K 10 6 2   ◇ 3 2   ♣ 9
       1D   1S
       1NT   3H

But a simple reverse by the responder may be temporarily employed to avoid crowding when slow exploration may be desirable:

(30) ♠ A Q J 2   ♡ A K 10 6 2   ◇ 9 5 4   ♣ 6
       1D   1H
       2C   2S

When responder holds a hand that is rigidly built and therefore designed for play at only one or two denominations, he wastes no time after his initial response but bids game at once:

(31) ♠ K Q J 8 4 3   ♡ Q J 10 9 5 4   ◇ 2   ♣ Void
       1D   1S
       2D   4H

(32) ♠ A K Q 9 8 6 2   ♡ 8   ◇ Q 3 2   ♣ 9 5
       1H   1S
       2C   4S

In example (31) the opener is given a choice of suits at the four level.

The bid of a second suit by the responder may be gainfully employed to give the opener ample room to show the precise nature of his hand, particularly where his bid and rebid may not have sufficed for that purpose.

(33) ♠ 7 ♡ K J 2 ◇ A Q 9 5 3 ♣ A 7 3 2
  1S 2D
  2H 3C

If North rebids 3H, South will proceed to the heart game. Nothing is lost by giving North room to disclose the important characteristics of his hand. It is by making these fine waiting bids that experts are able to select suit denominations when they make the best contracts, and no-trumps when a dominant suit is lacking.

SECOND RESPONSE OVER A STRENGTH REBID

To show a hand better than minimum, the opener may rebid 2NT or 3NT; he may skip a level of bidding; he may reverse; or he may bid a new suit at the three level. He may urge game or command it. If game is forced, responder is charged with the obligation to define his distribution and high cards precisely so that the partnership may select its best game contract and go on to slam in proper cases.

SECOND RESPONSE OVER A REBID OF 2NT

When the opener's rebid is merely chance-giving, responder's task is simple:

(34) ♠ K J 5 4 ♡ K J 2 ◇ 8 3 ♣ 10 9 5 3
  1D 1S
  2NT 3NT

Responder adds his 8 points to opener's 19 and bids 3NT, being certain that the partners possess 27—28 points.

(35) ♠ K Q 5 4 ♡ 9 3 2 ◇ 7 6 5 ♣ J 8 3
  1H 1S
  2NT No Bid

Since the partnership holds 25—26 points only, game must be rejected. With most of the points in one hand, and very few in the other, 26 will rarely produce a no-trump game.

On the way to a no-trump game, responder should check back with the opener and offer him a choice between major-suit play and no-trumps:

(36) ♠ Q 5 4   ♡ A 7 6 3   ◊ Q 8 7 6   ♣ 10 5
    1S   1NT
    2NT   3S

(37) ♠ 9 5   ♡ K 7 6   ◊ A Q 10 9 2   ♣ Q J 4
    1H   2D
    2NT   3H

The opener, opposite responder in hand (36), knows that the delayed spade raise is not a very stout one, for otherwise South would have responded 2S initially. Nevertheless, North may prefer to play the hand at spades, and a choice between 3NT and 4S is thus offered to him. Note that *the raise of opener's suit* after opener rebids 2NT is a game acceptance.

When the responder simply rebids a suit that he bids initially at the one level, he says that there is no game in the partnership and demands that the opener pass:

(38) ♠ K J 10 9 6 3   ♡ 7 3   ◊ 10 5 4   ♣ 9 2
    1H   1S
    2NT   3S

Similarly, when responder bids a suit after an initial response of 1NT, he urges that he remain undisturbed at that auction:

(39) ♠ 9 5 4   ♡ 8   ◊ K 7 2   ♣ Q J 10 8 6 5
    1H   1NT
    2NT   3C

unless partner has exceptional consolidation for that suit.

SECOND RESPONSE OVER A REBID OF 3NT

When the opener bids 3NT on his rebid, any move by the responder indicates that suit play is preferable, or that slam may be in the cards. When the responder moves into a major-suit game, he merely states that the partnership is apparently better off at suit play; and the opener must pass:

(40) ♠ K 9 5   ♡ J 10 9 8 6 4   ◊ Q 3 2   ♣ 6
    1C   1H
    3NT   4H

When the responder moves out of 3NT into four of a minor, he indicates his interest in a minor-suit game or—particularly at duplicate—a slam. Once the partnership has reached game in a constructive bidding sequence, no bid short of game may thereafter be passed. Accordingly, do not make things worse by bidding 4D with hands like the following:

(41) ♠ 9 6 2   ♡ 8 5   ◇ K J 10 9 5 4   ♣ Q 7
       1C   1D
       3NT   *No Bid*

SECOND RESPONSE OVER A JUMP REBID, RESPONSE HAVING BEEN MADE AT THE ONE LEVEL

The jump rebid, when made over a response at the one level, shows a count of 19—20 and urges partner to proceed to game if he has a good minimum hand. Inasmuch as opener indicates a six-card suit when he bids it three times (as when he jump rebids), responder may support the opener with as little as a worthless doubleton when he has enough strength to accept the chance-giving offer:

(42) ♠ K Q 5 4   ♡ 9 4   ◇ K J 6 5   ♣ 9 7 6
       1H   1S
       3H   *4H*

or may bid 3NT with scattered strength and a singleton of partner's major suit:

(43) ♠ A 7 6 3   ♡ 10   ◇ K 10 5 4   ♣ Q J 3 2
       1H   1S
       3H   *3NT*

The opener may properly construe the second response of 3NT as a denial of two-card support for his major suit. It is incumbent on the responder to raise with a doubleton if he decides to act on opener's offer of game.

It is proper for the responder to rebid a good six-card spade suit, if his hand permits a second action.

(44) ♠ K J 10 9 6 5   ♡ 7   ◇ K 3 2   ♣ 8 5 4
       1H   1S
       3H   *3S*

It is quite possible that opener may be able to provide adequate support for a suit that can be emphasized by the responder. Mere dissatisfaction with opener's suit is no justification for further responsive action, however.

When the jump rebid is in a minor, the responder is urged to bid 3NT with an intermediate or good minimum hand and stoppers in unbid suits.

Since responder is not bound to make a second response, a second suit bid may be construed as strength-showing.

(45) ♠ Q J 10 8 6 3 ♡ A 9 5 ◇ 6 ♣ J 10 2
          1D   1S
          3D   3S

When the responder has more than 9 points in high cards, he generally should take some constructive action over a jump rebid.

SECOND RESPONSE OVER A JUMP REBID, RESPONSE HAVING BEEN MADE AT THE TWO LEVEL

Since the responder who bids a new suit at the two level as his initial action is required to bid again, the jump rebid becomes an *absolute force* to game in the Stayman System. If the opener has a good hand and the responder holds 12—13, it is clear that a game must be reached. This being so, the responder's second call involves problems of selection only.

Inasmuch as the jump rebid urges game at opener's suit, responder should raise when he has two or more cards to offer in support of the opener. (We omit from present consideration those hands with which responder must be concerned about a slam, leaving them for later treatment.) So the raise is given or refused, depending on responder's ability to provide adequate trump support:

(46) ♠ 8 5 ♡ A K 8 5 3 ◇ K J 6 ♣ 10 9 2
          1S   2H
          3S   4S

The bid of a second suit at the three level suggests the lack of a stopper in the unbid suit and impliedly urges opener to bid 3NT if he guards that suit:

(47) ♠ 9 5 ♡ K Q 5 4 ◇ 3 2 ♣ A Q J 7 2
          1D   2C
          3D   3H

(48) ♠ Q J 2 ♡ K Q 5 4 ◇ 8 7 ♣ A 10 9 3
          1D   2C
          3D   3NT

With hand (48), the second response of 3H would serve no purpose except to deceive opener into thinking the partnership lacked a spade stopper.

SECOND RESPONSE AFTER A JUMP-RAISE

Since the jump-raise of a major-suit bid at the one level indicates 19—20 in the opener's hand and strongly urges game, responder should go on when he has any reason for optimism. A count of 8 or better will generally combine with a jump-raise to produce game. The following is a typical hand:

(49) ♠ K Q 8 3 2 ♥ 9 5 4 ♦ K 7 6 ♣ 8 5

1C	1S
3S	4S

With a four-card suit only, but with *delayed* stoppers in unbid suits (where four top card tricks may have to be lost), responder should bid 3NT rather than four of the major:

(50) ♠ K J 5 3 ♥ Q J 7 ♦ 7 5 ♣ Q 10 9 2

1D	1S
3S	3NT

But since the jump-raise will almost invariably contain four-card trump support, responder should not bid 3NT merely to cry out about the shortage of his trump suit.

The jump-raise of the response of one diamond is not forcing, but is strongly invitational:

(51) ♠ A 6 3 ♥ 6 5 ♦ K Q 10 8 4 ♣ 6 4 2

1C	1D
3D	3S

(52) ♠ 9 5 4 ♥ 10 8 7 ♦ K J 8 6 ♣ Q 9 5

1C	1D
3D	No Bid

The bid of 3S with hand (51) is an acceptance of opener's chance-giving raise but asks opener to supply the missing heart stopper. Since the opener has not bid 1S over the response of 1D, it is extremely unlikely that he will support responder's spade bid, but if he does, responder will now carry on to the sound diamond game.

The double raise over an initial response of 2H places the partnership in game. Any subsequent action by responder must be interpreted as a slam try. The double raise of a minor-suit response at the two level presents responder with questions relating to slam bidding also, and we shall discuss these situations in a chapter devoted to constructive bidding beyond game.

SECOND RESPONSE OVER A JUMP-SHIFT

When a jump-shift is made opposite a response at the two level, the partnership will almost invariably be involved in probing for slam because there is no necessity for crowding action by the opener when he knows that responder will bid again over a normal rebid. This being so, the responder should concern himself with revealing characteristics of suit length, possession of key cards in opener's suits and side-suit controls.

If the first response has been at the one level, however, the jump-shift is the only device by which opener may force responder to bid until game is reached. If responder's first bid has defined his hand with near-accuracy, responder must thereafter confine his action to distributional definition only. When the jump-shift occurs at the two level, the second response of 2NT is a sign of great weakness and does not guarantee a stopper in the unbid suit.

(53) ♠ K J 2   ♡ Q J 4 3   ◇ 8 6 5 4   ♣ 6 3
              1D   1H
              2S   2NT

but a second response of 3NT does promise such a stopper.

If responder has adequate support for one of opener's suits, he should show it rather than rebid a fair five-carder of his own, but when opener has offered two minor suits, it is generally best for responder to rebid a major before showing a mild preference.

(54) ♠ K Q 10 8 6   ♡ Q 6 4   ◇ J 8 3   ♣ 3 2
              1D   1S
              3C   3S

But if responder has important cards in consolidation of opener's minor suit, their disclosure must be considered of first importance:

(55) ♠ K 10 9 6 2   ♡ 8 5   ◇ K Q 3   ♣ 8 6 4
              1D   1S
              3C   3D

When the responder holds a balanced hand appreciably better than a minimum, a jump response into 3NT is extremely informative and may enable opener to visualize a slam:

(56) ♠ K 10 6   ♡ A J 8 3   ◇ Q J 5   ♣ 8 3 2
              1C   1H
              2S   3NT

With dominant trump support, the responder raises, and the number of raises will depend on the general strength of his hand:

(57)   ♠ K 10 8 6   ♡ A 9 5 4   ◇ Q J 2   ♣ 6 3

1H	1S
3C	4H

Since the jump-shift over a response at the one level shows a minimum of 21 points, the responder with 11 or 12 must make some slam move, particularly when he holds adequate support for one of opener's suits.

When the responder holds a solid suit of his own, he may jump his response over the jump-shift. This unusual bid is made on a hand of this type:

(58)   ♠ 9 2   ♡ A K Q J 8 4   ◇ 7 6   ♣ 10 5 2

1D	1H
3C	4H

It will obviously be of tremendous importance for the opener to know that responder's suit will yield six tricks without loss. Frequently, on the basis of this information, opener may be able to go on to slam.

SECOND RESPONSE OVER A REVERSE OR NEW SUIT AT THE THREE LEVEL

Since a reverse shows about 19—20 points, the responder with a balanced hand and stoppers in the unbid suits should bid 2NT to show 9—10 points, and 3NT with greater strength.

A reverse over a response at the one level, though strength-showing, is not forcing. The opener may, therefore, construe any second response other than a preference as advancing:

(59)
♠ 8		♠ A Q 7
♡ A K 7 4		♡ 9 7 5
◇ A Q 10 9 3		◇ K J 6
♣ A 9 5		♣ 8 7 6 2
1D		1NT
2H		2S
3NT		

(60)
♠ K 5 4		♠ A Q 7
♡ A K 7 4		♡ 9 7 5
◇ A Q 10 9 3		◇ K J 6
♣ 5		♣ 8 7 6 2
1D		1NT
2H		2S
3D		4D
5D		

Having denied a biddable spade suit with his first response, the responder indicates he is willing to proceed to game and can offer spade stoppers.

The bid of a new suit at the three level by the opener (when it is not a jump rebid) occurs only when the first response has been at the two level. This sequence is, accordingly, forcing to game and the responder's problems are of selection only. He will have to bid again and it is important, in the narrow confines of one bidding level, that he respond in such a way that the contract of 3NT will not be viewed longingly by the partnership in a backward glance. The following hands present problems of selection as the responder will generally meet them:

(61)　♠　9 5　　♡　A K 10 8 3　　♢　A 7 6　　♣　9 5 4
　　　　　　　　　　1S　　　　　2H
　　　　　　　　　　3C　　　　　3D

(62)　♠　8 5　　♡　A Q 8 7 6　　♢　9 8 5　　♣　K Q 2
　　　　　　　　　　1S　　　　　2H
　　　　　　　　　　3C　　　　　3H

With hand (61) the bid of 3D leaves room for opener to support hearts and yet shows the diamond stopper at the same time, thus permitting opener to select the best game contract for the partnership.

With this we consider the treatment of lower-level bidding finished and we go on to a detailed discussion of no-trump bidding.

8

THE OPENING BID OF 1NT

THE OPENING bid of 1NT is one of the most respected weapons in the arsenal of the offensive pair. Even when the bid requires no greater strength than an opening suit bid, the initial no-trump call somehow cows the adversaries and keeps them silent. Traditionally, the initial bid of 1NT is a hand of more than nominal opening strength. In those systems that employ the 4-3-2-1 count, as does ours, the requirements are generally stated to be 16—18, and when the bid of 1NT carries the authority of so much count, there is sufficient reason for the opponents to lean back in their chairs and ponder only about what suit to open against the final contract. For with massed strength in one hand, and the other partner an unknown force to be reckoned with, the chances of scoring game against a strong 1NT opening bid are extremely slight.

There are, of course, certain disadvantages to the opening bid of 1NT. Consuming, as it does, the entire bidding space of the one level, it makes approach bidding all but impossible. There is also the danger that the opening may be exposed to severe penalties if the opponents possess the major share of the remaining high cards. But this is a hazard that can be discounted, not because it does not exist, but because it lurks in every decision to embark on a bidding journey. Certainly the risk in bidding is warranted by the game or slam bonus which is the bidder's objective. The opening bid of 1NT has great intimidating value and the barrier set up against the opponents is difficult to surmount because it involves a substantial risk for the player who is bold enough to challenge for possession of the bidding field.

The establishment of 16—18 as the requirement for the opening bid of 1NT recognizes several factors. The range is not an accident; as a matter of fact, if one accepts the doctrine that the bid should be safeguarded by strength, the range of 16—18 follows logically in the light of the function it discharges in an integrated bidding system.

In spite of the fact that there is a gap in the normal bidding system which is filled in by fixing the range of the opening no-trump bid at 16—18, there is much to be said for establishing its strength as 12—14. At first blush, it may seem that a bid of 1NT with a hand no stronger than an opening suit bid of one is insupportable. But on analysis, many sound reasons may be discovered to buttress the claims of those who hold it to be a very effective bidding tool.

As against the argument that it exposes the bidder to serious penalty is the answer that the bid makes contention difficult for the opponents, who must step into the auction at the two level. The adversary who sits to the left of an opening no-trump knows that if he bids he may find himself caught between a sledge-hammer and an anvil, and the havoc may be tremendous. If he bids, he faces disaster; if he passes, he may be surrendering with a hand that might yield game. The opponent to the right of the opener is no better off. Even when the responder has passed the bid of 1NT, there is no assurance that he does not hold 11 or 12 points, in which case the defenders will expose themselves as badly if they read his silence as weakness.

The Stayman System takes a position in the centre of the two popular standards by advocating the use of either or both. Not vulnerable, the requirements may be set at 12—14; vulnerable, 16—18. With this dual range, you may enjoy the advantages of the weak no-trump as a barrier when the risks of penalty are slight; and take refuge in the strong no-trump when punishment may be severe.

It is our belief that there is much to be said for the employment of either standard throughout the system to the exclusion of the other, and we urge the reader to use the no-trump he feels is best for his style and temperament. Another logical compromise would be to use the weak no-trump at match-point play where a bottom on one board is offset by a top on another regardless of the swing in terms of aggregate points; and to use the weak no-trump or strong no-trump according to vulnerability when aggregate points govern the play.

If we had to choose one range to the exclusion of the other, we should select the weak no-trump as the more effective and the no-trump best designed to give mobility to the offensive pair.

In the presentation of the material that follows, it would be confusing constantly to jump from the weak to the strong no-trump and attempt to give the requirements for the opening bid, the response, the rebid, etc., in terms of both. For the sake of clarity, we shall devote ourselves to the strong no-trump alone, although the same bidding principles and technique apply to both. Certain simple adjustments must be made if the weak no-trump is used and we dispose of them now.

The range of the weak no-trump, 12—14, is 4 points lower than the strong no-trump, 16—18. Since we shall be dealing exclusively with the

16—18 no-trump in the following pages, we ask our readers to translate point count requirements into the lighter no-trump by adding 4 points to the strength demanded of the responder for the actions taken by him. For example, when we state that the responder requires 9 points for a certain bid, the reader may properly assume that 13 are needed for the identical action if the weak no-trump is being used. For purposes of amplification, we publish tables showing the point count requirements for all bids made in response to or in connection with an opening bid of 1NT and we state the requirements in terms of weak no-trump openings and strong ones. These tables appear at the end of Chapter 11.

DISTRIBUTIONAL REQUIREMENTS

Any hand that is balanced qualifies for the opening bid of one no-trump. We may accordingly employ the bid with the following hand patterns: 4-3-3-3; 4-4-3-2; 5-3-3-2. Some variation is permissible when the hand contains a five-card suit, although the 5-3-3-2 distribution is a very favourable one for no-trump play.

The following are mostly typical opening bids of 1NT:

(1) ♠ A Q 5 4   ♡ A 6 2   ◇ K J 5   ♣ A 7 2   (18)

Here is a classical hand with all suits guarded and the most balanced hand pattern. Although the hand is a maximum in terms of high cards, it has poor distribution for suit play. In other words, its entire strength lies in its high cards.

(2) ♠ K Q 9 5   ♡ K J 10 2   ◇ K 9   ♣ K Q J   (18)

Do not hesitate to bid 1NT merely because your hand contains two four-card majors. If there is a four-four fit in spades or hearts, future bidding will reveal it. Observe that 1 point is deducted because the hand is Aceless.

(3) ♠ 9 5 4   ♡ A Q 10   ◇ A K 9 5   ♣ A 4 2   (17)

The possession of one worthless three-card suit is permissible. If a doubleton is held, it should be as good as K x, although many experts reduce this to Q x when the hand otherwise qualifies for the bid. (*NOTE*: Not vulnerable, the hand may even contain a worthless doubleton as:

(4) ♠ 9 5   ♡ A 9 5 4   ◇ K Q 8 3   ♣ A 10 8   (13)

but the bid of 1NT vulnerable should provide at least Q x or x x x in the weakest suit.)

(5) ♠ K 7   ♡ A J 5 4   ◇ K Q 8 6 3   ♣ A 10   (18)

Bid 1D, not 1NT. With a 5-4-2-2 distribution, there are many advantages to suit play that should not be obscured in an opening bid of 1NT. Notice that the rebid of 2H (over any normal response) is a reverse in adjacent suits, and this bid as well as no-trumps will be available for a strength rebid. There is no prohibition against the bid of 1NT with 5-4-2-2 distribution, but in general the suit bid will bring better results.

(6) ◇ 10 8 5 2   ♡ 9 6 4 3   ◇ A K   ♣ A K Q (16)

Bid 1C. With two suits containing no stoppers, the hand should be opened with a suit bid. The opening bid of 1NT vulnerable guarantees high cards *in three suits at least*; not vulnerable, this requirement may be occasionally honoured in the breach.

(7) ♠ A   ♡ K J 10 5   ◇ A Q 4 3   ♣ K 5 4 3 (17)

You may not bid 1NT with a singleton. You must first explore for a suit fit in order to capitalize on your fine trump distribution. You will, of course, fall back on no-trumps if no dominant trump suit is uncovered.

(8) ♠ A 5 4   ♡ K Q 6   ◇ A Q 9 4 3   ♣ K 10 (19)

Bid 1D. Do not bid 1NT when you have more than 18 points. No-trump bidding is precise and a departure from your system, even by a point, may cost you a game or slam.

The opening bid of 1NT is not proscribed simply because a hand contains a five-card major; but since the major-suit game is the best high-road to game, the suit opening bid should be made if the hand provides a definitive rebid. For example:

(9) ♠ A Q 9 5 4   ♡ A 7 6   ◇ K J 5   ♣ K 10 (18)

Bid 1S. If partner responds, no bidding problem exists for the opener; and if partner passes 1S, the partnership will probably be in its best contract.

(10) ♠ A Q 9 5 4   ♡ K 7 6   ◇ K 10 5   ♣ K 10 (16)

Bid 1NT. The opening bid of 1S is not made with this hand because if responder has a count of 10 or 11 points, he may be able to bid no more than 1NT: in which case opener will be unable to make a strength rebid and a game may be missed. The opening bid of 1NT covers the gap.

The reader will discover that his most exact bidding sequences will be generated by the opening of 1NT and it is, accordingly, one of his bidding tools that should be treated with great affection.

9

NO-TRUMP RESPONSES AND LATER REBIDS

THE REASONS for the popularity of no-trump bidding are not far to seek. The opening *suit bid* is a bid of very wide range, and imposes on the responder the difficult task of defining his own hand within the bidding limits imposed by the combined power of his own cards and the uncertain power of his partner's. When the opening bid is 1NT, however, the responder leans back in his rocking-chair, and, at a glance, is able to decide within very narrow limits what the combined hands will produce. To put the case simply, the responder, opposite a suit bid, has no immediate way of knowing whether his partner's suit is three cards in length or seven; and whether his point count is 13 or 22. Opposite 1NT, only a Queen represents the margin of possible variance.

Since the upper and lower limits of the opening bid of 1NT are immutably fixed by the partnership, it is comparatively easy for responder to make certain decisions. He may have bidding problems of a minor nature, and, with a weak hand, he may have to decide whether his pair is better off at no-trumps or at two of a suit. He will face this decision only when he holds a five-card suit. With no suit longer than four cards, there is no good reason for him to think that he can provide a suit that will play a trick better than no-trump. With a six-card suit, on the other hand, the chances of the opener doing better at no-trumps than the responder at his suit are very slim—so much so that we state *as an absolute rule* that the responder must bid his suit when, as in Stayman, his system permits him to play the hand at a part-score.

When the responder holds hands where game is a virtual certainty, his problems are again limited to those of selection only, but the steps he must take are uncomplicated, as we shall see shortly.

In this chapter, we shall confine ourselves to the treatment of responder's hands when game, from his point of view, is either definitely out or definitely in. (We shall discover that in rare cases, opener may succeed in changing responder's mind about the possibility of game, but generally the opener will rely on responder's disclaimer of game and leave him at a comfortable part-score.)

THE RESPONSE OF 2D, 2H OR 2S

The response of 2C is artificial in the Stayman System and is generally known as the Stayman Convention. Our next chapter deals exclusively with this.

Since the opener is marked with a maximum count of 18, composed of at least 16 points in high cards, the responder who holds less than 8 points must rule out the desirability of game. This being so, the sole question facing the responder is: "Shall I bid or pass?" In the Stayman System, the responses of 2D, 2H or 2S demand a no bid from the opener unless certain exceptional circumstances prevail. For practical purposes, the responder may assume that his bid will be the last one in his side's voluntary offensive.

When responder's distribution is 4-3-3-3, 4-4-3-2, or even 4-4-4-1, the chances are that the opener is as well off at 1NT as responder would be in a suit—and he may be better off. It is true that with two or three suits of four-card length, there is more than a little likelihood that a four-four suit fit exists somewhere; but the chances of finding it in one random response are not great enough to warrant raising the contract. With a count of 7 points or less, the partnership possesses 25 at most, and with most of the strength in one hand, 25 will rarely produce game. With the following hands, the responder passes opposite an opening of 1NT:

(1) ♠ K 10 5 2   ♡ K 9 5   ◇ J 6 2   ♣ 5 4 3 (7)

(2) ♠ K 5 4 3   ♡ 9   ◇ Q J 7 5   ♣ J 10 8 5 (7)

When the responder has a five-card suit, he should generally pass with very weak hands, his one hope being that the opponents will slumber and fail to take penalty action. Since, with no strength, it is apparent that any contract is doomed to defeat, it is pointless to make a call the effect of which may be to alert the defenders to the possibility of imposing a penalty. Remember that one opponent has already passed and only one remains to reckon with if responder also passes. But, if responder bids, both adversaries remain in the bidding contest. So, with the following hand, responder passes:

(3) ♠ A 8 6 5 4   ♡ 9 8 2   ◇ 7 6 5   ♣ 5 4

There is no point in bidding with a worthless hand. If one no-trump is doubled you will bid because your fourth and fifth spades will probably yield tricks at spades and not at no-trumps. But wait until the axe falls before crying for the casket.

Of course, with unusual distribution, even a weak hand will produce tricks in combination with one which virtually guarantees support. So, it is proper to respond with hands like this:

(4) ♠ Q 10 8 4 2   ♡ J 10 9 5   ◊ 9 8   ♣ 4 3
　　　　　1NT　　　　　　2S

When the responder's hand contains a count of 6 or 7, a bid should always be made if the hand is unbalanced:

(5) ♠ K 10 8 4 2   ♡ 2   ◊ 9 8 5 4   ♣ A 9 5
　　　　　1NT　　　　　2S

With 5-3-3-2 distribution and a count of 6 or 7, a pass should be preferred if it is likely that the suit will be brought in at no-trumps; otherwise a bid is the sounder course.

Holding a six-card suit, the bid is always to be preferred. In the first place, the partnership may well make eight tricks with the dominant trump suit. Secondly, even when the hand does not make, the penalty will not be great:

(6) ♠ 9 8 7 6 4 2   ♡ A 7 6   ◊ 5 4 3   ♣ J
　　　　　1NT　　　　　　2S

As prevously stated, the response of 2D, 2H or 2S commands a pass from the opener except in unusual circumstances. In spite of the responder's request that he be permitted to play the deal at a part-score, the opener may raise responder if:

(A) He has a maximum hand and A K x, A Q x or K Q x in partner's suit.

(B) He has a maximum no-trump and a four-card fit for partner's major suit response.

There is, accordingly, always a possibility that the opener will raise to three, but this is the worst fate that can befall the responder since the opening bidder is prohibited from taking game action over a sign-off. Below are examples of hands with which the opener raises a response at the two level:

(7) ♠ A 9 5   ♡ Q 5 4   ◊ A K 7   ♣ A J 4 2   (18)
　　　　　1NT　　　　　2D
　　　　　3D

The diamond raise informs the responder that the suit is, for all practical purposes, a solid one if responder holds *any* high honour. With a hand like the following, responder would, of course, go on to game.

(8) ♠ A 7   ♡ 9 5   ◇ Q 8 6 5 4 2   ♣ 7 5 4
        1NT   2D
        3D   3NT

(9) ♠ K 10 7 5   ♡ A Q   ◇ A 7 6 5   ♣ K J 4 (17)
        1NT   2S
        3S

Note that the opener, with hand (9), may value his hand for spade play at 19.

(10) ♠ A 7 6   ♡ K Q 7   ◇ A 10 9 8   ♣ A 9 5 (17)
        1NT   2H
        2NT

The rebid of 2NT, as in hand (10), is a declaration by the opener that his hand is a maximum and qualifies for a raise to 3H, but proclaims that the raise is the three-card control type. Note that the requirements for the raise are fulfilled: *a maximum no-trump and two of the top three heart honours.* If responder now bids 3H, opener will not disturb him. The unusual rebid of 2NT is designed to permit responder to make a choice of final contracts according to the structure of his hand. In the following examples, the responder is able to make a sound election by reason of the precise information conveyed in the rebid:

(11) ♠ A K 7   ♠ Q 9 8 6 3 2
     ♡ A 5 4   ♡ 9 3
     ◇ K J 7 5   ◇ 10 9 6
     ♣ K 8 4   ♣ 9 5
        1NT   2S
        2NT   3S

(12) ♠ A 5 4   ♠ 9
     ♡ K Q 8   ♡ J 10 9 5 4
     ◇ A J 5   ◇ K 7 6 4 2
     ♣ A 10 8 5   ♣ 9 2
        1NT   2H
        2NT   4H

FREE RESPONSES AT THE TWO LEVEL

As we have seen, the responder shows a lack of interest in game when he responds 2D, 2H or 2S. The meaning of his response is not altered in that respect if an overcall intervenes, but there are certain inferences the opener may draw that are different from those that would be warranted had the opponent remained silent. He knows the responder is not bidding in order to take the 1NT out of trouble, because the opponent's bid has already accomplished that. Therefore, the responder's action may be construed as at least a willingness to contest a part-score. This being so, it is almost a certainty that game exists for the opener if his was a maximum no-trump with dominant major-suit trump support, or two of the top three cards in responder's suit. Nevertheless, opener handles the response in the same manner as he would have had there been no contention. Responder will almost certainly carry on the game:

(13) ♠ A 9 5   ♥ K Q 4 3   ♦ A J 7 5   ♣ A 2
      1NT   2C   2H   No Bid
      3H

If the responder has 8 or more points, the suit response at the two level cannot be made; with that amount of strength game possibilities must be investigated. We shall discover that there are chance-giving methods available to the responder who holds 8—9 points; and with 10 or more, the responder will, of course, make a bid that cannot be dropped short of game, since the partnership certainly possesses 26 at the least. Suffice it to say, for the present, that the response of 2D, 2H or 2S, whether in competitive bidding or not, is an unqualified denial of game from the reponder's point of view.

THE RESPONSE OF 2NT

The responder shows a count of 8—9 and no four-card major suit by responding 2NT. This response requests the opener to proceed to a no-trump game with 17—18 points.

When we come to the Stayman Convention, we shall demonstrate how the responder, with intermediate or game-going strength, institutes a sequence that will check on the major when he holds four hearts or four spades. The response of 2NT states that the investigation of major suits would be profitless.

THE 2NT RESPONSE OVER CONTENTION

When the responder has 8—9 points, he should take one of the following three actions over an intervening overcall. (We assume that the penalty double does not appear attractive on the hands we now consider.)

        (1) A response in a suit at the two level.
        (2) A forcing bid at the three level.
        (3) A response of 2NT.

With a singleton in the opponent's suit and a good major, the slight stretch to three of the major is preferable to 2NT:

(14) ♠ K J 9 5 4   ♡ J 5 4   ◇ 9   ♣ Q 10 3 2
      1NT   2D   3S

or the opponent's suit may be bid in lieu of three of a major when responder has hearts and spades.

Two no-trumps is generally best with balanced distribution:

(15) ♠ K J 9 5 4   ♡ K 5   ◇ J 3 2   ♣ 10 9 7
      1NT   2D   2NT

The fact that the responder's right-hand opponent inserts a bid does not alter the responder's course very much. If the responder thinks that penalty action will be as rewarding as the contract that appears to be makable, he will double rather than bid, particularly when the opponents are vulnerable and he is not.

(16) ♠ 7 6 5   ♡ K 5 4   ◇ K Q 5 4 2   ♣ 9 5
      1NT   2C   2NT

The reader will note that the response of 2NT, with hand (16), is made although responder holds no club stopper. With 9 points, responder must take chance-giving action and he depends upon the opener to provide the stoppers.

THE RESPONSE OF 3NT

With 10 or more points and not enough strength to be concerned about a slam, the responder's only job is to steer the partnership into the best game contract. When the responder has four or more cards in a major suit, he will probably employ the Stayman Convention. Since the slam zone begins at about 33, the responder with 13 points definitely rules out a slam and simply proceeds to game:

(17) ♠ A 9 5   ♡ K 10 3   ◇ Q 8 4 2   ♣ A 7 6
      1NT   3NT

THE RESPONSE OF 3NT OVER CONTENTION

As a general rule, when the responder has a choice between the response of 3NT and three of a minor, the bid of 3NT should be reinforced by some strength in the suit that will probably be attacked, unless, of course, responder's suit is solid and his hand is so strong that defeat at no-trumps is only remotely possible:

(18)   ♠   8 7 6   ♡   10 3   ◇   K Q 8 5 4 2   ♣   K 5
         1NT   2C   *3NT*

(19)   ♠   A 9 5   ♡   10 3 2   ◇   K Q 8 5 4 2   ♣   9
         1NT   2C   *3D*

THE CHOICE BETWEEN 2NT OR 3NT AND A PENALTY DOUBLE

Whether game is doubtful or a sure thing from the responder's point of view, an overcall requires that he decide whether to try for game or for a penalty. Needless, perhaps, to say whatever we state here is qualified by a player's knowledge of his opponents and their bidding habits. To paraphrase Oliver Wendell Holmes, a page of experience is worth a volume of logic. If the person who overcalls is one who can boast that he never bids unless he has them, the decision of the responder will be governed largely by his willingness to accept a small penalty or to risk the opponents making his contract doubled. On the other hand, if the intervener is a player who frequently steps out of line, doubts should be resolved in favour of the double. For our purposes, we must assume that the player who overcalls is employing sound judgment.

Responder's action will often depend on whether aggregate or match-point scoring is being used. At match points, to settle for plus 100 when a pair should be plus 140 may be a major disaster. At aggregate scoring, however, small losses do not generally figure in the final result.

In match-point play, therefore, it is vital that responder double whenever he holds 8—9 points and a well-balanced hand. This is especially true when the adversaries are vulnerable; but even when they are not, the odds favour penalty action as against a very doubtful game and an uncertain 2NT contract:

(20)   ♠   K 9 5   ♡   A 7 6   ◇   Q 5 4 2   ♣   10 9 5
         1NT   2C   *Double*

At rubber bridge, the double should be made when responder has strength in the bid suit, although the double is also sound on close hands when, if the opponent does fulfil his contract, no game is involved. Thus, at rubber bridge, the double with hand (20) would be the proper action, for the penalty will generally compensate for the plus-score that might have been produced offensively. But a double with the following hand, though a fine one at match points, would be quite unsound at total points:

(21)   ♠   K 9 5   ♡   10 9 5   ◇   A 7 6   ♣   Q 5 4 2
         1NT   2H   *Double* (at match points)
         1NT   2H   *2NT* (at aggregate points)

When responder has a hand *of general strength* and intends to bid 3NT immediately, an overcall presents an opportunity to double that should be seized invariably. There may be times when the opponents get away with a penalty less costly than the offensive team's potential, but ordinarily the penalty will prove the more rewarding course.

Of course, when the response of 3NT is to be based *on a long suit*, responder lacks the defensive strength for doubling, and proceeds to game at once:

(22) ♠ K 9 5   ♡ 10 2   ◇ K Q 9 5 4 3   ♣ 8 4
            1NT   2S   3NT

THE RESPONSE OF 4H OR 4S

When the responder holds a hand that is inflexibly built for trump play at a major suit, he bids the game immediately if his point count is sufficient for game and definitely inadequate for a slam. As in the case of the 3NT response, there is no point to delay or to the exposure of distributional information to the opponents when the final contract is a foregone conclusion:

(23) ♠ K Q 10 8 5 4   ♡ K 3 2   ◇ 9   ♣ 10 4 3
              1NT   4S

(24) ♠ K Q 8 5 2   ♡ 10 4   ◇ Q J 10 8 3   ♣ 9
            1NT   4S

Observe, in connection with hand (24), that there is no point to presenting a choice of suits to the opener. The final contract will be 4S even if the opener has better diamonds than spades; and the disclosure of two suits can only profit the opponents.

THE SUIT RESPONSE AT THE THREE LEVEL

THE RESPONSE OF 3H OR 3S

(A) A game-going hand with a five-card major and distribution seemingly better designed for suit play, or
(B) A slam-going hand with a five-card major, distribution immaterial. The response is forcing to game.

The following are typical jump responses in major suits:

(25) ♠ A Q 9 5 4   ♡ 8 2   ◇ K 10 5   ♣ Q 5 2
            1NT   3S

(26) ♠ A 8   ♡ J 10 8 5 3   ◇ K Q 5   ♣ 10 9 2
      1NT   3H

As with hand (25), the contribution of three-card support from the opener
is the factor upon which the choice of the heart contract will be made to
depend.

(27) ♠ A 8   ♡ K Q J 9 5   ◇ K 7 6   ♣ Q 3 2
      1NT   3H

There are slam possibilities that responder intends to investigate after first
disclosing his good heart suit.

(28) ♠ A K Q 8 2   ♡ 10 5 4   ◇ Q 3   ♣ J 7 5
      1NT   3NT (at match points)
      1NT   4S (at aggregate points)

The difference between 420 and 430 is meaningless at aggregate scoring,
but could be vital at match points.

THE RESPONSE OF 3C OR 3D

The response of 3C or 3D is more often a slam try than a desire for suit
play at game. The reader will recall that, with balanced hands and only
game in sight, responder bids 3NT at once, since that is the short cut to
game:

(29) ♠ K 5 4   ♡ 8   ◇ K Q J 8 5 3   ♣ 9 5 4
      1NT   3NT

Inasmuch as responder is probably interested in slams when he initially
bids 3C or 3D, opener's duty is to rebid in such a manner that the
strength of his hand is made manifest at once. This he does by rebidding
3NT with a minimum, and cue-bidding with a maximum:

(30) ♠ A 5 4   ♡ A Q 8 3   ◇ K 7 6   ♣ A 5 4 (17)
      1NT   3D
      3H

If, despite opener's cue-bid, responder merely carries on in his minor
suit, opener must not force a slam on the partnership. It is for the reponder to make the final determination about slam.

THE REBID OVER A RESPONSE OF 2NT

When the response of 2NT has been made in a non-competitive
auction, the opener passes or proceeds to game depending on whether his

hand is a minimum or a maximum. When the left-hand opponent has overcalled, however, the opener's decision to go on, although dictated by identical considerations, requires different bidding technique. The reader is reminded that the responder, with a four- or five-card major and only 8—9 points, must respond 2NT to show the chance-giving strength of his hand. In order to give the responder a chance to show major suits, the opener who decides to proceed to game should disclose a four-card major of his own, or make a waiting bid to provide responder with room to show a five-card major. For example:

(31) ♠ A Q 5   ♡ K 10 8   ◇ Q 9 5   ♣ A K 7 4
     1NT   2D   2NT   No Bid
     3C

The opener's rebid of 3C is a denial of a four-card major, but leaves room for responder to bid a five-card major if he has one. Responder, with no five-card major, will go on to the no-trump game.

(32) ♠ A Q 5 3   ♡ K 10 8 2   ◇ Q 9 5   ♣ A K
     1NT   2D   2NT   No Bid
     3D

When the opener has two four-card majors, the bid of the opponent's suit makes this clear to responder, who may now make an election between no-trumps and a major-suit game.

With one four-card major, the opener bids it.

(33) ♠ A 10 5 4   ♡ K Q 8   ◇ Q 7 5 2   ♣ A K
     1NT   2D   2NT   No Bid
     3S

Finally, with a maximum hand and the opponent's suit well stopped, the opener bids 3NT.

THE REBID OVER THE RESPONSE OF 3H OR 3S

The opener should carry on to the major-suit game, regardless of his own distribution, with any three-card support for responder's suit.

(34) ♠ A 9 5   ♡ K 10 3 2   ◇ A Q J   ♣ Q 3 2
     1NT   3S
     4S

(35) ♠ A 10   ♡ K Q 5 4   ◇ A J 10 6   ♣ Q 10 6
     1NT   3S
     3NT

When the opener rebids 3NT, the responder is told unequivocally that the opener holds A x or K x in responder's trump suit.

When the opener has adequate trump support for responder's major and, in addition, has a maximum no-trump rich in first- and second-round controls, he cue-bids. If responder merely bids the game, nothing is lost by opener's show of strength. But if responder intends to probe for slam, the cue-bid presents an immediate acceptance which will be used to generate a series of control-investigating actions. Thus:

(36) ♠ A J 8   ♡ K Q 5 4   ◇ A 7 6   ♣ A 10 4
          1NT   3S
          4D

Opener cue-bids to indicate good trump support, an excellent opening no-trump and a desire to go further. If responder merely returns to 4S, opener will bow out gracefully.

When responder first bids 3H or 3S and then returns to his suit over a rebid of 3NT, he indicates a hand with which he must have entertained hopes of slam. With only a major-suit game as his objective, he would have bid 4H or 4S at once. It follows, therefore, that the opener should make a slam move with a maximum no-trump rich in controls.

(37) ♠ A 5   ♡ A K 7 2   ◇ K 9 5 4   ♣ A 3 2   (18)
          1NT   3S
          3NT   4S
          5C

(38) ♠ K 5   ♡ K Q J 3   ◇ A 10 5 4   ♣ A J 9   (18)
          1NT   3S
          3NT   4S
          5D

ACTION OF OPENER WHEN RESPONDER MAKES AN IMMEDIATE GAME RESPONSE

The responder is the sole member of the partnership in a position to decide whether a slam is a possibility for his pair. When responder is looking at a hand that can produce a slam if opener has a maximum or if opener holds certain key cards, the Stayman System provides him with tools with which a sequence may be fashioned to permit the communication of vital information. *The bid of game by responder is a denial of a slam, and it tells opener that his best hand is not good enough for more than game.*

THE RESPONSE AT THE THREE LEVEL OVER CONTEN-TION

The inability to bid at the two level because the opponent has consumed the responder's bidding space sometimes forces the responder to resort to the response of 2NT instead of employing the Stayman Conventional bid of 2C. When the responder has sufficient strength to contract for game, a suit bid at the three level is, of course, permissible and is forcing to game.

(39)　♠ 9 5　　♡ A Q 8 5 3　　◇ K J 8　　♣ 5 4 3
　　　　　　　1NT　　2S　　3H

The responder with sufficient strength to force to game may bid the opponent's suit *to ask opener to show a four-card major*:

(40)　♠ K J 5 4　　♡ Q 3　　◇ A 10 5 2　　♣ 7 5 2
　　　　　　　1NT　　2H　　3H

Responder will now pass if opener bids 3NT.

RESPONDER'S METHOD OF CALCULATING POINT COUNT

The opening bid of 1NT proclaims that the opener has a balanced hand and it is more than ordinarily likely that the partnership will eventually wind up in a no-trump contract. For this reason the responder, in evaluating his hand, should give no weight to short suits until and unless a dominant trump suit is uncovered. The point count of his hand, opposite a bid of 1NT, will, therefore, consist of high cards and long cards only.

When, however, responder discovers a four-four major-suit fit, he may add point count for suit shortages. For example:

(41)　♠ K J 5 4　　♡ A 7 6 3　　◇ 9　　♣ 10 5 4 2
　　　　　　　1NT　　2C
　　　　　　　2S　　4S

Responder's hand, originally valued at 8 points, increases to 12 points by reason of suit valuation:

High cards	.	.	.	9 (spade King promoted)
Short suits	.	.	.	2
4-4-4-1 distribution	.	.	.	1
Total count	.	.	.	12 points

IO

THE STAYMAN CONVENTION

IN THE 'thirties and early 'forties almost every bridge book contained the admonition, often repeated, that the opening bid of 1NT should be given very sparing use. At that time, the advice was sound, because any sequence that started with 1NT ended at 1NT or at game. The bid did have one important function: it permitted a player with more than modest pretensions to make it perfectly clear in his first call that he intended to play the hand, come hell or high water, and would brook no interference from his partner. As a result, the partner of such a player was put on notice that if he held a hand requiring delicate delineation, he could resign himself to being dummy at 1NT or 3NT, unless he held a hand with a tremendously long suit of his own. The following series of bids could be heard in every bridge club in the land:

1NT	No Bid	2H	No Bid
2NT	No Bid	3H	No Bid
3NT	Double	4H	Double
Down 800!			

We do not mean to suggest that it was only obstinacy that inspired the opening bidder to cling to the selection of the final contract. Actually, the opener never could be quite sure whether the responder used 2H as a weak bid, a strong one or a slam try; and there were plenty of advocates of each.

This was to change in 1945, when we published the Stayman Convention. For some time, we had been working on the problem of reaching game contracts or part-scores when the partnership possessed a four-four major-suit trump fit, while at the same time communicating information about general all-round strength so that no-trump or suit games might be reached when the opener had a maximum, and rejected when he did not.

In the last nine years, the Convention has become a very precise tool and has accomplished all we ever hoped for it. The method has spread around the globe. In America it is used by over 85 per cent. of the tournament players and increasingly large numbers of players in Europe and other parts of the world have found it an indispensable adjunct to their bidding systems. We present here the Convention as we recommend that it be used, as we have tested it and polished it in the competition of national and international play.

When your partner opens the bidding with 1NT, the hands you may hold may be classified as follows:

(1) No possible game . . . . . 0—6 points
(2) Game possible . . . . . . 7—9 ,,
(3) Game certain, but no slam . . . . 10—14 ,,
(4) Game certain, slam possible . . . 15—16 ,,
(5) Game certain, slam probable . . . 16—17 ,,
(6) Game and slam certain . . . . 18— ,,

From the weakest category of hands to the strongest, the Stayman Convention has an important application that may be understood more perfectly after an explanation of what the Convention accomplishes. The science of bidding involves the two factors of power and direction. A fine bidding system is one that enables two players to find their best denomination at their best level.

The central bid of the Stayman Convention is the response of 2C, an artificial bid employed by the responder to signify his interest in the opener's—

(1) Major-suit distribution.
(2) General strength.

The response of 2C puts into effect a programme of rebids and second responses that have precise meanings, and these can best be examined and learned by a study of hands that demonstrate the scope of the Convention and the problems it eliminates. But first, a short preliminary schedule of function and meaning of the conventional responses and rebids:

The bid	The sequence	The meaning
2C	1NT—2C	The Convention is operative.
2D	1NT—2C 2D	A denial of four hearts or four spades; strength of hand undefined.
2H	1NT—2C 2H	Affirms four-card heart suit and denies four spades; strength of hand undefined.
2S	1NT—2C 2S	Affirms four-card spade suit and does not deny possibility of four-card heart suit also; strength of hand undefined.

The bid	The sequence	The meaning
2NT	1NT—2C 2NT	A rare rebid to indicate an absolute maximum opening 1NT with exceptional fillers and/or a running suit.
No Bid	1NT—2C 2D—No Bid	A weak hand with which responder had hoped to strike a suit fit.
2H, 2S	1NT—2C 2D—2H	A five-card suit and a count of at least 8 points. Forcing for one round.
2S	1NT—2C 2H—2S	A five-card spade suit and a count of at least 8. Forcing for one round.
3H	1NT—2C 2H—3H	A four-card heart suit and a count of at least 8. Chance-giving.
3S	1NT—2C 2S—3S	A four-card spade fit and a count of at least 8. Chance-giving.
2NT	1NT—2C 2D—2NT	8—9 points. Chance-giving.
3D	1NT—2C 2S—3D	10 plus points. Game-forcing and may set stage for slam bidding.
3C	1NT—2C 2S, 2D, 2H—3C	A weak hand and a desire to play at 3C part-score.
4H	1NT—2C 2H—4H	Game in hearts; no slam.
4S	1NT—2C 2S—4S	Game in spades; no slam.
3NT	1NT—2C 2H—3NT	Game in no-trumps; no slam.

The player who uses the Convention will have one of the following types of hands:

(1) Very weak, with a six-card or longer club suit. He wishes to play the hand at 3C rather than at 1NT.

(2) Very weak, with good length in spades, hearts and diamonds. Responder intends to pass the opening bidder's rebid whether it is 2D, 2H or 2S. This bid has great usefulness at match-point play.

(3) A sound chance-giving hand with 8—9 points, often with ambitions in the majors.

(4) A game-going hand containing some major-suit length.

(5) A game-going hand with possibilities of a slam.

(6) 4-3-3-3 distribution and sufficient strength to suggest a slam. "Sheer Power" hand, later defined.

As may be seen, the range of responder's strength is extremely broad. His target may be anything from a part-score to a slam. Control of the bidding, while it is theoretically shared by both partners, is largely in the hands of the responder, since the opener has already closely limited his strength and will add the missing details in his first rebid.

THE 2C RESPONSE WITH WEAK HANDS

As responder, you believe that 3C will make a better contract than 1NT. You bid 2C. At your next turn you bid 3C and almost certainly buy the contract. Requirements: six-card or longer suit and less than a count of 8.

(1) ♠ 9   ♡ 10 5   ◇ K J 3   ♣ 10 8 6 5 4 3 2

Bid 2C. This hand will almost certainly play better at 3C than at 1NT. However, if your partner persists to 3NT, he will do so only with a maximum and very fine club consolidation, in which case there should be a fine play for game.

(2) ♠ 9 5   ♡ K 8   ◇ 7 6 2   ♣ Q 9 6 5 4 2

No Bid. There is no reason to believe that 3C will be better than 1NT. If opener is doubled, the response of 2C is proper and can only be construed as a rescue.

Your weak hands may contain distributional advantages that make the prospect of suit play decidedly more attractive than no-trumps. Not infrequently, your hand, as responder, will provide a safe haven at 3C or a major-suit partial, as in the following:

(3) ♠ 10 8 6 5   ♡ 3   ◇ 6 2   ♣ K J 9 5 4 3

Bid 2C. If partner bids 2S, you will pass. Over any other rebid, the second response of 3C will purchase the contract.

(4) ♠ Q 8 5 2   ♡ 10   ◇ 8 6   ♣ K J 9 5 4 3

Bid 2C. If your partner bids 2S, you will raise to 3S. If he bids 2D or 2H, you will go on to 3C and play the hand there.

Since the rebid will almost certainly be in a suit, your response may be based on a very weak hand if, distributionally, the advantages of suit play are substantial:

(5) ♠ 10 8 6 2   ♡ J 10 5 4   ◇ J 9 6 3   ♣ 7

Bid 2C. A very fine bid. You are willing to pass the rebid of 2D, 2H or 2S. This bid is an excellent move, since it may well keep opponents out of the bidding.

(6) ♠ K Q 5 4 2   ♡ Q 8 6 3   ◇ 10 5 4 2   ♣ Void

Bid 2C. An excellent play for game in a major exists if partner rebids 2H or 2S. If the rebid is 2D (a denial of spades or hearts), the responder intends to pass and take his chance. He could not bid 2S over a rebid of 2D, because that second response would confirm the possession of full chance-giving strength (8—9). At duplicate, however, the second response of 2S should be made notwithstanding the one point shortage, since it is essential that the hand be played in a major suit at match point.

(7) ♠ 9   ♡ 8 5 4   ◇ K 10 5 4 2   ♣ Q J 8 6

Bid 2D. Since there is no chance of finding a major-suit contract, the 2C response would be pointless.

THE 2C RESPONSE WITH CHANCE-GIVING STRENGTH

When the responder holds a hand that contains 8—9 points, he is aware that game is a proper undertaking for the partnership if opener has 17—18; but that a part-score only should be engaged for if opener has 16. If the responder has 9 points and no four-card major, he may put the question of game to the opener in a very simple manner: by responding 2NT.

Strictly speaking, therefore, the Stayman Convention is used with responding hands of chance-giving strength only when the question of a major suit is involved collaterally with the problem of ascertaining that sufficient strength is held for game. This is not to say that the expert always uses his conventions according to the book. He may respond 2C when he has no four-card major, in lieu of 2NT or 3NT, merely to "keep the opponents honest"—that is, to keep them uncertain as to what his hand contains. But the response of 2C will generally be employed in this range of hands where a major-suit trump fit is sought.

(8) ♠ K J 8 3   ♡ K J 7 2   ◇ 8 6 5 4   ♣ 2

Bid 2C. If your partner has four cards of either major, this hand will increase in strength tremendously for trump play. If opener's rebid denies a four-card major, responder will proceed to 2NT, having lost nothing in the process of investigating trump possibilities.

(9) ♠ K J 8 3   ♡ A 5 2   ◇ J 5 4 3   ♣ 7 2

Bid 2C. Here, the responder has only one four-card major, yet he is

careful not to overlook the possibility that opener has four spades also
and that a superior spade game (or spade part-score) exists for the pair.
The hallmark of the expert is the careful selection of underbids that permit
the investigation of every possibility that may give him an advantage,
however slight, over less thoughtful players.

(10) ♠ K Q 8 5 4   ♡ K 7 6 5   ◇ 4 3 2   ♣ 10

Bid *2C*. Even though responder has a five-card major, he properly
probes opener's hand to discover whether a four-four heart fit exists.

(11) ♠ 10 8 6 2   ♡ 9 5 4   ◇ A K 9 3 2   ♣ 8

Bid *2C*. Even though your four-card major is very weak, it is quite
possible that the opener has a fine spade suit. Your hand will gain tremendous power at spades and the possibility of a four-four fit must be
explored.

RESPONSE OF 2C WITH GAME-GOING STRENGTH

When the responder has 10 points or more and one or two four-card
majors, he employs the conventional response of 2C to check on the
distribution of opener's hand before committing the partnership to 3NT.

(12) ♠ K Q 8 5 3   ♡ K Q 2   ◇ 9 5   ♣ 8 4 3

Bid *2C*. If opener bids 2S, responder will bid 4S. If opener bids 2D or
2H, responder will bid 3NT. In neither case will opener go beyond game,
since the responder indicates that game only can be produced.

(13) ♠ K J 5 4   ♡ A 7 6   ◇ A 3 2   ♣ 9 5 4

Bid *3NT*. No-trumps is the shorter road to game and there is little point
to spade play even if partner has four cards in that suit.

(14) ♠ K J 3 2   ♡ Q J 4 3   ◇ A 7   ♣ 5 4 2

Bid *2C*. The ideal hand for the check-back: if opener bids 2D, denying a
four-card major, responder will bid 3NT at once. Likewise, if opener bids
2S or 2H, responder will bid the suit game immediately.

(15) ♠ 10 6   ♡ 9 4 2   ◇ K Q J 5 4   ♣ A 10 3

Bid *2C*. Although the responder has no real interest in the majors, he
camouflages his weakness in those two suits by using the Convention
instead of bidding 3NT at once. The hand occurred in the 1954 World's
Team Championship and resulted in a swing of 730 points. This was the
deal:

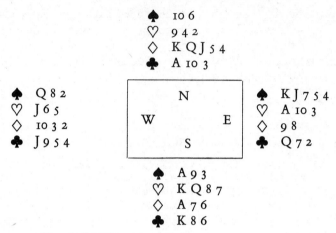

At one table, the bidding proceeded:

South	North
1NT	3NT

West, on lead with no attractive opening, and having a sound aversion to opening from a Jack, selected the two of spades for a lead. When the smoke cleared, East and West had collected five tricks for plus 100.

At the other table, a shrewd North threw a red herring across the trail:

1NT	2C
2H	3NT

West could not be criticized for his opening lead of the club four. To him, it appeared that North certainly held a four-card spade suit and had gone on to 3NT only after making certain that South did not also hold four cards of that suit. Under those circumstances, the spade lead did not appear attractive.

STOPPING SHORT OF GAME

In the illustrations that follow, the opener has a minimum no-trump and the responder less than game-going strength. Note how the partners exchange information without getting beyond their depth:

SEQUENCE 16

Opener	Responder	Opener	Responder
♠ A J 9 5	♠ K 4	1NT	2C
♡ K Q 5 4	♡ 7 3 2	2S	3C
◇ A 7	◇ 10 8	No Bid	
♣ K J 2	♣ Q 10 8 6 4 3		

Opener shows a four-card spade suit and is prepared to reveal his heart suit also until the second response of 3C tells him that responder has a long club suit in a more-or-less worthless hand.

SEQUENCE 17

Opener	Responder	Opener	Responder
♠ A J 9 5	♠ K 4	1NT	2C
♡ K 8 5 4	♡ Q 7 6 2	2S	2NT
◇ A 7	◇ K 10 5 3	3H	4H
♣ K J 2	♣ 8 6 3		

While the play for game is a little short of adequate, the stretch is warranted, particularly at rubber bridge.

SEQUENCE 18

Opener	Responder	Opener	Responder
♠ K 9 5	♠ A 7 6 4	1NT	2C
♡ Q 7 6	♡ K 9 5 3	2D	2NT
◇ A K 4	◇ Q 8	No Bid	
♣ A 10 7 2	♣ 9 5 4		

Opener's 2D rebid reveals that he holds no four-card major. Responder states with the bid of 2NT that he has a count of 8—9 and asks opener to pass or go on to game, depending on the strength of his hand.

SEQUENCE 19

Opener	Responder	Opener	Responder
♠ A Q 7	♠ 8 6	1NT	2C
♡ 9 5 4	♡ Q J 8 3 2	2D	2H
◇ A Q 3	◇ K 10 5 4	2NT	No Bid
♣ K J 10 2	♣ 9 7		

Responder's bid of 2H, in the face of opener's denial of four hearts, indicates that he would still like a heart contract if opener can contribute Q x x or better. With only three small hearts, opener signs off at 2NT. Opener is forced to bid over 2H, one of the second responses that cannot be passed.

SEQUENCE 20

Opener	Responder	Opener	Responder
♠ Q 7 3	♠ 8 6	1NT	2C
♡ A 5 4	♡ Q J 8 3 2	2D	2H
◇ A Q 3	◇ K 10 5 4	3H	No Bid
♣ K J 10 2	♣ 9 5		

Compare this with Sequence 19. Opener, holding adequate support for responder's heart suit, raises to three, and thus shows a minimum no-trump containing a heart raise. He cannot jump to four hearts, because responder alone can determine whether there is a play for game. Responder, with a minimum chance-giving hand, wisely declines to go on.

SEQUENCE 21

Opener	Responder	Opener	Responder
♠ A Q 2	♠ 9 5	1NT	2C
♡ K J 5 4	♡ Q 10 3 2	2H	3H
◇ K 10 2	◇ A Q 5 4	No Bid	
♣ K 9 7	♣ 10 8 6		

Responder raises to 3H, showing four-card trump support and urging opener to go on to game if he holds a maximum. Opener, with the awareness that the partnership is lacking game strength, declines the invitation.

SEQUENCE 22

Opener	Responder	Opener	Responder
♠ 9 5 4	♠ Q J 8 6 3 2	1NT	2C
♡ K Q 10 7	♡ 9 5	2H	2S
◇ Q J 3	◇ K 2	2NT	3S
♣ A K Q	♣ 7 6 3	No Bid	

Responder shows a strong five-card suit or a six-carder in a hand that is not strong enough opposite a minimum to jump to game. Opener's second rebid of 2NT denies K x x or A x x.

GAME SEQUENCES WHEN RESPONDER HOLDS LESS THAN 10 POINTS

Game will be reached when the opener has a maximum no-trump if responder's 2C bid was being employed in its conventional manner with a hand of chance-giving strength. We have already noted that the opener shows his maximum in his second rebid, since his first rebid gives distributional information only. Responder may show adequate strength by confirming a full 8—9 points, and he does this by taking action other than 3C on his second response.

SEQUENCE 23

Opener	Responder	Opener	Responder
♠ A J 9 5	♠ Q 3 2	1NT	2C
♡ K Q 5 4	♡ A 7 6 3	2S	2NT
◇ A 7	◇ K 5 3 2	3D	3H
♣ K J 10	♣ 9 8	4H	No Bid

Responder's bid of 2NT confirms 8—9 points and suggests the posses-sion of four hearts. Opener shows a maximum no-trump and probes for the four-card heart suit, which responder now shows, whereupon opener goes on to the heart game.

SEQUENCE 24

Opener	Responder	Opener	Responder
♠ A 9 5	♠ Q J 8 4 2	1NT	2C
♡ K Q 4	♡ 8 6	2D	2S
◇ A J 10 7	◇ Q 9 5 4	3D	4S
♣ A 6 2	♣ K 3		

With adequate trump support and a maximum hand, opener shows game by bidding a minor suit at the three level. Had opener lacked adequate spades, his rebid would have been 3NT. Opener does not jump to 4S at once, for the reason that responder may prefer to play the hand at 3NT when he discovers that opener has a high honour in the suit. Further-more, it is always possible that responder's 2S bid is psychic and it is safer to communicate the fact of trump support and permit responder to make the final election about where game should be played.

SEQUENCE 25

Opener	Responder	Opener	Responder
♠ A 9 5	♠ 6 4	1NT	2C
♡ K Q 4	♡ A 10 7 6	2D	2S
◇ A J 10 7	◇ K 9 8 4 3	3D	3NT
♣ A 6 2	♣ Q 5	No Bid	

Since opener has already told responder about his maximum no-trump and adequate spade support, he properly leaves it to responder to make the last decision. Observe that although responder does not have a spade suit, the sequence might still be a genuine one, inasmuch as responder, after ascertaining that opener had the Ace, King or Queen of spades and a maximum, could very well decide on no-trump play even though he held a five-card spade suit, as in the following sequence:

SEQUENCE 26

Opener	Responder	Opener	Responder
♠ K 9 3	♠ A Q 8 4 2	1NT	2C
♡ A 10 8	♡ Q 9 5	2D	2S
◇ A J 10 7	◇ 2	3D	3NT
♣ K Q 4	♣ 10 9 8 6	No Bid	

Once the responder knows that the opener has the King of spades, diamond strength and a maximum no-trump, he is perfectly satisfied to play the hand at no-trump.

SEQUENCE 27

Opener	Responder	Opener	Responder
♠ 9 5 4	♠ Q J 8 6 3 2	1NT	2C
♡ A Q 8 2	♡ 9 5	2H	2S
◇ A 8 6	◇ K 2	2NT	3S
♣ A K 5	♣ 7 6 3	4S	

Opener first discloses a heart suit and then shows a minimum no-trump. Responder, at this point, is bound to reveal the full strength of his hand and his 3S bid indicates a willingness to stop at a part-score. But opener ventures to game on the basis that every high card in his hand is efficient and there should, accordingly, be a fair play for it.

SEQUENCE 28

Opener	Responder	Opener	Responder
♠ A J 5	♠ K 9 6 4 2	1NT	2C
♡ K 4 2	♡ Q J 3	2D	2S
◇ A J 7	◇ 8	3S	4S
♣ Q J 9 5	♣ K 7 6 4		

Opener's raise of spades, though marking a minimum no-trump, enables responder to revalue his hand upwards. With unbalanced distribution, responder soundly elects the spade game.

GAME SEQUENCES WHERE RESPONDER HAS 10—13

When the responder has a count of 10, the partnership has a combined count of 26 at least, and game-forcing steps are mandatory. With less than 14 points, and so about a Queen short of a safe slam contract, responder's sole task is to make certain that a major-suit game is reached if it lies in the cards and appears to present a more desirable contract. The following sequences indicate the manner in which the Stayman Convention is employed to give authority to the game selection:

SEQUENCE 29

Opener	Responder	Opener	Responder
♠ A J 5 2	♠ K 7	1NT	2C
♡ Q 10 6 5	♡ K 8 4 2	2S	3D
◇ K Q 6	◇ A 9 5 3	3H	4H
♣ A 2	♣ 6 5 4		

When the opener's rebid is 2S, it is always possible that the opener has four hearts as well as four spades, and responder makes allowance for this with a forcing underbid of 3D.

SEQUENCE 30

Opener	Responder	Opener	Responder
♠ A J 5 2	♠ K 7 6	1NT	2C
♡ Q 10 6 5	♡ 3 2	2S	3NT
◇ K Q 6	◇ A J 10 9 5		
♣ A 2	♣ Q J 4		

Although it may be stated as a general rule that a responder using the Convention has one of the two majors, responder must not be disturbed when he jumps to 3NT over opener's rebid. If he were interested in a four-heart contract, he would have made the forcing bid of 3D. Compare Sequence 29. His use of Stayman has perhaps been tactical.

SEQUENCE 31

Opener	Responder	Opener	Responder
♠ 7 5 2	♠ K Q J 8 3	1NT	2C
♡ A K 2	♡ Q 8 4 3	2D	2S
◇ A 8 5 4	◇ 9	2NT	4S
♣ K Q 5	♣ A 7 6		

Responder employs the Convention to uncover a possible four-four heart fit, but when the 2D rebid reveals the absence of majors in the opener's hand, responder goes on to the spade game, knowing that opener will produce A x or x x x as support.

Perhaps you have noticed that many of the game contracts that were reached in the illustrative hands were not "lay-down", but required some skill or some luck or a little of each. This is not unintentional on our part. We have already stated many times that there is an adequate play for game when the combined hands count 26 points. It may not be amiss to point out again that as the strength of the combined hands tends towards balance between the partners, the declarer has more flexible play. When the requirements of the opening no-trump are 16—18, close games will require the full 26 points, but when the lighter no-trump requirements are employed, 25 will often yield a fine play for game, particularly when the division is 13/12.

THIRD AND FOURTH HAND NO-TRUMP

Although the requirements for the opening bid of 1NT are about the same in third or fourth position as they are first or second hand, the opener may, occasionally, shade his bid a trifle after his partner has passed.

Before leaving this chapter, we should like to devote a few more words to the process of counting the responder's hand. The reader will recall that opposite a suit bid, the responder counts short suits in his total valuation. When the opening bid is 1NT, however, the responder may not give the same value to singletons and doubletons. There are two reasons for this: first, since the opener has great general strength, there is more than the usual chance that the responder's shortage is duplicated by the opener's high cards, and both cannot be given value simultaneously without distorting the combined total; second, the hand may play at notrumps where short suits have no value at all.

Accordingly, until a suit fit is found, and pending the exploratory steps that will reveal a dominant trump suit if it exists, the responder must value his hand in high-card and long-card points only. With the discovery that opener will contribute strong trump support, or that responder will contribute fine support for the opener, the responding hand must be revalued with full weight given to distributional elements of strength.

II

THE WEAK NO-TRUMP

EXCEPT FOR a few references to the weak no-trump in Chapter 8, we have confined our discussions in the last three chapters to bidding sequences and principles as they relate to the strong, 16—18 point count, no-trump. We do not, thereby, wish to leave the impression with the reader that the strong no-trump has our preference. We have, up to this point, dealt exclusively with one standard merely in order that there would be no confusion in the text; and we selected the strong no-trump because more players have been accustomed to using it.

The weak no-trump, distributionally, is almost identical with its big brother. The hand patterns supporting the bid of 1NT will generally be 4-4-3-2, 4-3-3-3 and 5-3-3-2, the so-called balanced distributions. In point count, the weak no-trump has a range 4 points below the strong no-trump: 12—14 as against 16—18. Since 26 points are needed to produce game, the responder with 11 points or less will not generally seek a game contract, because he knows that the partnership has 25 at best and may have only 23 or 24. With 12—13, responder will urge game and with 14 points he will demand it. The reader will find that every principle that we have gone to great lengths to explain applies, with necessary changes in point count, to the weak no-trump.

The 12—14 no-trump has decided advantages. The one level is ordinarily employed for the investigation of hand distributions, the aim being to uncover a trump suit—preferably a major—in which the partnership stands its best chance of producing game or a part-score. When the bidding starts at the very lowest level—at 1C for example—a great deal of information may be exchanged by two players before they have reached 1NT, the terminal point of the one level. This is all highly desirable when exploration is necessary, because the players have distributions that require delineation. But there is one great disadvantage to the initial low-level bid. It permits an opponent to make an overcall on a hand of marginal strength, and this liberty of action that he enjoys leads frequently to a bidding contest that puts the opening bidder and his partner out of business.

No great harm results from competition when the defenders are badly outclassed, because the offensive pair will merely roll over the bid and continue on its way to a selected contract. When, however, the strength of a deal does not give the opener and his partner a decisive superiority, there is a tremendous advantage in being able to keep the opponents silent. The opening bid of 1NT accomplishes this many times where an opening suit bid of one might not. Faced with the necessity of entering the two level, if he wishes to contest, and aware of the fact that his left-hand opponent may be loaded for bear, the defender may decide it is safer to stay out of the bidding and thus many hands will be purchased economically by the declarant pair. And often, when he feels reluctant to sit back with a strong hand, the defender will step out into the two level to be caught between two good hands and severely mauled.

The opening bid of 1NT, based on a balanced hand of 12—14 points, has little or no distributional assistance to offer partner. Almost invariably, the opener would rebid 1NT if he were to open with a suit bid of one. By bidding 1NT at once, he informs his partner that his 12—14 points are largely in high cards scattered through the four suits. This makes penalty action by responder a lot easier when an overcall intervenes, for he need not fear that a large part of the opener's hand will be valueless defensively. Another advantage is that close no-trump games may be reached when the combined hands hold 25 points divided almost evenly between two hands neither one of which contains a full opening bid.

There is, of course, greater risk in the 12—14 no-trump than in the 16—18, but this increased vulnerability to penalties is largely illusory. If responder has 6 points, the pair would have reached 1NT in any event; and if the responder has less than 6 points, a pass to an opening suit bid would have revealed opener's plight and exposed him to a bad penalty. The opening bid of 1NT provides a certain amount of protection when the responder is very weak. His pass may contain as much as 11 points and the opponent who bids after him cannot tell whether he has just short of game strength or a very poor hand. Furthermore, if the opponents do take penalty action, responder may frequently be able to rescue when he holds a five-card or six-card suit, with confidence that the opener will furnish some consolidating strength in his suit.

THE OPENING BID OF 1NT

The following hands are illustrative of the 12—14 opening bid of 1NT:

(1)   ♠ A Q 5 4   ♡ 9 6 2   ◇ K J 5   ♣ A 7 2
             (14)   A maximum

(2) ♠ K Q 9 5   ♡ K J 10 2   ◇ K 9   ♣ Q 6 3
(14) A maximum

(3) ♠ 9 5   ♡ Q 10 2   ◇ A K 9 5   ♣ A 4 3 2
(13)

(4) ♠ A 7   ♡ K 10 5   ◇ A Q 9 5 4   ♣ 10 8 2
(14) A maximum

(5) ♠ K 5 4   ♡ K 3 2   ◇ A 10 8 4   ♣ Q 10 8
(12) A minimum

Observe, in connection with hand (3), that the weak no-trump may contain a worthless doubleton. In this respect, the requirements differ from those relating to the strong no-trump.

RESPONSES AND LATER BIDS

(6) ♠ K 10 5 2   ♡ A K 9   ◇ J 6 2   ♣ 5 4 3
1NT   *No Bid*

(7) ♠ 9 8 6 5 4   ♡ A 4 2   ◇ J 8 3   ♣ Q 5
1NT   *No Bid*

(8) ♠ Q 10 8 4 2   ♡ J 10 9 5   ◇ A 8   ♣ 4 3
1NT   2S

(9) ♠ A J 8 6 4   ♡ Q 8 5 4 3   ◇ 9 5   ♣ 4
1NT   2H

(10) ♠ 9 8 6 5 4   ♡ A Q 7   ◇ A 5 3   ♣ 6 4
1NT   2S

(11) ♠ A 7   ♡ 9 5   ◇ Q 8 6 5 4 2   ♣ A 7 5
1NT   2D
3D   3NT

Note, in connection with hand (11), that the rebid of 3D promises 14 points containing the A K x of diamonds.

(12) ♠ A K 6   ♡ 10 5 4   ◇ K J 7 5   ♣ K 8 4   (14)
1NT   2S
?

Bid 3S. A maximum 14 with two of the top three honours (or four excellent cards in a major-suit bid by responder) requires a raise despite responder's sign-off.

(13)   ♠ K Q 7   ♡ 10 8 6 5 2   ◇ 7 6   ♣ A Q 7 (11)

          1NT   2H

          3H   ?

Bid *4H.* Opener's raise guarantees 14 points and excellent heart support. You may now value your fifth heart at 1 point and your doubleton diamond takes on a plus value.

(14)   ♠ K 9 5   ♡ A J 7   ◇ A J 5   ♣ 9 8 3 2 (13)

          1NT   ?

Bid *3NT.* This response requires some explanation. When the responder held a count of 9 opposite a strong no-trump, the recommended response (no major being contained in his hand) was the chance-giving bid of 2NT. If the opener held only 16 points, the partnership possessed a total of 25 only, and the game was stated to be beyond the expectations of the pair. Opposite the weak no-trump, the possession of 13 points gives the partnership the same total of 25 when the opener's hand is a minimum, but with the important difference that the 25 points are now split 12 and 13. With the ability to play to or from either hand at will, 25 points will produce game often enough to warrant bidding game.

(15)   ♠ K J 9 5 4   ♡ Q J 5 4   ◇ 9   ♣ K Q 2 (13)

          1NT   2D   ?

Bid *3D.* Responder forces to game by bidding the opponent's suit. Opener will now bid a four-card major if he has one.

(16)   ♠ 7 6 4   ♡ A 3   ◇ K Q 8 5 4 2   ♣ K 5 (14)

          1NT   2C   ?

Bid *3NT.* The force in a minor should be reserved for slam hands or for hands unsuited for no-trump play by reason of distributional characteristics, as in the hand below:

(17)   ♠ A 9 5   ♡ A 10 3   ◇ K Q 8 5 4 2   ♣ 9 (15)

          1NT   2C   3D

(18)   ♠ K 9 5   ♡ A 7 6   ◇ A Q 5 4   ♣ 10 9 5 (13)

          1NT   2C   ?

Double. The penalty action is certainly a sounder course than a close game. You have a sure profit that will generally equal or exceed the value of your game (if one can be made).

(19)   ♠ 9 5   ♡ A Q 8 5 3   ◇ K J 8   ♣ A 5 4

          1NT   2S   ?

Bid *3H.* This bid is forcing.

(20) ♠ Q 5   ♡ K J 5 4   ◇ A 10 3 2   ♣ A 7 2
        1NT   2S   ?

Bid *3S*. The bid of the opponent's major suit asks opener to bid the other major if he holds four cards of the suit, otherwise 3NT.

THE STAYMAN CONVENTION

CLASSIFICATION OF HANDS

Responder holds		Partnership capabilities
0—10	. .	No possible game.
11—13	. .	Game possible.
14—18	. .	Game certain, but no slam.
19—20	. .	Game certain, slam possible.
21—22	. .	Game certain, slam probable.
23—	. . .	Game and slam certain.

NOTE: When we state that a game or slam is certain, we mean that the chances are so overwhelming in its favour that it must be bid.

SEQUENCE 21

♠	A J 9 5	♠	K 4	1NT	2C
♡	Q 5 4 3	♡	A 8 2	2S	3C
◇	K 7	◇	10 8	*No Bid*	
♣	K J 2	♣	Q 10 8 6 4 3		

SEQUENCE 22

♠	A J 9 5	♠	K 4	1NT	2C
♡	J 8 5 4	♡	K Q 7 6	2S	2NT
◇	Q 7	◇	K J 10 5	3H	4H
♣	A J 2	♣	10 9 7		

SEQUENCE 23

♠	9 7 5	♠	K 10 8 2	1NT	2C
♡	K 9 7	♡	A J 5 4	2D	*No Bid*
◇	A 10 3	◇	9 8 6 5 2		
♣	K Q J 7	♣	Void		

SEQUENCE 24

♠	K 9 5	♠	A J 6 3	1NT	2C
♡	Q 7 6	♡	K J 9 5	2D	3NT
◇	K 4 2	◇	A 8		
♣	A 10 7 2	♣	9 5 4		

A slight stretch when the opener is found with a bare minimum, but it will be brought home a fair share of the time with good declarer play and a little luck.

SEQUENCE 25

♠ Q 7 6	♠ A 5	1NT	2C
♡ 9 5 4	♡ Q J 8 3 2	2D	2H
◇ A Q 3	◇ K 10 5 4	2NT	No Bid
♣ K J 10 2	♣ 9 7		

Opener shows a minimum with less than adequate heart support.

SEQUENCE 26

♠ K 9 5	♠ Q J 8 4 2	1NT	2C
♡ K Q 4	♡ A 8	2D	2S
◇ Q J 10 7	◇ 8 5	3D	4S
♣ A 6 2	♣ K Q 8 3		

Opener shows a maximum no-trump and normal spade support by bidding a side suit. The immediate double raise to 4S is not permitted, since responder's 2S bid may be psychic.

SEQUENCE 27

♠ Q 6 2	♠ K 9 5 4	1NT	2C
♡ K J 5 4	♡ A 10 2	2H	2NT
◇ K 10 2	◇ Q J 8 3	No Bid	
♣ K 9 7	♣ Q 3		

Responder signs off at 2NT when opener denies a four-card spade suit.

SEQUENCE 28

♠ K 9 5	♠ 7 4	1NT	2C
♡ K 4 2	♡ A 10 7 6	2D	2S
◇ A 10 7 6	◇ K 9 8 4 3	3D	3NT
♣ A 6 2	♣ K Q	No Bid	

Responder makes the tactical bid of 2S to deter a possible spade lead against the ultimate 3NT contract. Opener bids 3D to show a maximum no-trump and adequate spade support.

SEQUENCE 29

♠ 8 5 4	♠ K J 10 9 2	1NT	2C
♡ K 10 8 2	♡ Q 5	2H	2S
◇ A Q J	◇ K 10 5 4	3NT	
♣ K Q 10	♣ J 9		

Opener shows a maximum that lacks adequate spade support.

SEQUENCE 30

♠ J 8 5 2	♠ 9 7 6	1NT	2C
♡ K 10 6 5	♡ 2	2S	3NT
◇ J 10	◇ A K Q 9 5 4		
♣ A K 2	♣ Q 8 5		

Responder puts up a smoke screen by implying heart strength.

We hope that the presentation of the foregoing examples will be helpful to those readers who intend to use the weak no-trump either exclusively or under particular conditions of vulnerability. What we have done, in effect, is to reduce the opener's hand by the equivalent of an Ace and strengthen the responder's to compensate for the reduction. Thus, the combined strength of the partnership hands remains the same as in the hands presented in the last three chapters, wherein the strong no-trump was used as a standard. While the transfer of 4 points from the opener's to the responder's hand does not alter the sum total, it does make for greater facility in declarer play; and we reflect this difference by recommending game-forcing action when the responder holds 13 points in a hand that has fillers or some distributional merit.

In summary of both the strong and weak opening no-trump and their responses:

The bid	With strong no-trump	With weak no-trump
Opening 1NT	16—18	12—14
Responder's No Bid . . .	0—7	0—11
Responder's bid of 2D, 2H, 2S .	0—7	0—11
Responder's bid of 2C-Stayman .	8—	12—
Responder's bid of 2NT . .	8—9	12—
Responder's forcing series to game .	10—	13—
Responder's forcing series to slam .	17—	21—

HIGHER OPENING BIDS IN NO-TRUMPS

HANDS THAT are distributed 4-3-3-3, 4-4-3-2 and 5-3-3-2 are generally described as "balanced", which means that winning tricks will come in the main from high cards rather than from long cards or ruffing.

For players who choose to use the weak no-trump, a count of 12 points scattered through three suits permits him to launch the bidding with 1NT. The strong no-trump school will wait for 16 points before making the same bid. Whether the opening 1NT is 12—14 or 16—18, the 2NT opening is identical for all players: 20—22 points. In higher opening no-trump bids, no suit may be weaker than Q x x or K x. If a hand counts 20 or more and contains a weaker suit, an opening suit bid is mandatory.

When the opening bidder holds a hand that contains 20 points or more and no suit is weaker than Q x x or K x, he must open the bidding with a call that will put the responder on notice that very few, if any, high cards are needed to produce game. The desirable range for any limited bid is 2 points at the outside, and this principle is applied in fixing the ranges of opening no-trump bids that are used to portray balanced hands of 20 to 28 points in strength. Holding 20—28 points, stoppers in all suits and balanced distribution, the opener makes one of the following bids:

20—22 points	.	.	.	2NT
23—24 ,,	.	.	.	2C, followed by a minimum rebid in no-trumps
25—26 ,,	.	.	.	2C, followed by a jump rebid in no-trumps
27—28 ,,	.	.	.	3NT

We devote an entire chapter to the opening bid of 2C, which is used in the Stayman System to initiate the bidding on all hands that require less than a Queen from partner to produce game. In this chapter, we consider the opening bid of 2C as it is employed to implement no-trump bidding. So used, the initial call of 2C is merely a device to describe the size of the no-trump bid that the opener makes on his rebid.

The responses to the opening bid of 2C are conventional, but for present purposes it will suffice to say that the response of 2D is negative and may represent a complete washout, the opening 2C bid being a forcing bid. Any other response is constructive and guarantees specific high-card strength which will be set forth later. Accordingly, when the response to 2C is 2H, 2S, 2NT, 3C or 3D, the opener's task is merely to show the size of his no-trump so that the responder may take intelligent action. The rebid of no-trumps at the cheapest level shows 23—24 points; the jump rebid, 25—26. Thus:

2C	2D	
2NT		23—24 points
2C	2H, 2S	
2NT		23—24 points
2C	2NT	
3NT		23—24 points
2C	3C, 3D	
3NT		23—24 points
2C	2D, 2H, 2S	
3NT		25—26 points
2C	3C, 3D	
4NT		25—26 points

The following hands are examples of those where a choice must be made between a suit bid of one and 2NT:

(1) ♠ K J 5 4   ♡ A Q 7 6   ◇ A K   ♣ K 10 9 (20)

Bid *2NT*. The count is 20 points, a minimum hand. Don't worry about the four-card majors. Your partner will employ the Stayman Convention to probe for a heart or spade game if he is interested.

(2) ♠ Q J   ♡ A K 7 2   ◇ A Q J   ♣ A 10 9 5 (21)

Bid *1D*. You have no stopper in spades and cannot bid 2NT even though your hand qualifies for the bid in point count and distribution.

(3) ♠ K Q   ♡ A Q 9 5 4   ◇ K Q J 7   ♣ A 10 (22)

Bid *1H*. Do not open with 2NT on 5-4-2-2 distributions. The semi-two-suiter becomes a powerful hand when a trump fit is found, and search for it is best initiated with a suit bid followed by vigorous rebid action.

THE RESPONSE TO 2NT

When the responder has 5 points or more, he must make a response to an opening bid of 2NT, and with very good distribution the point count requirement may be shaded. If the opener is doubled (an extremely rare occurrence) responder may rescue in any five-card or longer suit provided his hand is otherwise worthless. With 5 or more points, a redouble would, of course, be in order. The following responses are available to the partner of the player who bids 2NT:

3D, 3H, 3S . .	Game lies in a suit or at no-trumps. Slam seems out of the question.
4H, 4S . . .	Slam is only remotely possible.
3NT . . .	5—10 points. Flat distribution at its higher level of strength (9—10).
4NT . . .	4-3-3-3 distribution with 11—12 points. Opener totals the combined hands and acts accordingly.
5NT . . .	4-3-3-3 distribution with 13—14 points. A small slam must be bid and opener will bid six of his best suit if he has a 4-4-3-2 or 5-3-3-2 hand before committing the deal to 6NT.
3C . . .	The Stayman Convention. Opener rebids at the three level precisely as he would at the two level had the bidding been 1NT—2C. Responder promises 5 points at least (or its equivalent) and his top strength is unlimited, but will be revealed later.

In general, the development of the bidding proceeds in accordance with principles almost identical with those governing the progression when the opening bid is 1NT. There is, of course, no sign-off by the responder except a pass. A suit response, other than 3C, indicates that responder wishes to be raised to a suit game if the opener has adequate trump support. A raise to 3NT is a limited bid that says that a slam is out of the question even if opener has the very finest 2NT opening bid. The jump to a suit game states that game is the objective of the responder, but opener may raise if he holds a maximum with good trump support and Aces and Kings making up the remainder of his point count. In constructing a bidding sequence, the responder may try to induce a narrower definition from the opener so that he, the responder, may make a final decision; or he may, where exact definition of his own hand is easy, give the opener the pleasure of naming the declaration.

SEQUENCE 4

♠ A K 10	♠ J 3 2	2NT	*No Bid*
♡ K Q 9 5	♡ 7		
◇ A J 7	◇ 10 6 5 4		
♣ K 8 2	♣ Q 9 5 4 3		

Although 3C would make a superior declaration, there is no practical way to stop there. Any call by the responder other than a pass will be construed by the opener to be progressive.

SEQUENCE 5

♠ A Q	♠ K 10 8 6 2	2NT	3S
♡ A K 7	♡ J 9 5 4 3	3NT	4H
◇ K Q 5 4	◇ 3 2	No Bid	
♣ K 9 8 3	♣ 7		

Responder, with excellent distribution, albeit only a high-card count of 4 points, offers opener a choice between the spade and heart game contracts.

SEQUENCE 6

♠ A Q 8	♠ K J 10 7 5	2NT	3S
♡ A Q 10 3	♡ 8 2	4C	4S
◇ A J 10	◇ 9 5 4 3	No Bid	
♣ A 10 5	♣ 7 6		

The opener states, with the rebid of 4C, that he has a maximum 2NT; 22 points, and good spade support. Having made his try for a slam, the opener subsides when responder can bid only 4S.

SEQUENCE 7

♠ A J 7	♠ Q 10 8 4	2NT	3C
♡ Q J 10	♡ K 9 5 2	3D	3NT
◇ A K 9 5	◇ 8 4 3	No Bid	
♣ A J 10	♣ 9 5		

With a count of 5 and four cards in each major, responder employs the Stayman Convention. When opener states that he has neither major, partner proceeds to the no-trump game. With 5 opposite 20, the play will be tight but it is adequate. Note how the 10's and 9's give added strength to the hands.

SEQUENCE 8

♠ A J 7 5	♠ Q 10 8 4	2NT	3C
♡ Q J 10	♡ K 9 5 2	3S	4S
◇ A K 9	◇ 8 4 3	No Bid	
♣ A K 10	♣ 9 5		

Responder seeks and finds a fit for a major suit.

SEQUENCE 9

♠ A J	♠ K 7 5 4 3	2NT	3C
♡ A Q 7 2	♡ 9 5	3H	3S
◇ K Q 3	◇ A 10 8 6 5	3NT	No Bid
♣ K Q 10 2	♣ 4		

Responder tries to find a major-suit fit. When opener shows four hearts (thereby denying four spades) responder nevertheless suggests the desirability of a spade contract if opener has Q x x or better. With only two spades, opener bids 3NT and the hand is played there.

SEQUENCE 10

♠ K Q	♠ J 9 8 7 5 4 3	2NT	3S
♡ A Q J 2	♡ 9 5 4	3NT	4S
◇ K Q 10 9	◇ 7 6 3	No Bid	
♣ A 10 7	♣ Void		

Although responder has only 1 point in high cards, the fifth, sixth and seventh spades are equivalent to high cards in trick-taking potential. Through plastic valuation, responder can figure that he will probably be able to hold his losses to one spade trick, one heart trick and one diamond trick.

SEQUENCE 11

♠ A 9 3	♠ K Q 7 6 5 4	2NT	4S
♡ A K 7 6	♡ Q 5 2	5S	5NT
◇ K Q J	◇ 9 5	6 NT	No Bid
♣ A Q 6	♣ 3 2		

The jump to game in a major is reserved for those hands that contain a six-card or longer suit and will produce slam opposite a maximum opening bid rich in Aces and Kings. With 22 points and very efficient high cards, opener suggests a slam and at the same time shows adequate spade support. Since there seems to be no particular advantage to suit play, responder returns to no-trumps so that the declarer may have the benefit of the opening lead running up to the powerful hand rather than through it.

SEQUENCE 12

♠ A 10 3	♠ K J 8 6 5 4	2NT	3C
♡ A J 10	♡ Q 5 4 2	3D	4S
◇ K Q J 5	◇ 9	No Bid	
♣ A J 2	♣ 6 3		

The Stayman Convention probes the heart suit before committing the partnership to a spade contract.

SEQUENCE 13

♠ A 10 7	♠ K J 5 3	2NT	3C
♡ K Q 10	♡ A 7	3D	4NT
◇ K J 5	◇ Q 10 6	No Bid	
♣ A K 9 2	♣ J 8 5 4		

Responder employs the Stayman Convention before showing the full strength of his hand. When opener's rebid of 3D rules out a major-suit contract, responder jumps to 4NT, showing 11—12 points.

SEQUENCE 14

♠ K 10 5	♠ A Q 4	2NT	4NT
♡ A Q 7 6	♡ K 8 5	No Bid	
◇ A J 10	◇ Q 5 4 3		
♣ A Q 9	♣ 8 3 2		

As in Sequence 13, responder asks opener to go on only if he has a maximum.

SEQUENCE 15

♠ A Q 5 4	♠ K J 2	2NT	5NT
♡ K 10	♡ Q 8 5	6D	No Bid
◇ K 10 8 6	◇ A Q J 7		
♣ A K J	♣ 10 3 2		

In this sequence, we illustrate the manner in which the superior suit slam is reached. Although the play for 6NT is adequate, the play for 6D is better. In duplicate, of course, match-point considerations may dictate the selection of 6NT even when the play for that contract is slightly inferior to the play at a minor.

SEQUENCE 16

♠ K 10 5	♠ A 7	2NT	3C
♡ A Q 7 6	♡ K 8 5 2	3H	6H
◇ A J 10	◇ K 9 8 6 4	No Bid	
♣ A Q 9	♣ J 7		

As soon as responder discovers the four-four heart fit, he revalues his hand and gives point count to his doubletons, added value to the heart King, and long-card value to the five-card diamond suit. With the original count of 11 augmented to 14, responder bids the heart slam on the basis of a minimum combined count of 34.

SEQUENCE 17

♠ K Q 4	♠ A 5	2NT	3D
♡ A K 7	♡ 2	3H	3S
◇ K 10 6	◇ Q J 9 5 4 2	5NT	6NT
♣ A Q 8 3	♣ J 10 7 5		

The response of 3D may generally be construed as a mild slam try, since responder would not offer a choice between 3NT and 5D if his hand were balanced and of moderate strength only. In general, the bid of 3D will reflect a six-card suit. There is a simple finesse for the slam.

THE OPENING BID OF 2C

The opening bid of 2C is forcing and artificial. Opener may have

(1) A no-trump hand that counts 23 or more; or
(2) A suit hand that is worth some game contract.

The opener may or may not have a club suit. When the 2C opening bid is used to describe a hand usually termed in other systems "the big two-bid", his first rebid will be in a suit. When, however, the opener has a hand balanced for no-trumps and containing a count of 23—26, his first rebid will be in no-trumps.

RESPONSES TO 2C

The responder may make a positive response (a bid other than 2D) only if he has—

(1) An Ace and King; three Kings; or King and Queen of one suit and King in another; or
(2) A five-card (or longer) suit headed by at least K Q or A J.

With the strength specified in (1) above and a biddable suit, the responder bids the suit. With the required strength and no biddable suit, responder bids 2NT with 7—8 points, and 3NT with 9—10. Holding 11 or more points, responder should bid a suit, biddable or not, but whatever his count, the initial response of 2D must be made if the specified high cards of (1) or suit described in (2) are lacking.

With the suit specified in (2), the response in that suit is made. When the suit is diamonds, the first response will be 3D, since 2D is the conventional denial of the required high-card or suit characteristics. There is, of course, no such thing as a raise of 2C, inasmuch as the opening bid is artificial and does not promise a club suit. The response of 3C promises a biddable club suit.

When the responder makes the negative bid of 2D and yet holds a count that seems important in the light of subsequent bidding, he may take more vigorous action in later bidding, particularly when the opener's rebid in no-trumps indicates that all of responder's high cards will be useful.

OPENER'S REBIDS IN NO-TRUMPS

When the opener's first rebid is in no-trumps, he shows he has a hand distributed 4-3-3-3, 4-4-3-2 or 5-3-3-2 and a count in excess of 22. The opener may have—

(1) 23—24 points, in which case he will make a minimum rebid in no-trumps at his next turn.

(2) 25—26 points, in which case he will make a jump rebid in no-trumps at his next turn.

Coupled with the opening bids of 2NT and 3NT, the opener has four different bids (or bidding combinations) with which he defines his strength within a range of 2 points. This enables the responder to pass when he has less than is required to produce game opposite the less-than-game-going strength indicated by the opener when his first bid or rebid is 2NT. With less than 2 points, responder may pass; otherwise he carries on to game.

If responder's first bid is 3C or 3D, the minimum rebid is, perforce, 3NT; the jump rebid is 4NT. Both bids are quite safe, since in the first case the partnership will have a combined total of 30 points at least; and in the latter case, 32.

The Stayman Convention is used in its normal way except that it appears in responder's second response, the first having been used to disclose the presence or absence of specific characteristics set forth above. There is this difference, however, in its application. Since the responder may be looking for a suit for slam purposes, where majors and minors are equally effective, the Stayman Convention requests opener to bid his highest-ranking suit, major or minor. The following are typical Stayman sequences:

SEQUENCE 18

♠ K Q 5	♠ 9 6 3	2C	2D
♡ A Q 7 6	♡ J 10 2	2NT	No Bid
◊ A J 10	◊ 7 6		
♣ A K 2	♣ 9 8 6 5 4		

Without a count of 2 or more, responder lets the bidding die at 2NT. With another Jack, he would raise to game for a sketchy, but not hopeless contract.

SEQUENCE 19

♠ K Q J 2	♠ 10 7 6 5	2C	2D
♡ A K 7	♡ Q 8 4 2	2NT	3C
◊ A J 10 3	◊ 7	3S	4S
♣ A Q	♣ 10 7 3 2		

The second response of 3C is the Stayman Convention, and through its employment the partnership reaches the excellent 4S contract. The reader's attention is directed to the fact that, although the responder may pass opener's rebid of 2NT, his failure to do so will be construed as marking him with game-going strength, and all bids thereafter are forcing until game is reached.

SEQUENCE 20

♠ A Q 5	♠ K 7 3 2	2C	2D
♡ K 10 9	♡ Q 8 5 4	2NT	3C
◊ A Q J	◊ 9 2	3NT	No Bid
♣ A Q J 2	♣ 7 6 5		

The use of the Stayman Convention, when the opening bid is 2C followed by a rebid in no-trumps, is to elicit information about the biddable suit or suits possessed by opener, *minor or major*. In this respect, the function of the Convention is different from its function when used opposite an opening bid of 1NT or 2NT. When the opener has only one biddable suit, he bids it. When the biddable suit is clubs, he bids no-trumps at the

lowest available level, as in this sequence. When the opener has two biddable suits, he bids the higher-ranking first.

SEQUENCE 21

♠ A 6 5	♠ K Q J 7 6	2C	2S
♡ A Q 8	♡ K 9 5	2NT	4C
◇ K Q J 5	◇ 7 6 2	4NT	5NT
♣ A Q J	♣ 8 3	6NT	*No Bid*

With a high-card count of 9 points and an excellent five-card suit,
responder commits the partnership to a slam with his bid of 5NT, which
demands 6NT and no more. Responder can count five tricks that his
hand will add to the opener's. Since a count of 23—24 will generally
produce 7—8 tricks, he feels there will be better than a 50—50 play for
the slam. Observe responder's use of the Gerber 4C bid to check on the
number of Aces held by the opener. It is possible, though unlikely, that
opener has two Aces only, in which case the slam will not be bid.

SEQUENCE 22

♠ A Q 5 4	♠ J 10 8 6	2C	2D
♡ A K J	♡ 8 7 6 3 2	3NT	4C
◇ A K	◇ Void	4S	No Bid
♣ K Q 7 6	♣ 9 5 4 3		

Opener shows a game-going hand and responder uses the Convention
to search for a four-card heart or spade suit, intending to bid 4H if opener's
rebid is 4D. Opener bids the highest-ranking suit, *minor or major*, when
the Convention is used following the opening bid of 2C. Responder
passes at 4S, being satisfied with this fine contract.

SEQUENCE 23

♠ A J 5 4	♠ K Q 2	2C	3C
♡ A K 10	♡ 9 5 4	6NT	7NT
◇ A K 10	◇ 3 2	No Bid	
♣ A Q 3	♣ K J 10 5 2		

Since opener can mark responder with the King and Queen of spades and
the King of clubs, opener jumps to 6NT for which there must be an
excellent play, and inferentially suggests a grand slam. Had opener
wished to reach the small slam only, his rebid of 5NT would have so
indicated. The jump to 5NT whether by an opening bidder or by a
responder, invariably demands a small slam, and is forcing.

SEQUENCE 24

♠ A 10 9 5	♠ 7	2C	2D
♡ A Q J 2	♡ K 9 5 4	3NT	4C
◇ A K 7	◇ J 9 8 3 2	4S	5D
♣ A K	♣ Q J 10	5H	6H
		No Bid	

Although the responder has a very fine hand opposite what turns out to be a 25—26 point count, he must first respond 2D to indicate that he lacks the specific holdings which would warrant positive action. Having discharged that obligation and now free of that restraint, responder uses the Convention to uncover opener's distribution. When the four-card heart suit is revealed, responder proceeds to the excellent suit slam.

THE OPENING BID OF 3NT

Most American players use the opening bid of 3NT to indicate a balanced hand of enormous power distributed throughout all four suits. There is some authority for employing the bid when opener has a long running suit and a smattering of high cards outside, but it is our experience that it is unwise to use the bid both ways, and we feel that the ortho-dox usage is the soundest. The initial declaration of 3NT announces game in hand opposite a wash-out and its strength, in terms of point count, is 27—28. With so much high-card power, the reader is cautioned against using the bid for hands that contain five-card or longer suits; for long cards buttressed by such great top-card strength put the hand of 27—28 into the slam zone. So responder may assume that the player who bids 3NT has a 4-3-3-3 or a 4-4-3-2 hand.

Since the opener will have a hand that will produce nine tricks without assistance, every high card above a Jack in responder's hand may be rated by him as a winner, and a long suit containing a Queen or higher card will generally be the source of many tricks. A few sequences may illus-trate the kind of action the responder will be called upon to take oppo-site an opening bid of 3NT.

SEQUENCE 25

♠ A K 3	♠ Q 8 7 6 2	3NT	5NT
♡ A Q 10	♡ 9 5 4	6NT	No Bid
◇ A K J 7	◇ Q 6		
♣ A Q 7	♣ 8 3 2		

Responder's two Queens may be counted as trick-winners, and in addi-tion the fourth and fifth spades should prove tremendously valuable. Since opener promises 27, the partnership has a combined count of 31 in high cards plus a five-card suit—enough, ordinarily, to produce a small slam. Responder's bid of 5NT demands six and precludes grand slam action.

SEQUENCE 26

♠ A K 2	♠ 9 8 6 5 4 2	3NT	4S
♡ K Q J 9	♡ 7 6	No Bid	
◇ A K Q	◇ 5 2		
♣ A J 5	♣ 10 7 6		

The response of 4H or 4S over 3NT asserts that the hand may be unproductive at no-trumps (see the next sequence).

SEQUENCE 27

♠ A K 7	♠ Q 8 6 5 4 2	3NT	4S
♡ A K 7 2	♡ 9 5 4	5S	6S
◇ A 9 5	◇ 10	No Bid	
♣ A K Q	♣ 8 7 3		

The power of the long suit opposite the great strength of the 3NT opening is manifest here. Responder's Queen of spades and the fourth, fifth and sixth cards in that suit are winning tricks under the wings of opener's Aces and Kings.

We proceed now to the consideration of other bids in no-trumps.

13

OTHER BIDS IN NO-TRUMPS

PRECEDING CHAPTERS have treated the opening bids of no-trumps and the manner in which bidding sequences are developed when the opening bid is no-trumps. It remains to consider no-trump bids that are injected into the auction, offensively or defensively, after the bidding has been initiated with a suit bid.

It may be stated, with certain minor reservations, that a bid in no-trumps, whenever made, represents a hand of balanced distribution and of narrowly limited strength. Because great reliance is invested in all no-trump bids, it is tremendously important that, wherever they occur during the auction, they be custom-tailored to fit the situations they cover.

Putting aside the opening bids, no-trumps may be bid under five different sets of conditions; in this chapter the requirements of the bid and the manner in which sequences are built upon it are defined. The bid in no-trumps may occur:

(1) As an overcall.
(2) As a response to suit bid.
(3) As a rebid after an opening bid of a suit.
(4) In unusual defensive situations.
(5) In competitive auctions where an informatory double intervenes.

THE OVERCALL OF 1NT

The player who, holding a good hand, hears an opening suit bid at his right faces an entirely different set of problems from those that he confronts when he makes the first bid. To begin with, if he assumes, as he may, that approximately 14 points are held in one hand against him, it is clear that the chances of producing game depend on his partner holding almost all the high cards that are missing. If we accept the fact that game will be made only a small part of the time against an opening bid, we must logically conclude that a player who takes action in the face of an opening bid is bound to take no risk that is disproportionate measured against the part-score that will generally be the ceiling of his team's capabilities.

Giving application to this conclusion, we are able to state the range of strength of the 1NT overcall. Since the opening lead of the opponents has already been marked for them to their advantage, the overcaller should be able to count on that point count which, on average, will give him better than half. To achieve this theoretical edge, opener will require a hand that we have previously defined as the strong no-trump, 16—18 points. We arrive at this figure by a simple calculation:

			Points
The entire pack contains			40
Opponent's opening bid equals		14	
With 16 in overcaller's hand	16		30
There are outstanding .			10
Divide them between partner and opponent .	5	5	
We shall have	21		
Opponents will have		19	

Thus our first requirement for the overcall of 1NT should be backed up by 16—18 points.

Almost needless to say, perhaps, the overcaller must have a stopper or stoppers in the suit bid by his opponent. Second- and third-round stoppers are more desirable than the Ace, because they gain strength through favourable position behind the bidder. A holding such as Q 10 x x, for example, will prove as effective as A K if the opponents persist in attacking the suit, and since only 2 points guard the opponent's suit, the remaining 14—16 will be useful in producing many additional tricks.

When an expert has a close decision to make in respect to overcalling with a bid of 1NT, the possession of third- and fourth-round strength in the adversary's suit generally inclines him to the selection of no-trumps because at a suit contract the value of the Queen and Jack in a suit bid against them is of little consequence, whereas at no-trumps the 3 points they represent may be as useful as 7.

As is almost invariably true, the bid of no-trumps shows that no singleton is contained in the hand. Actually, with important distributional advantages at suit play, the take-out double should be selected rather than 1NT. The overcall of 1NT is preferable with 4-3-3-3 hands, with hands in which there is no four-card major and whenever the opening bid is 1H or 1S, and the probabilities are, therefore, that partner's response will take the partnership beyond 1NT.

When partner overcalls with 1NT, it may be assumed that he has no great interest in suit play, and this is almost conclusively true when the opening bid is 1C or 1D. When the opening bid is 1S, however, partner may have to bid 1NT due to his inability to handle other equally likely responses to a double. Consider your partner's problems when he holds the following hand:

(1) ♠ K J 10   ♡ Q 10 5 4   ◇ K Q 9 2   ♣ A Q
              1S   ?

The opening bid is 1S. With a count of 17 and a 4-4-3-2 distribution, the hand above is well designed for play at hearts, but an informatory double would be very risky. It is true that a response of 2C could be passed, but we should not like to drop out of the bidding at this doubtful station. The immediate overcall of 1NT will be found to be the sounder action with hands of this kind against the opening bid of 1S. If partner does double first and then bid 2NT over your response at the two level, you may assume that his hand was too strong for 1NT. His range, for such bidding, is 18—20.

The Stayman Convention is employed opposite an overcall of 1NT almost precisely as it is opposite the opening bid of 1NT. With chance-giving strength only, overcaller's partner will bid 2C if he has major-suit interest and 2NT with 8—9 points and no four-card length in unbid majors. With sufficient power to force to game, the bid of the opponent's suit (when it is diamonds, hearts or spades) may purchase room for slow investigation of suit possibilities before engaging for 3NT. The following hands are illustrative of those in which the overcall of 1NT is among the bids available to the prospective bidder:

(2) ♠ A J 10   ♡ Q 10 5 4   ◇ K Q J   ♣ A 10 9
              1H   ?

Bid 1NT. This is the classical overcall of 1NT. A count of 17 points, two potential stoppers in the adversary's suit and only 2 points involved in guarding the threat suit, hearts.

(3) ♠ 9 5   ♡ Q 10 5 4   ◇ A K 8 3   ♣ A K J
              1H   ?

Bid 1NT. Observe that the overcall of 1NT may contain a worthless doubleton in one of the unbid suits. The defender cannot always find the perfect defensive call among the limited actions that are available to him.

(4) ♠ Q 10 5   ♡ Q 8 6   ◇ A 4   ♣ A K Q 5 3
              1S   ?

Bid 1NT. The five-card near-solid club suit makes this type of hand very attractive for no-trumps.

(5) ♠ A 10 5 4   ♡ A J 8 2   ◇ 5 3   ♣ A Q J
             1C   ?

Double. If the response is 1D, the Doubler may then bid 1NT, having lost nothing in his investigation of major-suit possibilities.

(6) ♠ A 10 5 4   ♡ A J 8 2   ◇ 5 3   ♣ A Q J
             1H   ?

Bid *1NT*. Partner, with 8—9 points and strength in spades, will use Stayman to ferret out a four-four trump fit, so there is no risk that a game at no-trumps will be reached without probing the spade suit.

(7) ♠ 3 2   ♡ A 7 6   ◇ K 10 8   ♣ A K Q 3 2
         1D   No Bid   1H   ?

Bid *1NT*. The overcall of 1NT may be made second or fourth hand and has the same requirements: a balanced hand, stoppers in all bid suits and 16—18. There is this cautionary word of advice, however. With both opponents bidding, there is increased danger in the overcall of 1NT; and, especially when vulnerable, it should be used only when, as in the hand above, there is a suit that should produce a large number of tricks and when the penalty loss, therefore, cannot be catastrophic. It is much better to delay action with a hand like the following, although it counts 16:

(8) ♠ K J 3   ♡ A J 7 2   ◇ K Q 8   ♣ Q 7 5
         1D   No Bid   1H   *No Bid*

The chances of producing more than a part-score are very slight, and the bid of 1NT could conceivably cost 1,100 or 1,400 points.

(9) ♠ Q 10 9 2   ♡ A J 5   ◇ K 9 4   ♣ K 3 2
         1S   No Bid   No Bid   ?

Bid *1NT*. Here we have an exception to the rule specifying a count of 16—18 for the overcall of 1NT. Since the opener's partner has marked himself with a worthless or near-worthless hand, fourth hand is bound to protect his partner's pass. This action is often termed "balancing". There would be little point in doubling with a hand perfectly balanced for no-trumps and containing stoppers in the opponent's suit. The pass by opener's partner practically eliminates the risk of penalty action. In this fourth-hand protective position, the requirements for the bid of 1NT are 12—14 and the bid is handled precisely as is the weak no-trump opening bid. The range of 12—14 is not affected by the size of the no-trump in general use by a partnership nor does vulnerability alter its requirements.

(10) ♠ K J 5 4   ♡ 3 2   ◇ A 7 5   ♣ K 10 7 6

South	West	North	East
1H	1NT	2H	?

Bid 3H. With sufficient strength to warrant game-forcing action, the bid of the opponent's suit is made to tell partner that game must be reached (or a penalty double imposed) and that East is interested in checking up on the possible presence of a four-four spade fit. In this type of sequence, the bid of 2NT by East would be chance-giving and 2S, 3C or 3D sign-offs.

THE OVERCALL OF 2NT OR 3NT

The overcall of 2NT or 3NT is best reserved for hands that contain a long running suit and a scattering of intermediate high cards elsewhere. The bid should not be rescued, and any bid other than game made opposite the overcall of 2NT is to be interpreted as constructive and forcing. With any interest in suit play, the overcall of 2NT or 3NT would not have been made. A bid of a five-card suit opposite a 2NT overcall is rather pointless, and the overcaller will, therefore, assume that partner's suit is six cards in length and will support him on that basis.

(11) ♠ K 9   ♡ Q 3 2   ◇ A K Q J 5 4   ♣ 9 5

	1S	?

Bid *2NT*. Your partner can take action on the basis that you will take seven tricks without his assistance and will need a couple of quick winners to produce game.

(12) ♠ K J 5   ♡ A Q 2   ◇ A K J 7   ♣ Q 10 4

	1S	?

Double. Your next bid will be 2NT and partner will thus be informed that you have about 20 points well distributed throughout the four suits.

(13) ♠ A Q 9 8 5 3   ♡ 7 2   ◇ 5 4   ♣ J 10 6

	1H	2NT	No Bid	?

Bid *3NT*. Partner has seven running tricks and you may give him two more. The bid of 3S would accomplish nothing worth while. There is a reasonable play for the no-trump game; there is probably no play for 4S.

THE RESPONSE OF 2NT AND 3NT TO A SUIT BID OF ONE

As already covered in Chapter 5 the Stayman System utilizes the range of strength that is in current use by many other systems for the direct responses of 2NT and 3NT. The whole range of bids in no-trumps is in the smaller segment of the game of contract bridge that may be described as "scientific". Even this description is only appropriate as contrasted with the larger segment of the bidding scope which is far from scientific and loses substantially when approached with that frame of mind.

The opener has bid 1D. The responder holds:

(14) ♠ K 8 7   ♡ A J 6   ◇ K J 6   ♣ K 10 6 5

Bid *2NT*. With this bid you describe a hand of 13—15 points, with even distribution (no singleton, only one doubleton) and all unbid suits stopped. Such definition should take your side to its best final contract, and tell the enemy as little as possible to aid them in the defence.

(15) ♠ A 7   ♡ K 7   ◇ A 9 7 6   ♣ K 8 7 6 5

Bid *2C*. Though your point count is within the 13—15 point range, a bid of 2NT is not best, in view of the 5-4-2-2 distribution. The pre-emption of bidding space may act against your side, preventing your reaching a superior minor-suit slam or game contract instead of a contract of 3NT that may even be defeated, occasionally.

(16) ♠ K 9 5   ♡ A 7 6   ◇ 5 4 3   ♣ A J 3 2
No Bid   No Bid   1D   No Bid
2NT

When the bidding is opened third or fourth hand, the 2NT response indicates a balanced hand and a count of 12—13 (occasionally 11 points with excellent fillers). Naturally, this action is not forcing on opener. It is strictly descriptive and, of course, invitational. Opener passes only with a dead minimum or a shaded third-hand opening.

OPENER'S REBID OF NO-TRUMPS

THE REBID OF 1NT

After opening the bidding with one of a suit, the response being in a suit at the one level, the rebid of 1NT tells several things about the opener's distribution and about the general size of his hand. We recall that the rebid of 1NT is a minimum rebid. But there are bad minimums and good ones, and it is desirable to provide ourselves with methods which give responder the least possible guesswork.

If your bidding methods call for the use of a 12—14 opening 1NT, the rebid of 1NT states that the opener has a hand ranging from 15 to 17. This imposes little hardship on us, because with most hands counting 12—14 the opening bid of 1NT would have been made; and with other hands counting 12—14 with which we chose not to open with 1NT for distributional reasons, we disdain the rebid of 1NT in favour of a suit rebid or the bid of a second suit. Thus

    1D   1H   (system calling for 12—14 opening 1NT)
    1NT

states that opener has 15, 16 or 17 points.

If your bidding methods call for the use of a 16—18 opening no-trump, the rebid of 1NT states that the opener has less than 16 points, or a weak 16 (with no good intermediate cards). Accordingly, we assume that when the bidding has proceeded

    1D   1S   (system calling for 16—18 opening 1NT)
    1NT

the opener has 13, 14 or 15 points. Here again it is true that the opening bidder will have to eliminate the rebid of 1NT when his hand counts 16 or 17 and did not qualify, for one reason or another, for an opening 1NT. With that much strength, the opener will either rebid his suit or bid another suit, thus avoiding the implications of the 1NT rebid.

An examination of a few hands may be helpful in reviewing the action of the opener that enables him to differentiate between weak and strong minimum hands.

  (17) ♠ A Q 5   ♡ K 6 2   ◇ 3 2   ♣ A K 7 6 2
            (with 16—18 no-trump)
               1C   1D
               ?

Bid 2C. The rebid of 1NT would convey the idea that opener had less than 16 points. He bids 2C to avoid that implication.

  (18) ♠ K 5 4   ♡ 3 2   ◇ A K 7 5 4   ♣ K J 3
       (with 12—14 no-trump or with 16—18 no-trump)
             1D   1H
             ?

Bid 1NT. If you use the 12—14 no-trump, partner will assume that you have 15 or better. If you use the strong no-trump, he will assume that you have less than 16 points.

  (19) ♠ A 5 4   ♡ Q J 7 6   ◇ K 9 5 4   ♣ 10 2
            (with weak no-trump)
             1C   1H
             1NT   ?

Bid 2NT. With a count of 10 points, your action as responder is dictated by your assurance that the opening bidder has a count of 15, 16 or 17 points. The chance-giving bid of 2NT is made to permit opener to proceed to game if he has 16 or 17.

THE REBID OF 2NT OVER A RESPONSE AT THE ONE LEVEL

When the opener jump rebids 2NT, he states that he has a point count, coupled with what the responder promises, sufficient to produce eight tricks at no-trumps. Since 24—25 are required for this purpose, and since the responder may be counted on for 6 points only, we establish the range of the rebid at 18—19. In addition, the opening bidder indicates that his hand is balanced and that stoppers are held in unbid suits. The opener may have a count of 20 in a hand that did not qualify for an opening bid of 2NT because it lacked a stopper in the suit responder has bid.

(20)　♠ A J 9　　♡ K Q 8 6　　◇ A 10 2　　♣ A J 6　(19)
　　　　　　1C　　　　　1D
　　　　　　2NT

With a count of 19, opener was too good for 1NT and a point shy of 2NT. With such in-between hands, the jump rebid serves perfectly to give precise definition to his great strength.

(21)　♠ K Q 8 6　　♡ 9 5　　◇ A K Q 2　　♣ A J 4
　　　　　1D　　　　　1H
　　　　　1S

The one-over-one bid of 1S is preferred to the jump rebid of 2NT, following the principle that major suits should be investigated before the bidding is directed into no-trump channels. Since 1S is 90 per cent. forcing and will not be passed by responder unless he has a bare 6 points or less, there is no danger that a game will be missed. It follows that when the bidding has gone

　　　　　1C　　　　1D or 1H
　　　　　2NT

the responder may assume that the opener does not hold a biddable major suit, and accordingly responder need not embark on any further exploration of major-suit possibilities that require four-card support.

THE REBID OF 3NT OVER A RESPONSE AT THE ONE LEVEL

When the opener rebids 3NT over a response at the one level, he shows a full 20 points and may run as high as 24. As with the rebid of 2NT, opener also promises a hand distributed 4-3-3-3, 4-4-3-2 or 5-3-3-2 and all side suits stopped. Inasmuch as opener did not start the bidding with 2NT (or 2C), it is almost certain that he was prevented from doing so by the lack of a stopper in the suit bid by responder.

(22)   ♠ A K 9   ♡ 5 4   ◇ A Q J 5 4   ♣ A Q 10
            1D   1H
            3NT

When the opening bid is one in a major suit, the jump rebid of 2NT or 3NT marks the opener almost certainly with a 5-3-3-2 distribution, since the major-suit opening bid guarantees a five-card suit. The opener may, occasionally, make the jump rebid of 2NT with 5-4-2-2 distribution, but the tremendous slam possibilities inherent in a hand counting 20 or more make it undesirable to rebid 3NT when the opener's hand is a semi-two-suiter:

(23)   ♠ A Q   ♡ K J 5 4 2   ◇ Q 8 6 3   ♣ A Q
            1H   1S
            2NT

The opener's club holding is such as to incline him to the rebid of 2NT. Furthermore, he has no better bid available; 3D would be forcing to game, and opener, with 19, cannot assume that responder has more than 6 points. The bid of 2D would be a tremendous underbid.

(24)   ♠ A Q   ♡ K J 5 4 2   ◇ A Q 8 3   ♣ A Q
            1H   1S
            3D

With a count of 23, there are great slam possibilities and they may lie in diamonds if responder has adequate support for that secondary suit. The rebid of 3D leaves freedom to move in one of many directions and conveys to responder the idea that opener's hand is shaped better for suit play than for no-trumps.

    As with hand (21), major suits should be probed in advance of bidding no-trumps, and when opener is strong enough to force to game, a jump rebid in the major is a better action than *3NT*:

(25)   ♠ A K 9 5   ♡ 4 2   ◇ A K Q 5   ♣ A J 3
            1D   1H
            2S

Example hands (21) and (25) illustrate a principle that we have reiterated many times in this book: *Do not carelessly by-pass the trump road to game.*

There will be times, of course, when a suit bid cannot be made because it does not adequately reflect the strength of your hand, but when a major-suit bid does the job as well, do not forsake it.

THE REBID OF 3NT OVER A RESPONSE AT THE TWO LEVEL

The rebid of 3NT over a response at the two level shows 18—19 points, just as does the rebid of 2NT over a response at the one level. However, since responder shows at least 12 points when he enters the two level, the chances of a slam are not insubstantial and the rebid of 3NT should be made only when support for partner's suit is no better than fair. With good support, especially for hearts, cue-bidding may pave the way for a better sequence:

(26) ♠ A Q 10 5 4   ♥ A 9   ♦ A 9 7   ♣ K J 2

1S	2H
3NT	

Responder knows that opener has a count of 18—19 and a five-card spade suit. The rebid of 3NT suggests that opener's heart support is moderate at best.

THE UNUSUAL NO-TRUMP OVERCALL

When a player overcalls with a bid in no-trumps in a situation where it must be apparent that he does not hold the strength required for that bid, the Stayman System assigns to that overcall the functions of a limited informatory double. When only one major suit has been bid, the unusual overcall asks partner to bid his better minor suit.

(a)	1S	No Bid	2S	No Bid
	No Bid	2NT		

or

(b)	1S	No Bid	1NT	No Bid
	2S	No Bid	No Bid	2NT

or

(c)	No Bid	No Bid	No Bid	1S
	1NT			

In rare cases, the overcall of 3NT may be used similarly, but the reader must be careful not to confuse the standard no-trump overcall with the unusual one. If the 2NT or 3NT overcall may be standard, it must be so construed. In general, a prior pass by the overcaller will be the distinguishing feature of the unusual no-trump overcall.

THE BID OF 1NT IN COMPETITIVE AUCTIONS WHERE AN INFORMATORY DOUBLE INTERVENES

There are three situations in which the bid of 1NT may be employed in a competitive auction after a double has been injected into the bidding:

(1)	1D	Double	1NT	
(2)	1D	Double	No Bid	1NT
		or		
	1D	Double	1H	1NT
(3)	1D	No Bid	1H	Double
	1NT			

We cannot consider the treatment of no-trump bidding complete without devoting a few lines to each of these sequences.

The immediate response of 1NT over an intervening double indicates, of course, that the responder has taken a constructive action and we are warranted in assuming that he hopes to make seven tricks at no-trumps if he is permitted to play the deal at that contract. Since the opening bidder promises 13—14 points, we should expect to find responder with sufficient strength to give the offensive pair more than half the 40 points contained in the pack. This would require his contribution of at least 8 points. Because, frequently, delay in bidding may leave responder trapped by his own initial inaction, the range of the immediate response of 1NT is set at 8—11. With 12 points or more, a redouble communicates the fact of great strength to the opener and sets the stage for penalty action. The following hands are typical 1NT responses over intervening doubles:

(27)　♠　A 10 4　　♡　K J 2　　◇　Q 8 5 3　　♣　9 6 2　(10)
　　　　　　　　1C　　　Double　　　1NT

When your partner doubles an opening suit bid, he does so because he has great distributional advantages in his hand that make suit play desirable. He asks that you bid your best suit and implies that he will furnish enough trump support to give safety to your action. A bid in no-trumps opposite an informatory double is generally the last call he wants to hear, and it should be avoided, accordingly, unless the doubler's partner lacks an unbid four-card major and has enough strength in high cards to stand off the opponents in their suits. The range for this bid of 1NT is the same as in a response to an opening bid over an intervening double: 8—11.

(28)　♠　A J 9 5　　♡　A 7 6　　◇　J 10 3　　♣　6 5 4
　　　　　1S　　Double　　No Bid　　1NT

Should partner move out into a suit of his own, you have three-card support.

(29) ♠ A 5 4   ♥ K 3 2   ♦ 9 5 3   ♣ 10 6 4 2

      1S   Double   No Bid   2C

With only one guard against the adversary's suit, the bid of your four-card suit is preferable. More than half your point count will promote only one trick.

Finally, the opener's rebid of 1NT after a double intervenes on his right. Here, again, the bid must be interpreted as constructive. The floor of this rebid is 15 and its ceiling 17. The following are examples of this "free" rebid of 1NT:

(30) ♠ K 10 2   ♥ Q 3   ♦ A J 10 9 2   ♣ K Q 5   (16)

      1D   No Bid   1H   Double

      1NT

(31) ♠ Q 10 9 2   ♥ 7 5   ♦ K Q J 7 6   ♣ A K   (16)

      1D   No Bid   1H   Double

      1NT

Since, with greater strength, the opener may well be able to penalize the adversaries, a redouble is the better action when opener holds 18 points or more, after which a decision will be made either to penalize the enemy or go on towards a game or part-score.

14

PRE-EMPTIVE BIDDING AND PSYCHICS

A PRE-EMPTIVE action is a bid made at a level higher than necessary, often with the expectation of suffering a penalty, and designed expressly for the purpose of making it difficult or impossible for the opponents to reach their most favourable contract. The effectiveness of this move depends on the skill with which it is employed and on the division of the outstanding high cards at the time it is used. Under certain conditions, the effect on the adversaries can be devastating, as when—their joint strength being evenly divided—the risk of severe penalty inhibits each opponent from entering the auction at the high level offered him. Not infrequently a vulnerable slam or game may thus be taken from the enemy at a trifling price.

OPENING BID OF FOUR IN A SUIT

Commonest of these "shut-out" bids are those made at the level of four. Pre-emptive three bids are also common, and the weak two bid, while not precisely the same form of action, shares some of the characteristics of the "shut-out" bid. Since accurate bidding sequences ordinarily require the use of the lower bidding levels, a player who deliberately disdains to use them does so because his own hand is of a type that is easily defined in one call, and because he is fearful that if the opponents are permitted to communicate freely with each other, it will be costly for his side.

It is only when he may reasonably foresee that the opponents will take command of the bidding that a player may offer a penalty to them in advance of any assertion of strength on their part. With the elements of an opening bid in his hand, no player has just cause to be fearful of his adversaries; for with 13 or 14 points accounted for, the normal division of the remaining 26—27 points will give his pair a decisive preponderance, and it is to his advantage that the lower levels remain open to his own pair so that they may carefully assess their combined potential.

When, on the other hand, a player holds a hand that will yield one or

142

no defensive tricks, he cannot be unaware of the likelihood that the opponents will chalk up a game or perhaps a slam if the bidding is allowed to take its normal course, and it is at this point that he must do everything possible to interfere with their lines of communication. With a hand that contains a seven-card or longer suit, consideration must always be given to a manœuvre that can force the opposing pair into a hasty and inaccurate decision.

We formulate two rules that constitute the chief pillars of pre-emptive bidding:

(A) The pre-emptive hand should usually contain no more than $1\frac{1}{2}$ likely defensive winners,

(B) The bidder should not offer his opponents a penalty in excess of their probable potential on the deal.

In connection with (A), when a suit is seven cards in length or longer, we arbitrarily assume that only the Ace of that suit will provide a defensive winner, since it is quite unlikely that each opponent will have two cards of the outstanding six. Thus K Q J 10 9 8 7 is a suit of six offensive winners, but cannot be counted on to win a single trick if the opponents name the final contract.

Regarding Rule (B), it makes good sense to offer your adversaries a maximum of 500 points when you think they have a sure 620 or 650 and a possible 1,430. But it rarely makes sense to offer them a sacrifice at the six level before they have reached a slam. Generally, it is time to pay the top price when the opponents' bidding drives us to it; furthermore, no matter how worthless your own hand may be, you are hardly in a position to know what tricks your partner's hand may win.

Both sides vulnerable:

(1) ♠ K Q J 9 8 6 2   ♡ 8   ◇ Q J 10 5   ♣ 7
4S

(2) ♠ Q J 10 8 6 5 3 2   ♡ J 10 9 4   ◇ Void   ♣ 6
4S

(3) ♠ J 5   ♡ A K Q 8 6 5 4 3 2   ◇ 6   ♣ 2
4H

Hand (1) will yield eight probable winners and it is doubtful that it will produce a single winner defensively. We call this hand the perfect pre-emptive type, because it contains a definite number of offensive tricks and, therefore, presents a risk of known and limited proportions; and it is worthless in defence. With hand (2) we seemingly violate one of our rules by offering the opponents a penalty greater than the value of their game. This is permissible when a hand contains *no* defensive winners and the overbid involves only 100 or 200 additional points. The chances of opponents holding sufficient power for a slam are very great when a hand such as (2) is held, and any bid less than 4S would be a half-measure. Hand (3) contains a nine-card suit, and its owner cannot count on a single defensive winner. In this case, there is an excellent chance that the contract will be fulfilled.

Both sides vulnerable:

(4) ♠ K J 9 5 4 3 2   ♡ A 6 5   ◇ 9 5 4   ♣ Void

This hand contains one sure defensive winner, with another doubtful trick represented by the spade King. There are five quite certain winners —probably six; but we are too weak for a pre-emptive bid of four. We shall find, later on in this chapter, that this hand does qualify for shut-out action, but of a different kind.

Now that we have skimmed over the surface of the pre-emptive opening bid of four, it may be helpful to retrace our steps and summarize the advantages of shut-out action. Not infrequently, your pre-empt will keep the opponents out of the auction and permit you to steal the deal at a small loss. Once in a while you will even succeed in making your contract in circumstances where, but for your crowding action, the adversaries might have scored. Even when you do not accomplish your primary objective of keeping them silent, by taking away the exploratory levels of bidding you force them to find their contract in a very confined bidding space. Not uncommonly, the confusion and despair that result impel them into a bad contract, and you get a plus-score when your loss might have been considerable had you given them exclusive occupancy of the bidding premises. Finally, the pressure of pre-emptive tactics keeps the opponents in a constant state of unease that takes its toll on hands where you have no intention of participating in the auction. A player who is known to use harassing methods is a "brooding omnipresence" at the card table.

While it is perfectly sound to bid 4H or 4S with a solid suit, the opening bid of 4C or 4D is almost always rejected as a shut-out when the suit is solid, for with seven sure immediate winners, very little scattered strength in partner's hand will suffice to bring in a 3NT contract. In the American Summer Nationals of 1953, the following deal swung the entire match:

(5) Both sides vulnerable. South dealer.

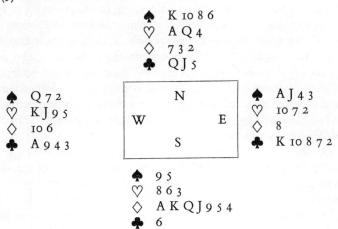

```
                    ♠ K 10 8 6
                    ♡ A Q 4
                    ◇ 7 3 2
                    ♣ Q J 5
♠ Q 7 2                                 ♠ A J 4 3
♡ K J 9 5          N                    ♡ 10 7 2
◇ 10 6          W     E                 ◇ 8
♣ A 9 4 3          S                    ♣ K 10 8 7 2
                    ♠ 9 5
                    ♡ 8 6 3
                    ◇ A K Q J 9 5 4
                    ♣ 6
```

At one table, North and South using the weak no-trump, the bidding was very simple: North bid one no-trump after two passes and South raised to three no-trumps. East led the club 7 and North-South scored 630 points.

At the other table, South opened the bidding with 4D and went down one for no score—a swing of 630 points on the deal, the result of a bad opening pre-emptive bid. Examination of South's hand will reveal that it does not require a very strong hand opposite a running seven-card suit to make a no-trump game, and for that reason the opening four bid should be shunned unless partner has already passed.

Since the bid of 4C or 4D denies a solid suit, the ideal suit for the minor shut-out is Q J 10 x x x x.

(6) ♠ A 7   ♡ 8   ◇ A J 10 8 6 5 4 2   ♣ 5 3
            4D

(7) ♠ 5   ♡ 3   ◇ K Q 10 9 8 7 6   ♣ Q J 10 2
            4D

Because the minor-suit four bid permits the opponents to bid either major suit at the four level, it is not quite as effective a barrier as the bid of 4H or 4S, and accordingly the risk taken by the bidder should be on the conservative side. As the effectiveness of a manœuvre diminishes, it is obviously not worth as great a peril.

RESPONSES TO OPENING FOUR BIDS

When the opening bid is 4H or 4S, the responder's only problem is faced when he thinks he holds sufficient strength to be concerned about a slam. With game already bid, no purpose is served in pushing a contract higher unless a slam is the objective. It is a losing cause, generally, to bid your suit in a contest with your partner to name the final declaration. If you have a very long spade suit, for example, it is quite likely that his major objective was to prevent the opponents from bidding spades and you may merely drive him one level higher. Your silence will be feared more by the opponents than a bid that will merely convey additional distributional information to them; and bear in mind that when your partner's shut-out bid has reached you, one opponent has already passed. Your bid re-establishes him as a live unfriendly force.

Granted, then, that partner of the pre-emptive bidder will move voluntarily over 4H or 4S only to probe slam possibilities, let us consider under what circumstances responder should make a slam move.

Pre-emptive bids work just as effectively against partner as they do against the opponents, and all the responder can do is apply a few simple rules and hope things come out right. If you are vulnerable and the opponents are not, it is quite clear that your partner thinks he will win eight tricks with no assistance from you. If both sides are vulnerable, he hopes to win seven or eight. If neither side is vulnerable, he hopes to win seven or eight. If you are not vulnerable and the opponents are, he may hope to win only six.

Perhaps the best way of estimating your chances of a slam is to combine your hand mentally with a typical one you visualize to be held by your partner. You will then be able to determine whether you can hope to produce twelve tricks between you.

All pre-emptive bids of four are not necessarily overbid to their permissible maximum and, accordingly, responder may raise to the five level if he wishes the opener to proceed to a slam when his hand has been overbid less than the allowable limit.

   (8) ♠ 9 5 4   ♡ A K 8 7 3 2   ◇ A 7   ♣ K 4

        Not vulnerable against vulnerable opponents

           4S   No Bid   ?

If opener has a solid spade suit, there is a good chance that a small slam will make, but there are many hands he may hold that, even with your great strength, will make 4S and no more. All in all, the chances of game being jeopardized by a 5S bid make any action but a pass inadvisable. He may, for example, have

      ♠ K Q J 10 8 6 3   ♡ 9   ◇ 3 2   ♣ 8 5 3

or

      ♠ Q J 10 9 6 3 2   ♡ 6   ◇ 6 4 2   ♣ 9 5

or even

♠ Q J 10 8 7 6 3 2   ♡ 9   ◊ 6 3   ♣ 5 2

in which event there is no play for slam and the play for 5S is, in two cases, almost hopeless.

(9) ♠ 9   ♡ A Q J 3   ◊ A K 7   ♣ A Q 5 4 3
     Vulnerable against non-vulnerable opponents
     4S   No Bid   ?

Your partner's vulnerable bid of 4S promises eight winners and his hand may be visualized to look like this:

♠ A K Q J 8 6 3 2   ♡ 9 5   ◊ 7   ♣ 6 2

Your response is 6S. It is unlikely that the play for slam is worse than a finesse.

THE RAISE TO GAME OF 4C OR 4D

Since only a part-score is jeopardized in a single raise of 4C or 4D and, because game is worth bidding if it will be successful about four times out of ten, the raise to a minor-suit game should be made with a hand rich in controls which rates to produce ten or eleven tricks.

(10) ♠ A K 9 4 2   ♡ Q J 7   ◊ K 7   ♣ A 5 4
     Neither side vulnerable
     4D   No Bid   5D

(11) ♠ A Q 8 7 6   ♡ K Q J 4   ◊ A K 2   ♣ 9
     Vulnerable against non-vulnerable opponents
     4C   No Bid   5C

THE RESPONSE OF 4H OR 4S

The responses of 4H and 4S must be construed as a desire to play the deal at the major-suit game.

THE OPENING BIDS OF 3H AND 3S

The opening bids of 3H and 3S are governed by practically the same rules as their bigger brothers. Being at a lower level, they require one less trick than do the four bids. Where a hand contains no defensive winners, and there is a choice between three and four, the latter should be preferred, for it is a bid of much greater effectiveness. So, with the following hand, neither side being vulnerable,

(12) ♠ Q J 10 9 8 6 5 4 2   ♡ 8 5   ◊ 6 2   ♣ Void

the opening bid is 4S, not 3S. The extra bidding level taken from the opponents is well worth the additional risk of 200 points.

The raise of the pre-emptive three bids depends on responder's ability to contribute consolidating cards that will limit the losses to three tricks. If you always visualize opener's hand as something like this

(13) ♠ K Q J 9 5 4 2   ♡ 6 4   ♢ 9 3   ♣ 10 2

you will be able to decide very easily whether a raise to game is warranted and when slam exploration should be undertaken.

THE OPENING BIDS OF 3C AND 3D

We do not particularly favour the opening bids of 3C and 3D. They have some pre-emptive value, but can often give away decided advantages to an opponent whose declarer play is simplified by the disclosure that the opening bidder is short-suited. The following is a sound opening 3C bid not vulnerable:

(14) ♠ 9 5   ♡ 8 6   ♢ 3 2   ♣ K Q J 10 8 6 4
                            3C

If partner bids 3NT, he should be permitted to play the hand there.

THE WEAK TWO BID

The opening bid of 2D, 2H or 2S suggests a game-forcing hand to many players. But long experience with these bids as mild shut-outs has convinced us that they have much greater utility as pre-emptive bids than as forcing bids. In a succeeding chapter, we explain the use of the opening 2C bid as the sole forcing two bid.

The requirements for the weak opening two bid are:

(1) A hand that does not qualify for an opening bid of one.
(2) A good suit, generally six cards in length, or longer.
(3) A total of five to seven playing tricks depending on vulnerability.

(15) ♠ A Q J 5 4 3   ♡ 2   ♢ 8 5 4   ♣ K 7 6
                          2S

(16) ♠ K Q 9 8 5 4 2   ♡ 9   ♢ 8 3 2   ♣ 6 3
                            2S

(17) ♠ 9 5   ♡ A 6 2   ♢ Q J 10 9 8 5   ♣ 7 4
                          2D

(18) ♠ K Q J 9 5 4   ♡ A Q   ♢ 7 5 3   ♣ 8 2
            1S (2S may be bid third or fourth hand)

RESPONSES TO WEAK TWO BIDS

A raise to three, whether over an intervening bid or not, is pre-emptive in nature and should not be interpreted as a move to invite game. Since the responder's hand may be one of many types and since he may, conceivably, be laying a trap for the opponents, he alone should decide about sacrificing if and when the adversaries reach game.

(19) ♠ K 9 5 4   ♡ 8   ◇ Q 9 5 4 3   ♣ 7 6 3
                2S   P   3S

Any bid other than a single raise (except a game bid) is forcing on the opener for one round. Responder may drop the opener's rebid, particularly if it is a rebid of his suit. Hence, responder's initial bid can be a psychic.

SEQUENCE 20

Opener	Responder	Opener	Responder
♠ K Q 10 8 6 4	♠ A 7	2S	2NT
♡ 9	♡ K 9 5 3	3D	4S
◇ A 7 4 2	◇ K Q 8 6		
♣ 6 3	♣ 5 4 2		

The rebid of 3D indicates that opener has a good hand (within the limits of the weak two bid, of course). With the assurance that his diamond strength will be of significant value to the opener, responder moves directly into game.

Not vulnerable against vulnerable opponents, the opening two bid may be made with a light hand, but for the sake of partnership confidence and in order that game and slam sequences may be built on a foundation that does not crumble, the opener should have as good as a trick and a half *in high cards*. Rarely, of course, will it contain more than two quick winners, because with so much high-card power and the strength of a six-card suit, an opening bid of one should be made.

SEQUENCE 21

Vulnerable

♠ A K J 9 5 4	♠ 8 6	2S	3H
♡ 8 2	♡ A K 10 7 5	3S	No Bid
◇ 7 5	◇ A 4		
♣ 6 4 3	♣ J 10 6 5		

Responder can afford one constructive bid because opposite a seven-trick hand, game is a good gamble. His bid is never a rescue. Opener has poor distribution and shows a minimum hand by simply rebidding his suit.

SEQUENCE 22

♠ 8	♠ A 5 4	2H	3D
♡ K Q J 10 8 5	♡ 9 2	4H	
◇ 8 3	◇ A K Q 7 4		
♣ K 10 6 3	♣ 9 5 4		

Opener, with six playing tricks and an aggressive distribution, jumps to game over partner's constructive response. If opener had rebid 3H, responder would probably pass. Compare with Sequence 21.

SEQUENCE 23

♠ 9	♠ A 5 4	2H	2NT
♡ K J 10 6 5 4	♡ 9 2	3H	No Bid
◇ K 9	◇ A Q 8 5		
♣ 10 8 3 2	♣ K J 5 4		

The response of 2NT ostensibly indicates a willingness to reach game if opener has better than a bare minimum. When the response is 2NT, the opener rebids his suit to show a minimum and bids another suit to show a good hand. The final decision as to game must be made by responder. Compare with Sequence 22. Note that when the response is in a suit, opener may jump to game with a maximum. But when the response is 2NT, it is possible that responder is fooling, and opener conveys the message of strength by bidding a second suit.

SEQUENCE 24

♠ K Q 10 8 6 4	♠ 2	2S	3H	Double
♡ 9	♡ Q 10 8 6			
◇ K 8 2	◇ A Q 9 5			
♣ 9 5 4	♣ K Q J 2			

The opponents often find the weak two bid an irresistible inducement to overcall and not infrequently the responder is given an opportunity to take attractive penalty action. Since responder has full knowledge that opener's hand is weak defensively, opener should not make the mistake of nullifying his action. Respect your partner's judgment. When you have told him what your hand contains, let him make the decision. He sees your hand perfectly; you know absolutely nothing about his.

PRE-EMPTIVE RESPONSES

So far we have discussed opening bids that are made at a level higher than one with the purpose of taking bidding space from the opponents. We shall now consider jump responses that are made to opening suit bids of one and that represent less strength than is depicted by similar bids in most systems.

When the bidding has been opened by your partner and the next hand remains silent, there is little reason to fear that the opponents will wrest the bidding from you. If you hold great balanced power, you will welcome an overcall because you may either go on to a declaration of your own selection, or double for penalties. With little general strength, the contest for the auction may be spirited, but there is nothing you can do to deter action by your left-hand opponent that may not cost more than it is worth; so you respond normally. It is only when you have great offensive strength in a suit of your own, or unusual consolidation for partner's suit and no substantial outside strength, that you are in a position to erect a barrier against the adversaries without great risk to your pair. And it is best that you do so.

When no contention has been offered at your right, there are two types of pre-emptive action that may be available to you:

(25)   ♠ K Q J 9 5 4 3   ♡ 8 2   ◇ 9 5   ♣ 4 3
            1D   No Bid   ?

Bid *3S*. Here we have the classical pre-emptive response at the three level: a seven-card suit nearly solid and an otherwise worthless hand, which (1) perfectly defines your hand as an inflexible one-suiter needing no support and guaranteeing six winners, and (2) makes it difficult for the opponents to enter the bidding.

SEQUENCE 26

♠ 2	♠ K Q J 10 9 5 4	1C	3S
♡ A 10 5 4	♡ 8 3	4S	
◇ K Q 3	◇ 9 5 4		
♣ A K 8 5 4	♣ 2		

Opener has no hesitancy in raising to a spade game with a singleton, since he knows that responder is independently impregnable in that suit.

SEQUENCE 27

♠ Q 7 4 3	♠ 9	1C	3H
♡ Void	♡ A Q J 10 8 6 2	No Bid	
◇ A 9 5 2	◇ 8 6 4		
♣ A K 8 4 3	♣ 5 2		

Opener does not fight his partner for the contract. Observe that had responder bid 1H initially, his second response would be a difficult selection. In this form of responsive pre-emption, it is sometimes possible to be more definitive by skipping a few levels of bidding than it is by preserving them for slower portrayal.

The pre-emptive raise to game in partner's suit, which we have treated in earlier pages, is common to practically all systems.

(28) ♠ 9   ♡ Q J 8 5   ◇ A 10 6 5 4 2   ♣ 8 6
        1H   No Bid   4H

Responsive pre-empts are unlike opening shut-outs in a very important particular: *the bidder hopes to bring in the contract,* but anticipates the possibility of contention and guards against it by bidding his limit at once. It would, of course, be pointless to overbid your hand and offer a penalty to the adversaries when your own partner has started the offensive and the enemy may have neither the ammunition nor the fortitude to start a bidding argument.

PRE-EMPTIVE RESPONSES IN COMPETITIVE SITUATIONS

The entrance of an opponent into the auction introduces an element that alters the function of the immediate double raise. Whether that action by your adversary is a bid or a double, there has been an assertion of strength by him and he has sounded the tocsin for his partner to rally round and challenge your pair for the right to name the final contract. Under these circumstances, any direct raise is an overbid and is not forcing. It is intended, as is any shut-out, to make communication between the opponents difficult and confused.

(29) ♠ 9   ♡ Q 10 6 2   ◇ A J 9 5 4   ♣ 6 3 2
        1H   2C   3H

The double raise may make it extremely difficult for the opponents to find a spade contract if, as seems likely, they have preponderant strength in that suit. It is one of the cornerstones of the Stayman System to fill the bidding space with action and with obstacles when the opponents should be feared. To give only a single raise with the hand above might make the difference of many hundreds of points.

The advantages of the weak double-raise are:

(1) If the opponents can make some contract, they will not be permitted to exchange information at comfortably low levels, and may thus be unable to discover where their combined strength lies.

(2) If the opponents are not in fact strong enough to outbid you, the pre-emptive action may occasionally induce a reckless overcall born of frustration, and it may be severely punished.

(3) If the opponents are crowded out of the bidding, you get away with the deal at a very small loss. You may even make a game when the opponents have most of the top cards and could themselves score a game had they been permitted to communicate freely.

(30) ♠ Q J 9 5   ♡ 8   ◇ K 10 5 3 2   ♣ 8 7 6
               1S   2C   ?

Bid *3S.* This hand is quite weak in high cards, but it has good distribution and there is reason to try to shut out heart bidding.

(31) ♠ Q 8 6 5   ♡ 9 2   ◇ K 10 5 3 2   ♣ 8 6
               1S   Double   ?

Bid *2S.* The single raise over the double is a sign of weakness and cannot mislead your partner. While it is true that the opponents will not be misled either, your bid does deny them one level of bidding and this may be productive of mischief.

(32) ♠ J 9 5 4   ♡ K Q 10 8   ◇ 6 3   ♣ 5 3 2
               1S   Double   ?

Bid *2S.* The double of one major often implies strength in the other, and your concealment of hearts may ambush the opponents.

(33) ♠ Q J 8 5   ♡ K 2   ◇ A Q 10 9 4   ♣ 7 6
               1S   2C   ?

Bid *2D.* Holding a hand with which you would have made a game-forcing double raise (1S—No Bid—*3S*) had no overcall intervened, you must now first bid a suit. This bid is forcing for one round and you can make a vigorous spade raise on your next turn.

Not vulnerable against vulnerable opponents, a pre-emptive raise to game can sometimes be used as a trap and is especially effective against an opponent who hates to be shut out of action.

THE PRE-EMPTIVE RESPONSE TO A TAKEOUT DOUBLE

Opposite an informatory double, holding a hand that is suitable for play in one suit only and that suit a major, a double jump response should be used to show five to six playing tricks and a very long suit. The following is illustrative:

(34) ♠ 9 5   ♡ K J 10 8 5 4 3   ◇ 6 5   ♣ 3 2
               1D   Double   No Bid   *3H*

This bid describes your hand in one call and makes it easy for partner to select his next action. If the contribution of such a suit as you describe will suffice to produce game, he will bid it. If his hand does not warrant game action, he may pass without fear that he may have left you in a bad denomination.

THE JUMP-SHIFT RESPONSE WHEN OPPONENT DOUBLES

As has been indicated in several other situations, the Stayman System gives different meaning to certain bids when an opponent has participated in the auction, as against the meaning when a partnership holds the auction unopposed. We believe so firmly in the value of pre-emption that many bids are used as "space-consumers", or pre-emptives that in an unopposed auction would be strength-showing.

Another such usage is the meaning of a jump-shift response in a sequence such as

1S   Double   ?

in which we define the response of 3C, 3D or 3H as a pre-emptive bid. With a hand of better than 10 points, responder can redouble to show his strength. Holding a good suit with good side strength but either insufficient strength for, or a tactical desire against, a redouble, responder may pass and later bid his suit.

To prevent being shut out, responder may make a minimum take-out to his suit. This leaves the jump-shift for its classical use as a strong bid or, as we prefer, as a pre-emptive. We have found at least four times as great utility for this usage and substantial profit as well.

THE JUMP OVERCALL

Currently, most players use the same methods to show a good hand when an opponent opens the bidding: they double informatorily, overcall in no-trumps, or make a jump overcall. This would be splendid, except that it keeps a fine bidding tool on a part-time job. We have found that there are few occasions to use the jump overcall with a good hand. And even when those occasions have arisen, a double followed by the bid of a suit has done the job as well or better. Since the jump overcall could not earn its keep as a strength-showing device, we have assigned a function to it that puts it to work much more frequently and usefully.

We use the single-jump overcall—

(1) as a pre-empt with equal vulnerability or when the opponents are vulnerable and we are not,

(2) to show a good hand when we are vulnerable against non-vulnerable pairs.

(35) ♠ 8   ♡ 6 3   ◇ Q J 10 8 6 5   ♣ K Q J 2
Neither side vulnerable
1S   ?

Bid *3D*. This hand should win six or seven tricks, so it is unlikely to be heavily penalized. By making your defensive manœuvre at a high level, you not only take a round of bidding from the opponents, but also place yourself in a position where you may subside thereafter and permit partner to make the remaining decisions.

(36) ♠ Q 5   ♡ 7 6 3   ◇ 5 4   ♣ K Q J 10 9 2
Opponents are vulnerable
1H   ?

Bid *3C*. You may win as few as five tricks, but your honours will reduce the loss to 600 points at the maximum. It would be unsound to bid 3C with any other conditions of vulnerability.

(37) ♠ 8   ♡ 7   ◇ A 10 9 8 6 5 4   ♣ Q J 10 5
Both sides vulnerable
1H   ?

Bid *3D*. This hand should produce seven winners and the bid is safe and descriptive. With a little help in the club suit, you may even make this contract.

(38) ♠ 5 4   ♡ K 7   ◇ A K Q J 5 4   ♣ A 5 4
You are vulnerable
1S   ?

Bid *3D*. The jump overcall in a minor suit *when you are vulnerable and the opponents are not* shows a good suit and a good hand.

(39) ♠ K Q 10 8 6 4   ♡ 9   ◇ Q J 10 2   ♣ 8 5
1H   ?
Neither side vulnerable

Bid *2S*. This is the classical jump overcall under these conditions of vulnerability.

(40) ♠ A J 10 9 5 4   ♡ A Q J   ◇ 8 6 3   ♣ 5
You are vulnerable
1D   ?

Bid *2S*. Your hand is strong enough to invite a raise with just a few winners. You have seven to eight possible tricks.

PARTNER'S ACTION OPPOSITE THE JUMP OVERCALL

When you have made a jump overcall, your partner can tell which side has most of the strength and whether or not a sound sacrifice is available. Whatever your partner holds, he is in the perfect position to control the action after you have told your story.

SEQUENCE 41

Neither side vulnerable

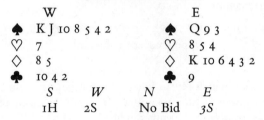

	W			E
♠	K J 10 8 5 4 2		♠	Q 9 3
♡	7		♡	8 5 4
◊	8 5		◊	K 10 6 4 3 2
♣	10 4 2		♣	9

S	W	N	E
1H	2S	No Bid	3S

The spade raise is purely pre-emptive and is not to be construed as urging partner to bid game. While East's shut-out efforts may not succeed in silencing South, South's task has been made more difficult. This is no chance-giving raise over a weak jump overcall. The raise to game should be made immediately if nine tricks seem certain and ten are possible.

SEQUENCE 42

East-West vulnerable

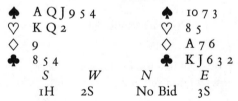

♠	A Q J 9 5 4		♠	10 7 3
♡	K Q 2		♡	8 5
◊	9		◊	A 7 6
♣	8 5 4		♣	K J 6 3 2

S	W	N	E
1H	2S	No Bid	3S

With these conditions of vulnerability, East's raise is designed to encourage game. Whenever a player detects a disposition on the part of non-vulnerable opponents to save against his vulnerable pair, he inclines to the overbid on close hands. This show of strength often induces a sacrifice and is sound tactics when a player really does not believe that his side can produce the game. Thus, had the bidding above proceeded:

S	W	N	E
1H	2S	3H	4S

East's best action is 4S. This bid takes the burden off himself and places it squarely on North-South who can hardly fail to sacrifice.

SEQUENCE 43

Neither side vulnerable

♠	Q J 10 8 6 5		♠	A 9 4 3 2
♡	8 5		♡	6
◇	K 10 5 4		◇	6 3
♣	7		♣	Q J 10 8 3

S	W	N	E
1H	2S	No Bid	4S

East's fine bid of 4S is made with the realization that there is probably no defence against a heart game or slam. This bid of 4S is called an "anticipatory sacrifice" and is made under a principle of the Stayman System to the effect that the safest and soundest time to sacrifice is before, not after, the opponents have reached their game or slam.

Let us see how a pre-emptive raise can fix your opponents. Here is a hand we played in England in 1949:

(44) Both sides vulnerable. West, dealer.

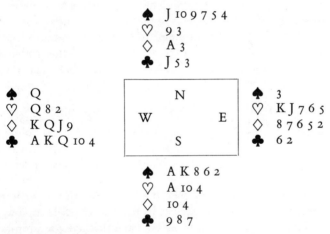

In the one room the bidding was as follows:

W	N	E	S
1C	No Bid	1H	1S
2D	2S	3D	No Bid
3H	No Bid	4H	

The bidding would probably be about the same at any total point tournament in America. North and South would lose 500 points at 4S, so the sacrifice would not gain much.

Now see what a swing was caused by the weak double-raise

1D	No Bid	1H	1S
2C	3S	4D	4S
5D	Double	All Pass	

Note how East is crowded by North's double spade raise. He must now either pass or bid 4D. For all he can tell, there may be a beautiful diamond save against a cold spade game. His action is a pure guess.

Poor West never gets a chance to show heart support. Instead, he must guess which side is sacrificing. South's "anticipatory sacrifice" bid of 4S makes evaluation difficult. The weak double-raise by North has fixed East, and South takes care of West by going along with the deception. The swing on the hand: 820 points, a fine example of confusion through pre-emption.

The jump overcall of 3H or 3S (over 1C or 1D; or over 1C, 1D or 1H in the case of the spade overcall) requires little discussion. Like the opening three bids, they show seven-card or longer suits and indicate overbids that will give the opponents no more than 500 points. They should not be raised to game except for purposes of sacrificing or when partner can contribute that strength that will combine to give his partner an adequate play for game. One important rule to remember in connection with jump overcalls: *Bid your proper maximum at once*, then never bid again except under compulsion.

THIRD AND FOURTH HAND PRE-EMPTIVE BIDS

After partner has passed, a player need not be fearful when holding a six- or seven-trick hand that there is a slam in the deal which may be jeopardized by crowding tactics. Accordingly, the third hand bidder may initiate the auction with a three bid; and it does not matter that his hand also qualifies for an opening bid of one. If a player feels that pre-emption will not make it difficult for his partner to reach a sound decision as to game possibilities, he may pre-empt with a hand that has good top-card strength. Needless to say, he may also pre-empt with hands that qualify under the general rules covering shut-out action.

Ordinarily, there is little reason to overbid when holding an opening bid of one and a long *spade* suit, the dominating suit:

(45)   ♠ A K Q 10 9 2   ♡ A 5   ◇ 9 6 3   ♣ 8 2
        No Bid   No Bid   1S

It is conceivable that the opponents may bid and make a 4H contract that might not have been reached had the opening bid been 3S, but you will find much more often that you can outlast the opponents in any bidding contest and that frequently the limit of your capabilities will be 2S, a declaration that can only be reached via normal channels.

For similar reasons, the opening 3H bid is rejected because the heart suit will outbid two suits at any level and gives way to the spade suit only. With four-card spade length, or high-card strength in the other major, the pre-empt should be discarded in favour of the normal opening bid of one; but when the structure of the hand is such as to suggest the likelihood of spade contention, the shut-out is sound:

(46) ♠ 9   ♡ K Q J 10 8 6   ◇ A J 10 9   ♣ 3 2
       No Bid   No Bid   *3H*

The minor-suit three bid should be made with hands qualifying for one bids only when they lack solidity or near-solidity in the long suit. Thus, partner need rarely face the problem of deciding whether he has sufficient consolidation for a 3NT contract. The following is a sound preemptive bid third-hand in spite of its point count:

(47) ♠ A 7   ♡ 9   ◇ Q J 10 8 5 4   ♣ A 10 3 2
       No Bid   No Bid   *3D*

With four-card length in either major, the bidder should start with a bid of one when his hand warrants that action, for the advantages of preemptive action in minor suits are not great enough to offset the games that are lost through failure to exploit the major-suit trump fit:

(48) ♠ 8   ♡ Q 9 5 2   ◇ A Q   ♣ K Q J 10 8 3
       No Bid   No Bid   *1C*

THIRD HAND ACTION. THE FOUR BID

Whenever a player can definitely rule out possibilities of a slam, or when the probabilities are slight, he may start the bidding with 4H or 4S, regardless of his point count or top-card strength, provided the rules of safety are observed. In general, the opening one bid should be preferred except when the bidder holds a hand with which game may be produced even though partner may not have what would be required to keep a one bid open:

(49) ♠ A Q 10 9 8 6 5   ♡ A 5   ◇ K 7 2   ♣ 2
       No Bid   No Bid   *1S*

There is no reason to throw away a part-score by overbidding. Unless partner will offer some assistance, game should not be reached.

(50)   ♠ 5   ♡ K Q J 10 9 5 2   ◇ A Q 9 8   ♣ 2
       No Bid   No Bid   4H

There is great likelihood of spade contention if the opponents are permitted to communicate at the low levels. Furthermore, the contribution of an Ace, or the diamond King, may suffice to bring home a game.

FOURTH HAND ACTION. THE THREE BID

Since the player, after three passes, may throw in his cards, and demand a new deal, no bid made by him would be sound if it were made with the idea of offering the opponents a profit, no matter how small. For this reason, the fourth hand three bids represent hands that are quite powerful and that would generally qualify for opening bids of one. There is ordinarily little point in the bid except where the bidder is vulnerable and there is danger of a save by a non-vulnerable pair. For example:

(51)   ♠ 8 3   ♡ A K Q J 9 6   ◇ A 7   ♣ K Q 3
                   Vulnerable
       No Bid   No Bid   3H

The responder is expected to reply if he holds that strength with which he would have kept a one bid open.

The minor-suit three bid, fourth hand, suggests a hand with a six-card solid suit and about a trick and a half outside. It urges a response with a hand that would have responded to a one bid.

(52)   ♠ Q 5   ♡ A 3   ◇ A K Q J 5 2   ♣ K 7 4
       No Bid   No Bid   3D

There is, of course, a possibility that the hand above may fail to make 3D, but it is unlikely that the opening bid of 1D would result in purchasing the hand at a lower level. It is very helpful for partner to know that opener's hand will produce seven to eight quick winners.

FOURTH HAND ACTION. THE FOUR BID

With nine tricks reasonably to be counted upon in his hand, the opener may often have the kind of distribution with which a slam is still not unlikely, and if he does hold that type of hand, the opening 2C bid will serve his purpose best. But occasionally, where only three quick winners would help for slam purposes, the opener may properly feel that the risk of a sacrifice is the more realistic consideration; and in such cases, with a rigid nine-trick hand, the pre-empt is sound.

(53)   ♠ 9   ♡ A K Q J 8 7 6   ◇ Q J 10 9   ♣ 2
　　　　Vulnerable *versus* non-vulnerable
　　　　No Bid　　No Bid　　4H

Partner with three Aces, or Ace King and Ace, or Ace Queen and Ace (having passed originally) is warranted in trying for a slam.

The fourth hand 4H or 4S bid is never made with a ten-trick hand, for the chances of a slam are great enough to explore with normal procedure.

PSYCHIC BIDDING

A psychic bid is one that is used for the purpose of misleading the opponents into believing that the bidder has greater strength than, in fact, he possesses; or that he has suit length where it does not truly exist; or both. The psychic bid is a deception as much of one's partner as of one's opponents: it would be unethical if it were otherwise.

As a tactical weapon, the effectiveness of the device lies in what it accomplishes, when it succeeds; and, when it fails, in the uncertainty it plants in the minds of the adversaries who may, for ever after, regard with suspicion every adverse action that has the appearance of irregularity.

Given a propitious set of conditions, a particular bid—it does not matter how unusual or risky—may so confuse the opponents as to result in a large swing against them. But the temptation to use unconventional and unusual actions must be resisted if the prospective loss is great.

Tremendous losses result when one partner plans a bidding sequence that ends up with a retreat to a suit bid by his partner, only to find that the suit does not exist. The psychic bid, when used intemperately, is an evil. When it is not used at all, a partnership gives away certain advantages that may make the difference between success and failure in top-flight competition. As is often the case, the proper use of psychics involves a compromise in which certain risks are eliminated at the price of restricting the bidder's liberty of action.

By virtue of the limitations placed on the opening bidder, we call this the "prepared psychic". If the opening bid is irregular, it must, nevertheless, conform to certain prescribed standards:

(1) Only hands containing 3—6 points qualify, of which at least 2 points must be in the bid suit.
(2) The suit that is bid must be from four to six cards in length, preferably at least a five-carder.
(3) The hand must contain no second suit with greater than four-card length.

By attaching specifications, two basic purposes are served. First, if the psychic is discovered and exposed, as is often the case, the bidder's partner may, nevertheless, make the indicated opening lead to strength, so important at no-trumps and of prime importance in duplicate where every trick saved has significance. Second, a player may occasionally embark on harassing manœuvres without taking the chance that he has made it impossible for his own pair to proceed to a sound contract.

The Stayman System makes allowance for the possibility of opening psychic bids in situations where the great strength in the responder's hand makes it appear a possibility that the opening bid is not of the genuine normal variety.

Whereas a psychic opener may pass responses that are ordinarily forcing such as one-over-one, two-over-one and 2NT responses, he is required to respond to a jump-shift response. The important thing is for both members of the partnership to be made aware directly that the opening bid was spurious.

When an opening bidder has received a jump-shift response, he shows that his opening bid is psychic by making a minimum rebid in no-trumps.

(54) ♠ K J 10 6 3 ♥ 5 3 ♦ 8 7 6 ♣ J 5 4
       1S   3C
       3NT

If the opening bid is normal, the rebid is anything other than the minimum in no-trumps. Thus the usual meaning of this bid—that the opener is a minimum—is changed.

(55) ♠ A 5 3 ♥ 5 4 ♦ A J 10 2 ♣ A 8 7 2
       1D   2H
       3C

Though you hold a minimum hand you are unable to bid 2NT for your second bid. This would tell partner you have a psychic. Instead, you show your second suit, anaemic as it is. Responder must make due allowance in his later action for the fact that the 2NT bid was not available to you.

(56) ♠ K 9 7 6 5 ♥ 5 4 ♦ A J 7 ♣ K Q J
       1S   3H
       3S

Since your opening bid has already shown a five-card suit, you would prefer to rebid 3NT the better to describe your hand. But this would show a psychic, so you rebid the spades and affirm that you have a real bid.

At this point it may be remarked that a response other than a jump shift shows less than 19 points. Accordingly, the total of the best psychic (6 points) and the best non-jump shift (18 points) will almost always afford an inferior play for game since the total of points held by the partnership will be less than 25. Holding 19 *or more*, responder must make a jump shift and if a genuine opening bid exists, a slam will be reached 95 per cent. of the time.

When responder has discovered through opener's minimum rebid in no-trumps that he is faced by a psychic, he can reassess the partnership position. If he chooses, he may pass. If the last bid was 3NT, he may choose this game. If the rebid by opener has been 2NT, he can even pass below game if he should so decide. Obviously, this would be most unusual, but possible. Almost always responder will bid again. Even so the partnership may stop below game, or go on depending upon the relative strength of each hand—within the already established limits.

(57)   ♠ 8   ♡ 10 6 5   ◇ K J 8 4 2   ♣ 7 5 3 2
                   1D   2H
                   2NT   3H
                   ?

Bid *4H*. Partner has 19 points at least and a fine suit. Though you have only 4 high-card points, you do have three trumps and a singleton which is valued at 2 points in support of hearts. You should never hang just below game in such situations. It is almost impossible that you will be doubled, and you should make the game over half the time.

If the responder has sufficient strength to insist on game even though opener is psychic, he can force another response by showing a new suit which is again forcing for one round.

(58)   ♠ A K Q J 6   ♡ A 6   ◇ K Q J   ♣ A K 7
                   1C   2S
                   2NT   ?

Bid *3D*. This hand is so strong that, despite the psychic which you have found opposite you, you intend to force to a slam, and wish to make a forcing bid while you find out whether it is better to play for spades or clubs—or even no-trumps. The bids of 3C or 3S could be passed. Therefore you select one that requires partner to keep going. 3H, 4C (forcing) or 4NT (Blackwood) are also quite possible second actions. *Chacun à son gout*—as long as it isn't 3C or 3S.

The limitations previously set forth relating to the strength and composition of the opening psychic bid refer to first and second hand only. As to vulnerability, it will be rare that a psychic opening bid will appeal to you when your opponents are not vulnerable. The risk of severe loss makes the venture unattractive. Even against vulnerable opponents, we cannot imagine a really sound vulnerable psychic. Shaded lead-directing bids in third position have already been discussed. No additional deviation of a psychic nature is recommended.

OTHER PSYCHIC BIDS

We must make passing reference to psychic bids made in response to opening bids and to those that are occasionally inserted with profit by the rebidder. These manœuvres are made in order to deceive the adversaries as to the structure of the bidder's hand. These bids can be extremely effective, and various illustrations may suggest an avenue of tactical adventure that may be entered with profit:

(59)   ♠   K J 5 4   ♡   Q 10 8 6 2   ◇   A 5 4   ♣   3
               1S

Bid 2D. Since you are going to play this deal at spades, the initial response may profitably be used to divert the opponents from leading diamonds. This would appear to be the one lead that may be damaging. The hand occurred in the Master's Pairs in the American Summer Nationals. The complete deal:

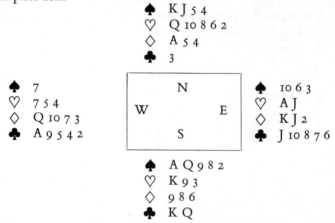

At most tables, the bidding proceeded 1S, 3S, 4S, and generally the diamond three was opened to defeat the contract. At one table the bidding went as follows:

1S	2D
2S	4S

The heart seven was opened and declarer made five spades for a top score.

Note that North has the *values* for his bid, so that the deception of his partner can rarely be costly.

Another hand:

(60)   ♠ A 10 5 3 2   ♡ K J 7 6   ◇ 9 8 5   ♣ 3
　　　　　　You only are vulnerable
　　　　　　　　1H

Bid *2C*. There is a strong temptation to respond 1S, but a little reflection will make it apparent that the spade bid serves no useful purpose, whereas the club bid may take away a possible sacrifice from your non-vulnerable opponents. Here, again, is an actual hand from a deal in a team match. The place: London. The time: 1953.

North-South vulnerable.   South, dealer.

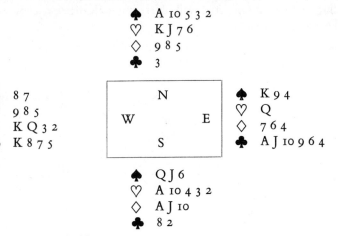

In one room, the bidding:

S	W	N	E
1H	No Bid	1S	2C
No Bid	3C	3H	4C
4H	5C	Double	All pass

The result: North and South plus 100.

In the other room:

S	W	N	E
1H	No Bid	2C	No Bid
2H	No Bid	3H	No Bid
4H	All pass		

The result: North and South plus 620.

The psychic bid may be used in the rebid where, the final contract already having been mentally decided upon, a red herring may be placed across the trail to the opening lead:

(61) ♠ A K 5   ♡ K Q J 8 2   ◇ 9 7 4   ♣ A Q

1H	2H
3D	3H
4H	

The 3D bid cannot cost anything and may divert the opponents into a lead more favourable to you. Observe that the responder has limited his hand by the 2H response, and we can thus be certain that the deception will leave him unharmed.

Thus we leave this important chapter on pre-emption and psychic bidding. Master this material well. Here is mobile defence, a cornerstone of the Stayman System.

15

THE OVERCALL

THE OVERCALL, to give it its broadest definition, is a bid made by a player whose side has not opened the bidding. In this chapter, we deal with every defensive bid, except the double, and these may be divided into three main classifications:

(1) The simple overcall:

　　1H—2C　　1H—1S　　1H—1NT

(2) The jump overcall:

　　1D—2S　　　1H—3C

(3) The pre-emptive overcall:

　　1C—3H

The simple overcall is a bid made in a competitive auction at the cheapest level available to the defender. The jump overcall is a bid made in a competitive auction at a level one higher than necessary. A pre-emptive overcall is a bid made competitively at a level one, two or sometimes three higher than necessary.

There are other defensive actions, and it may make for easier understanding if we complete our glossary of terms now.

A "defensive raise" is the raise of partner's overcall:

S	W	N	E
1C	1D	No Bid	2D

or

1H	1S	2H	2S

A "defensive jump shift" is the bid of a new suit at one level higher than necessary opposite partner's overcall:

1C	1S	No Bid	1D

A "protective overcall" (sometimes called "balancing") is a bid made after two successive passes under circumstances indicating that the defenders have enough combined strength to contest, as:

1H	No Bid	No Bid	1S

or

1D	No Bid	1NT	No Bid
2D	No Bid	No Bid	2H

A "delayed overcall" is an overcall not made at the bidder's first opportunity, as:

1D	No Bid	1NT	No Bid
2D	2S		

The "informatory double" and the "penalty double" are defensive actions that warrant an entire chapter of their own; they are examined in the next chapter.

The overcaller's position differs in significant respects from that of the opening bidder. When an adversary has initiated the bidding with any bid that evidences aggressive intent, the defender is bound to take notice of the implications. The opponent has proclaimed the ownership of about one-third of the deal's power and has embarked on a course that he hopes will lead to game. Furthermore, the overcaller enters the sphere of action against a pair with the advantage of a communication that has frequently set up unmistakable guide-posts for their future course. The overcaller is always one important step in arrears and the menace of penalty lies in every step taken by him. Since the player who bids after him has not yet disclosed his distribution or hand-size, there is considerable risk that the defender will find himself crushed between the hammer and the anvil.

The overcall offers a choice to the offensive pair of continuing on their way to a part-score or game; or of inflicting a penalty. The option is theirs, and it is a choice that must never be given gratuitously.

In discussing the overcall, we address ourselves at the outset to the element of safety.

Whatever the aims of the overcall—and we shall consider them in a moment—a realistic attitude forces us to adopt the view that only rarely will it lead to the successful engagement for game by the defenders. With more or less normal distribution and some high-card strength, we can never assume that our opponents will make more than game, and we must not, therefore, expose our pair to a penalty that is greater than the value of that game.

If the effect of an overcall were merely to give the adversaries the option of continuing their sequence or doubling for penalties, with impunity to them in either course, the overcall would be unworthy of serious consideration. To warrant the position of jeopardy, the overcall must contain the possibility of

(1) Producing a contract against which the opponents cannot compete successfully.
(2) Establishing a good and perhaps vital opening lead if the opponents buy the contract.
(3) Interfering with the opponents' communication so as to make it difficult for them to reach their best declaration.
(4) Setting the stage for an economical sacrifice.
(5) Pushing the opponents beyond the limits of what they can produce.

It will, of course, be rare that an overcaller may reasonably hope to accomplish every one of the possible objectives, but it may be stated without qualification that if the defensive bidder cannot look forward to the accomplishment of at least one of them, he has no reason to overcall and should pass.

There are certain factors that disincline the opponents to penalty action, and an overcall made under the cover of this aversion enjoys a measure of safety. It is rare, for example, that a non-vulnerable bid of one can be punished severely enough to make the penalty attractive to a vulnerable pair. Overcalls may gain a large degree of immunity when the suit that is bid has solidity. If a suit containing the Ace, King, Queen, Jack is held, it is only when an opponent has an unusually long trump holding that he will be inclined to double, whereas a broken suit is exposed both to suit length and to high cards held advantageously by the opponent behind the overcaller. The overcalls of 2C and 2D are, perhaps, the most punished defensive bids in bridge for they may be doubled without fear that a game will be scored if the double misfires; whereas the overcalls of 2H and 2S will sometimes escape unscathed only because the prospective doubler is fearful that a hidden distributional factor may permit the declarer to make his contract and chalk up game.

Before presenting examples of simple overcalls, we may, with profit, restate the reasons for taking defensive action and the reasons for abstaining.

You have a sound justification for bidding—

(1) If your hand is good enough to warrant the hope that you may ultimately outbid the opponents. This will generally be the case when you hold as good as an opening bid.
(2) If a bid from you will give your partner a good opening lead in the defence of a contract the defeat of which may hinge on his first play.

(3) If your bid will take bidding space away from your opponents and may create enough interference to disrupt their communication.

(4) If vulnerability conditions are such as to favour a sacrifice, and your hand provides reasons to believe that a good save may be found.

(5) If the strength and construction of your hand lead you to feel that you may, with safety, be able to push the opponents one level too high.

You should not overcall—

(1) When you have no bidding objective.

(2) When a bid will expose you to a penalty greater than 500 points.

(3) When you do not want to slow down the opponents, as when you know (and the adversaries don't) that the deal will break unsatisfactorily for them.

(1) ♠ A K J 9 8   ♡ 4 2   ◊ Q 10 8 3   ♣ 6 5
              1C   ?

Bid 1S. Many purposes are achieved by the overcall. First, you may, holding the highest-ranking suit, be able to outbid the opponents. Second, even if the adversaries succeed in taking the final contract, your partner has been provided with an excellent opening lead. Third, your overcall will take the entire one level from the opponents and may make their bidding task a bit more difficult. Under all but the worst circumstances, you should be able to win four to five tricks at 1S doubled.

(2) ♠ 5   ♡ K Q 10 8 6 2   ◊ K 10 8 3   ♣ 7 4
         1S   ?   (a) Vulnerable
                          (b) Not vulnerable

(a) No Bid. (b) Bid 2H. A possible suit for a sacrifice and a good opening lead are offered by the 2H bid, and the risk of loss, not vulnerable, should not exceed 500 points. The overcall has good interference value. There is not enough strength to come in vulnerable, however, for the penalty may run too high.

(3) ♠ A K Q 7   ♡ 10 9 5 3   ◊ 8 6   ♣ 9 5 4
         1D   ?   Not vulnerable

Bid 1S. There is very little likelihood that you will be doubled, and your overcall is effective in several respects. It inhibits a 3NT contract, for it is unlikely that either opponent will possess a spade stopper, and since your overcall *threatens* to capture the first *five* tricks at no-trumps, you will almost certainly push your adversaries into an unproductive suit contract. Generally, the overcall guarantees a five-card (or longer) suit, but there are times—as with this hand—when the bid is warranted as a tactical measure.

    (4) ♠ K J 10 8   ♡ 2   ◇ 9 5 4   ♣ K Q 10 9 3
       1S   ?   Non-vulnerable *versus* vulnerable

No Bid. While the overcall of 2C is tempting and perhaps within the limits of safety, it is much smarter to play possum and let the opponents bid without interference and without warning of the unfavourable distribution that is already apparent to the defender. An overcall might result in slowing them down or in giving them a penalty option on a deal where they could have only got into trouble had they been given enough rope.

    (5) ♠ A J 8   ♡ 9 5   ◇ Q 3   ♣ Q J 10 9 7 2
       1D   ?   Not vulnerable

Bid 2C. This overcall may cause tremendous communication problems for the opponents. The normal responses of 1H, 1S and 1NT have been taken from the responder, and he may not be able to enter the bidding over the barrier erected by the 2C bid.

    (6) ♠ 7 5   ♡ 4   ◇ J 10 8 6 4 3 2   ♣ K 8 3
       1S   ?

No Bid. Do not overcall in this situation. Admittedly, not vulnerable, 2D qualifies as far as safety is concerned. However, you would provide little interference in the bidding sequence and you might merely induce your partner to make a disastrous opening lead. The chances that a sound diamond sacrifice is available are slim. Finally, your bid may tip off the opponents to the distribution of your partner's hand and your own.

    (7) ♠ 6   ♡ 7 4   ◇ K Q 8 7 2   ♣ K Q 10 9 5
      Neither or both vulnerable
       1S   ?

Bid 2C. But you intend to bid only once, and if 2C is doubled you will move to 2D and thus give your partner a choice of the two suits. Not vulnerable against vulnerable opponents there are great possibilities for sacrificing, and the 2D overcall should be made initially to be followed by the club bid at your next turn.

(8)   ♠ J 10 9 8 5 3   ♡ K 7 4   ◊ A 5   ♣ 9 7
            1C   ? Not vulnerable

Bid *1S*. The spade bid makes an excellent barrier. In addition, you may, conceivably, be able to outbid the adversaries or force them to a contract that may be beaten.

(9)   ♠ 8 5 4   ♡ Q 5   ◊ K J 2   ♣ A K 7 6 5
            1H   ? Vulnerable

No Bid. A bid of 2C might be penalized 1,400 points. Your objective would be a part-score, worth about 150 points at most. Overcalls of this kind account for the greatest disasters at the bridge table; yet the average player finds it impossible to resist the temptation to take the plunge. Bear in mind that the bidding does not end with your pass. If the weakness of the opponents is indicated by the response and rebid, it is time enough to pick up the action then; and the risk of loss will no longer be present.

(10)   ♠ A 5   ♡ 10 8   ◊ Q J 10 8 7 6   ♣ K 9 3
            1S   ? Not vulnerable

Bid *2D*. Change the club holding to K Q x and the hand qualifies for a vulnerable overcall also. With this hand, there is reason to believe that you may be able to outbid the opponents, and your risk is slight.

(11)   ♠ A J 10 6 5   ♡ 5   ◊ 7 4   ♣ K Q J 6 4
            1D   ? Vulnerable

Bid *1S*. If you were not vulnerable, 2C would be the better overcall since it would probably enable you to come in with 2S on your next turn. Generally, the higher-ranking suit is bid first, as between suits of equal length, and especially when you cannot afford to make two bids. When, as with the hand above (not vulnerable), the bid of the lower-ranking suit offers the opportunity for an economical second overcall, a departure from the general rule is indicated.

(12)   ♠ 7 6   ♡ K J 9 7 4   ◊ A K 3   ♣ K J 2
            1S   ?

Double. This hand is too strong for you to stay out of the bidding. However, there is too much all-round strength for an overcall. For reasons of better hand definition, a takeout double is infinitely superior (see Chapter 16).

(13) ♠ 7   ♡ A Q J 4 3 2   ◇ A Q 4   ♣ K 4 3
            1S   ?

Double. Here again, a hand too strong for a simple overcall.

After both opponents have bid, the overcall can cause little interference, and a player who bids, under such circumstances, can have limited objectives at best. Consequently, an overcall following two adverse bids, must be immune to sizable penalty:

(14) ♠ K Q J 9 5   ♡ 8 4   ◇ 6 3 2   ♣ 10 8 5
        1C   No Bid   1H   ?   Not vulnerable

No Bid. The overcall of 1S will no longer be a barrier. Even its value as a lead-directing bid is diminished.

THE PROTECTIVE OVERCALL

When the partner of the opening bidder passes a suit bid of one, it is probable that the defenders hold enough strength to take command of the bidding or to punish the opener if he persists in contending for the final declaration. For this reason, and for the additional reason that penalty action is no longer seriously to be feared, the player in fourth position is generally called upon to "protect" his partnership with a reopening bid.

(15) ♠ A J 5   ♡ K 9 4   ◇ Q 10 4 2   ♣ Q 9 7
            1S   No Bid   No Bid   ?

Bid 1NT. Regardless of the type of opening no-trump you use, 12—14 or 16—18, and whether vulnerable or not, the protective overcall of 1NT shows 12—14 points. The bidding thereafter proceeds in accordance with methods previously discussed in connection with the weak no-trump.

(16) ♠ 9 5   ♡ K 10 8 5 4   ◇ Q 6 3   ♣ A J 2
            1S   No Bid   No Bid   ?

Double. With sufficient strength to take action, the double is preferred when fourth hand has 10 points or more and can stand any response his partner makes. A bid of 2H would be unsound; it might take the opponents "off the hook", and hearts might be the partnership's weakest suit.

When fourth hand has length in the opponent's suit, there are times when it may be more profitable to remain a defender. Thus:

(17) ♠ A J 10 9 2   ♡ K 7   ◇ 9 5 4 3   ♣ 3 2
1S   No Bid   No Bid   ?   Not-vulnerable *versus* vulnerable

No Bid. Your partner, presumably short in spades, was nevertheless unable to take any aggressive action over the opening bid. If you double, he will bid. Your best course is to try for the penalty.

THE DELAYED OVERCALL

A delayed overcall is one that is made after a player has initially passed. The bid is ordinarily inserted because there are signs that the offensive bidding sequence is grinding to a halt:

(18)	♠ K Q 10 8 6 3	♡ 9	◊ 7 6 4	♣ Q 3 2
	1H	No Bid	1NT	No Bid
	2H	?		

Bid 2S. With no apparent intention on the part of the opponents to go to game, the delayed overcall is made on the strength of partner's marked, though undisclosed, high cards; and therefore partner must not take further aggressive bidding action relying upon cards that have already been discounted:

(19)	♠ A 7 5	♡ K 8 5 3	◊ A 9 2	♣ J 8 5
	1H	No Bid	1NT	No Bid
	2H	2S	No Bid	*No Bid*

Remember that your partner could not overcall the first time.

(20)	♠ A J 8 7 6	♡ 9	◊ K 10 6 4	♣ Q 3 2
	1H	No Bid	1NT	No Bid
	2H	No Bid	No Bid	?

Bid 2S. The overcaller infers from the fact that the adversaries have quit at the two level that partner has enough strength to warrant a contest for the declaration.

DEFENSIVE RAISES AND OTHER RESPONSES TO THE SIMPLE OVERCALL

We must now devote some space to the action of the defender whose partner has made a simple overcall. By and large, plastic valuation and the application of the rule of the "two- and three-trick overbid" will enable him to estimate when game may be produced. He knows that his partner has a five-card or longer suit that needs only three small cards or a doubleton Queen to give his pair a dominant trump suit. However, a few guideposts may prove helpful.

Faced with a choice between a raise and a pass, the overcaller's partner raises (over a pass or over contention) with two or three playing tricks when vulnerable; and with three playing tricks not vulnerable. By providing the few tricks indicated by the raise, the partnership is placed in a contract that will either make or go down one trick—in short, a tight declaration.

(21) ♠ 9 5 4 3   ♡ 8   ◇ A 10 7   ♣ Q 9 5 4 2
         1D   1S   No Bid   2S

With twelve hearts unaccounted for, it appears that the 1S overcall crowded opener's partner out of the auction. The overcaller's raise continues obstructive tactics by giving the opener a very high hurdle to climb over. Here we have a fine example of harassment by the application of the principles of "action and pre-emption".

When overcaller's partner, with adequate trump support, can count nine tricks in the combined hands based on a minimum overcall, he raises to the three level; when he can see ten tricks, he raises a major-suit overcall to game.

(22) ♠ K 9 3 2   ♡ 7   ◇ A J 7 5   ♣ Q 9 5 4
         1C   1S   No Bid   ?   Not vulnerable

Bid 3S. With about five playing tricks opposite the promised four, nine tricks is a reasonable expectation.

(23) ♠ 7 5   ♡ 9 5 2   ◇ K Q 7 5 3   ♣ A 10 4
         1S   2H   No Bid   ?   Vulnerable

Bid 3H. Never bid a minor when you have adequate support for partner's major.

(24) ♠ 7 5 4   ♡ 3   ◇ K Q 6 5 4 2   ♣ K 5 4
         1S   2H   No Bid   ?   Vulnerable

No Bid. Do not rescue until you are doubled, and then only when, independent of partner, your bid is within the prescribed limits of safety. The bid of a minor opposite a major suit overcall is a constructive move, usually suggestive of no-trump possibilities.

With good hands opposite an overcall, a player selects his action according to the principles governing the highroads to game. Partner's major suit should be supported wherever possible; and no-trumps should be bid when major-suit support is lacking and stoppers in the opponent's suit are held:

(25) ♠ K J 5   ♡ Q 9   ◇ K J 9 4 2   ♣ Q J 3
         1C   1H   No Bid   ?

Bid 1NT. There would be no point in the bid of 2D. If there is game, it will lie in no-trumps or in hearts. The bid of no-trumps opposite an overcall is not an assertion of dissatisfaction with partner's suit. It is a constructive move implying that the bidder has at least two cards in partner's suit.

(26) ♠ A K J 7 5   ♡ A J 3   ◇ J 5   ♣ Q 10 4
     1H   2D   No Bid   ? Not vulnerable

Bid 2NT. The bid of 2NT reflects the great strength of your hand and
its balanced distribution. 2S would be a gross underbid; and 3S would
emphasize the spade suit at the cost of concealing the important heart
stoppers.

(27) ♠ A Q 5   ♡ J 5 4 3   ◇ 9 6   ♣ 10 9 8 2
     1H   1S   2D   ? Not vulnerable

Bid 2S. A very shaded raise, but it is important that you advise your
partner that a spade lead may be made against no-trumps or a suit contract.

(28) ♠ K J 7 5   ♡ A J 8 6 4 3   ◇ 9 5   ♣ 2
     1D   1S   No Bid   ? Vulnerable

Bid 4S. There is nothing to be gained by showing your heart suit. You
know you have a dominant spade suit. Bid game directly.

THE STRENGTH OVERCALLS

We have hitherto discussed the simple overcall, a bid that is generally
tucked into the auction with very modest pretensions so far as game is
concerned. We come now to those defensive actions which imply a
desire and an apparent capability to seize the bidding initiative from the
side that has opened the auction. There are three common types of
strength overcall (excluding the informatory double):

                (1) The jump overcall.
                (2) The No-trump overcall.
                (3) The bid of the opponent's suit.

The jump overcall has already been scrutinized in Chapter 14. We
remind the reader that when both sides are vulnerable, when neither
side is vulnerable, and when the opponents only are vulnerable, the jump
overcall is pre-emptive and bespeaks a hand that may be penalized 500
points unless partner reduces the loss by contributing winning tricks.
When your side alone is vulnerable, however, the jump overcall indicates
a seven- or eight-trick hand and invites a raise with a few winners:

(29) ♠ A J 10 9 5 4   ♡ 9   ◇ 7 4   ♣ Q 5 4 2
       1D   ? Not vulnerable

Bid 2S. This bid is purely pre-emptive, of course.

(30) ♠ A J 10 9 5 4   ♥ A K 5   ♦ Q J 2   ♣ 8
    1H   ? Vulnerable *versus* Non-vulnerable

Bid *2S.* A very strong hand is indicated—one that needs a couple of winners to produce game.

(31) ♠ K 5 4   ♥ 3 2   ♦ A 7   ♣ A K Q J 5 4
    1H   ? Vulnerable *versus* Non-vulnerable

Bid *3C.* The jump overcall in a minor suit, when made under these conditions of vulnerability, indicates a solid minor suit and about one and a half quick tricks outside.

With a side suit winner and a stopper in the opponent's suit, overcaller's partner accepts the invitation to contract for 3NT:

(32) ♠ A 7 3 2   ♥ Q J 5   ♦ 9 5 4 2   ♣ 6 3
    1H   3D   No Bid   *3NT*

The raise of the strength-showing overcall depends upon partner's ability to disclose a few winners:

(33) ♠ 9 5   ♥ K 4 3 2   ♦ Q 7 5 4   ♣ K 7 2
    1D   2S   No Bid   ? Vulnerable

Bid *3S.* With two Kings that may be useful, a single raise should be given.

(34) ♠ 9 5   ♥ K Q 3 2   ♦ A 9 5 4 3   ♣ 7 6
    1C   2S   No Bid   ? Vulnerable *versus* Non-vulnerable

Bid *3D.* The bid of a side suit opposite the strength-showing jump overcall is a one-round force and may be used either to indicate strength in that suit or, as with the hand above, to leave room for the overcaller to show a heart suit if his jump overcall was based on a spade-heart two-suiter. If the rebid is anything but 3H, overcaller's partner will proceed directly to 4S.

THE NO-TRUMP OVERCALLS

The overcall of 1NT over an adverse opening bid indicates a count of 16—18 (whether your standard no-trump is 12—14 or 16—18) and a hand that is balanced for no-trump play. There is one exception, as we stated previously, and that is where the overcall is protective, as in the sequence—

                1D   No Bid   No Bid   1NT

in which case the bid shows 12—14 points.

The overcall of 1NT by a vulnerable player should be buttressed by two stoppers in the opponent's suit or by a suit that will yield a number of tricks at once.

(35) ♠ A K 2   ♡ K J 5   ♢ K 10 9 4   ♣ A 7 6
               1S   1NT

(36) ♠ A 9   ♡ Q 9 5   ♢ K 4 2   ♣ A K Q 10
               1D   1NT

When the overcall of 1NT is deferred and the bidder's first action is a double, the implication is that the no-trump bidder sought first to discover whether partner held major-suit strength.

(37) ♠ A J 7 3   ♡ Q 10 9 6   ♢ A 10   ♣ A Q 2
               1C   *Double*

The responses to the 1NT overcall are almost precisely the same as opposite the opening 16—18 no-trump, except that the bid of the opponent's suit is available when responder wishes to engage in slow exploration and make certain at the same time that the bidding is not dropped short of game:

(38) ♠ A K J 5 4   ♡ Q 8 5 2   ♢ 4 3   ♣ 10 6
       1D   1NT   No Bid   2D

THE 2NT AND 3NT OVERCALLS

The overcalls of 2NT and 3NT simply express the overcaller's ability to win eight or nine tricks, respectively, by virtue of his possession of a long, solid suit. The raise from 2NT to 3NT should be made with a King or two Queens. Since these overcalls do not represent hands of well-distributed high-card strength, partner should not assume that normal support will be rendered to a five-card suit held by him. The 2NT overcall may lack a stopper in an unbid suit.

THE GAME-FORCE OVERCALL

The bid of an adversely declared suit indicates the possession of a hand that will produce game single-handed or that requires less than a count of 6 for its production. The bid is forcing until game is reached, and *the adverse suit may be bid without first- or second-round control of that suit.*

(40) ♠ K Q J 4   ♡ A K Q 7   ♢ 2   ♣ A Q J 10
               1D   2D

RESPONSES TO THE GAME-FORCE OVERCALL

With any five-card suit, or with a four-card suit containing the Queen or a higher card, that suit should be bid, particularly if it can be shown at the two level.

(41) ♠ Q 2   ♡ J 9 5 4 3   ◇ 8 7 6   ♣ 5 4 2
       1D   2D   No Bid   2H

Lacking such a suit, the bid of 2NT indicates the inability to take any constructive action:

(42) ♠ Q 8 5   ♡ J 8 6   ◇ 9 5 4 3   ♣ 10 5 2
      1H   2H   No Bid   2NT

Observe that the response of 2NT does not promise a stopper of the adverse suit. With a stopper and no biddable suit, the bid of 2NT may be followed by 3NT.

With two stoppers in the opponent's suit; or one stopper and some side strength, overcaller's partner may respond directly with 3NT:

(43) ♠ A K 7   ♡ 9 5 4   ◇ 8 7 3 2   ♣ 10 8 6
      1S   2S   No Bid   3NT

An intervening bid releases overcaller's partner from the obligation to respond. Accordingly, any "free" bid by him is a declaration of positive values:

(44) ♠ 9 5 3   ♡ Q 2   ◇ 8 6 5 4   ♣ K 10 5 4
      1C   2C   3C   3NT

OVERCALLS OF PRE-EMPTIVE OPENING BIDS

The overcall of 3NT to an opening bid at the three level indicates a desire to play the deal at that contract. Partner should not move out into a suit contract except with a very unusual unbalanced hand.

(45) ♠ K J 5   ♡ Q 10 7   ◇ A Q 10 9 5   ♣ A 8
      3S   3NT   Vulnerable *versus* Non-vulnerable

Observe that the 3NT overcall does not promise the strength of an opening bid of 3NT. Here the overcaller is forced by the pre-emptive action against him to make a stab in the dark.

(46) ♠ K J 5 4   ♡ A 7 6   ◇ A K Q 2   ♣ K 5
     Vulnerable *versus* Non-vulnerable
        3C

Double. Nothing is risked by investigating the majors before resorting to no-trumps.

The overcall in a suit at the three level should observe the rules of safety, but a little latitude is permissible in view of the fact that a pass might likewise expose the partnership to serious loss. The danger inherent in the overbid is reduced by virtue of the weakness advertised by one member of the opposing pair:

(47) ♠ A K J 9 2   ♡ 8   ◇ Q J 10 7   ♣ K 5 2
Neither side vulnerable
3H   3S

THE PRE-EMPTIVE OVERCALL

We have already gone into the subject of pre-emptive overcalls in Chapter 14.

To a large extent, the entire science of approach bidding deals with the development of bidding sequences in the one and two levels. When these levels are taken from a pair who own most of the high cards, they are forced to rely on hunch and guesswork rather than on precise hand-delineation; and guesswork will frequently cost them large sums of points.

The rule of the "two- and three-trick overbid" is an excellent one, but it cannot work for you unless you count your winners conservatively. When you are vulnerable and the opponents are not, you must base your calculations on the premise that the opponent who sits behind you has four or five cards of your suit and every honour card that is missing. That is not to say that you must always fear the worst. But if you hold a suit such as A Q 10 8 6 4, do not be amazed when the player behind you turns up with K J 9 3: it happens every day. On the other hand, it would be unduly pessimistic to refrain from pre-empting for fear that one opponent held six cards of your suit. The odds in favour of such a distribution are too small to be reckoned with seriously.

16

DOUBLES

THE EFFECT of a double, when it is followed by three consecutive passes, is to increase the rewards and bonuses that ordinarily accompany the fulfilment of a contract and to increase the penalties if the declarer falls short. When the bid is made by a player in the hope that it will stay affixed to the final declaration, it is called a "penalty" or "business" double, and amounts to an assertion by the defender that he does not believe that the declarer will make his contract. The double is also used for quite a different purpose: to show a hand of some strength and to indicate a desire that partner name his best suit so that the doubler's pair may put up a contest for the final declaration. The double so used is called an "informatory" or "take-out" double.

THE INFORMATORY DOUBLE

In general, we may say that a double is informatory when it is made at the doubler's first opportunity and before his partner has bid (a pass is not a bid). A take-out double has sometimes been called a transferred overcall, the doubler supplying the high cards and distribution and his partner selecting the suit. It is a bid that announces well-rounded strength and good support for any suit partner may elect to bid. Because the take-out double signifies an intention to seize the offensive there is a strong implication that the doubler is primarily interested in majors.

When the prospective defensive bidder has no long suit, but does have enough power to warrant the belief that his pair may be able to engage successfully for the final contract, his action will generally take the form of an informatory double. Furthermore, when no available overcall will reflect the great power of a player's hand, he may also employ the take-out double, not primarily for the purpose of eliciting information about his partner's hand, but rather in order that he may convey the fact that the strength of his hand is such that an overcall would not do it justice.

There are many types of informatory double, some simple and a few subtle. We now examine the general character of each common form of take-out double.

THE IMMEDIATE DOUBLE OF A SUIT BID OF ONE

The requirements for the simple take-out double of a suit bid of one are: about as good a hand, in high cards, as is indicated by the opening bid, with allowances for the state of vulnerability and for the level at which the doubler's partner will be forced to respond. A non-vulnerable double of 1C may, at its minimum, look like this:

(1) ♠ K 10 9 5   ♡ A 8 7 4   ◇ K J 3 2   ♣ 7

whereas a vulnerable double of 1S should resemble a hand like this:

(2) ♠ 9   ♡ A Q 8 4   ◇ K Q 5 3   ♣ Q J 10 2

Note that with hand (1) the distribution renders fine support for any suit bid by partner. There is almost no risk of a penalty double, being non-vulnerable, and the defenders may be able to exploit their distributional advantages to capture the contract or for an economical sacrifice. With hand (2), high cards must buttress the double, for partner must enter the two level and, being vulnerable, his bid will be subject to close scrutiny by two hungry opponents. The doubler, like the overcaller, must not expose his pair to a penalty in excess of 500 points. He may assume, for purposes of measuring the size of his risk, that his partner will be possessed of a four-card suit and about a King and a Queen for high cards. Observe that opposite hand (2), as weak a holding as

(3) ♠ Q 5 4 3   ♡ J 7 5 2   ◇ 7 6 2   ♣ 9 4

will almost surely permit the capture of at least seven tricks.

The comparative safety of the take-out double is well exemplified by the following example in which three possible North hands are arrayed opposite the South hand which presents a choice of actions:

(4)

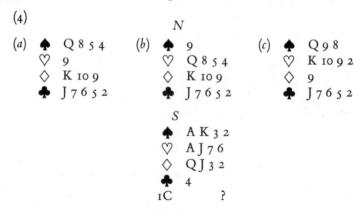

N

(a) ♠ Q 8 5 4   (b) ♠ 9   (c) ♠ Q 9 8
    ♡ 9   ♡ Q 8 5 4   ♡ K 10 9 2
    ◇ K 10 9   ◇ K 10 9   ◇ 9
    ♣ J 7 6 5 2   ♣ J 7 6 5 2   ♣ J 7 6 5 2

S
♠ A K 3 2
♡ A J 7 6
◇ Q J 3 2
♣ 4
1C   ?

If South overcalls, he has three suits from which to choose, and he tosses a coin as to whether he strikes North with support in the suit he selects. If he bids 1S, he may find North with hand (*b*). If he elects to overcall in hearts, he may find partner with hand (*a*). If he bids 1D, he may be unlucky enough to catch North with (*c*). And in no case may North do anything to improve the situation, since he is not strong enough to act independently. The take-out double ensures the partnership's selection of its best trump suit and thus increases its offensive potentialities while keeping the risk of penalty at a minimum.

The simple take-out double may be made, of course, with hands that do not offer outstanding support for all three unbid suits; but the doubler generally undertakes to provide a safe retreat of his own if he cannot consolidate the suit selected by his partner. He must, naturally, be prepared to handle any response induced by the double.

(5)   ♠ A Q J 8 2   ♡ K 10 5 4   ◇ A 5   ♣ 3 2
                    1C   ?

Double. The informatory double is superior to the overcall of 1S because it permits the investigation of the heart suit; whereas the bid of 1S might make it impossible to get into hearts. If doubler's partner responds 1D, doubler may still overcall with 1S. In the process he has lost no ground, for he is precisely where he would have been had he overcalled, but he has enjoyed the advantage of communicating important distributional information that may be used to great advantage in competitive auctions both in rubber and tournament bridge.

(6)   ♠ K 9 5 2   ♡ A Q 10 5 4   ◇ K 5 3   ♣ 2
                    1D   ?

Bid *1H*. Although it would be nice to probe the possibilities of spade play by using a take-out double, a response of two clubs would force the doubler either to remain mute in a bad contract or to bid 2H, a call that his limited strength does not warrant. The doubler must not project a bidding sequence that may well violate the rules of safety. Because the double may require a second-round bid of 2H, it must be forgone in favour of a simple overcall.

(7)   ♠ A Q 8 3   ♡ 8 2   ◇ A K 5 2   ♣ A J 5
                1C   ?

Double. No response can embarrass the doubler. If partner bids 1D, he strongly intimates, as we shall see later, that he lacks a four-card major,

and a single raise in diamonds will suffice to reflect the strength of the
doubler's hand. If partner bids 1H, the rebid of 1NT now perfectly defines the doubler's hand as one containing 16—18. The reader will note
that the doubler's rebid gives the size and distribution of his hand.

(8) ♠ A K J 9 5 4   ♡ K Q 2   ◇ 8 5 3   ♣ 6

1H   ?

Double, unless vulnerable against non-vulnerable opponents, in which
case bid 2S. The jump overcall is pre-emptive except in the one instance
stated above. That being so, the bidder employs a combination of two
actions—double followed by a suit bid—to show the great strength of
his hand. Compare with hand (7), where a similar combination gives
definition to the doubler's hand.

(9) ♠ A J 10 9 5   ♡ A Q 8 4 3   ◇ 5 2   ♣ 4

1C   ?

Bid *1S*. *In general*, a take-out double should be avoided when the prospective defensive bidder has two suits of five-card or greater length. With
the hand above, the bidding may get away from the player if he doubles,
with the result that he may never be able to show either suit, much less
both suits. Since the defender does not require four-card support in
spades or hearts, he should try to create a sequence that will give him
every opportunity to insert two-suit bids at a low level.

(10) ♠ A Q 10 9 2   ♡ A K 9 5 4   ◇ K 2   ♣ 3

Vulnerable *versus* Non-vulnerable

1D   ?

Bid *2S*. The reader will recall that with these vulnerability conditions the
jump overcall provides a method for ensuring a response from partner if
he has a few possible winners.

(11) ♠ A K J 9 5   ♡ A K 10 8 2   ◇ K 4   ♣ 5

1D   ?

Bid *2D*. With a hand that should provide an adequate play for game, the
immediate game force is made. Hands (9), (10) and (11) cover the range
of two-suited hands from which game may be made opposite a hand
containing one favourable characteristic.

THE IMMEDIATE DOUBLE FOLLOWING TWO ADVERSELY BID SUITS

The requirements for the two-suit double are the same as those for the
immediate double of a suit bid of one, because two suits have already been

bid by the opponents, the double promises good distributional consolidation in the remaining two suits and, as always, urges partner to bid a major suit if he has one (assuming that both majors have not been bid by the opponents).

(12) ♠ A Q 10 8 4 2   ♡ K Q 4 3   ◇ 8 7   ♣ 2
           1C   No Bid   1D   ?

Double. It is quite possible that doubler's partner lacks four-card length in both hearts and spades, but the doubler will rebid 1S even if the response to his double is 1H, thus describing his hand as containing a fine spade suit and implying good heart support. The immediate overcall of 1S would be sound from the point of view of safety, but might prove inferior if partner held a hand like the following:

(13) ♠ 3   ♡ A 10 9 5 2   ◇ 9 6 5 4   ♣ 9 7 3

Although the double after two suits have been adversely bid reveals great strength in the remaining suits, a series of two overcalls generally yields results superior to the take-out double when the defender holds two long suits.

(14) ♠ A Q 10 5 4   ♡ A K 7 6 5   ◇ 3 2   ♣ 6
           1C   No Bid   1D   ?

Bid *1S*. If the bidding does not mount too rapidly, you will show your heart suit at your next turn.

(15) ♠ K Q 5 4   ♡ K 10   ◇ A Q J 3 2   ♣ 10 4
           1C   No Bid   1H   ?

Double. Here is a classical example of a two-suit double: fine four-card support for the unbid major and a five-card suit offering sanctuary if partner has four cards in neither.

(16) ♠ 8 3 2   ♡ A K J 10 5 3   ◇ 5   ♣ A Q J
           1D   No Bid   1S   ?

Double. When a simple overcall will not adequately express the great power of his hand, the defender describes a strong one-suiter by doubling, followed by a bid of the suit held in length.

THE IMMEDIATE DOUBLE OF THE RAISED SUIT

Practically identical with the immediate double is the double made in fourth position after the opening suit bid of one has received a single raise. Since the level at which the doubler's partner must respond is higher, a slightly better hand is required of the doubler. However, when the bidding has proceeded

1C   No Bid   2C

or

1D   No Bid   2D

the prospective doubler has a right to assume that his right-hand opponent has a weak hand, and he may double with approximately the same strength required for immediate action over 1C or 1D. The known presence of a weak hand in the offensive pair gives a measure of protection against penalty action.

THE PROTECTIVE DOUBLE

When the partner of an opening bidder passes and thus reveals a hand that probably contains less than 6 points, the defender in fourth position will generally find that a double provides him with the best "balancing" action. His own distribution and top-card strength will usually permit him to predict what partner will do if he doubles, and the choice among an overcall, double or pass will depend on the visual picture he creates.

(17) ♠ A Q 8 5 4   ♡ K 3 2   ◇ 7 6 5   ♣ 8 4
1S   No Bid   No Bid   ?

No Bid. With a hand perfectly designed for defence, and of doubtful value offensively, the sound course is to pass.

(18) ♠ A 5   ♡ A Q 10 3 2   ◇ K 7 6   ♣ 5 4 3
1S   No Bid   No Bid   ?

Double. Whenever the opener's partner passes, it is fair to assume that the defenders have the major share of the high cards. A protective overcall of 2H would indicate merely enough strength to honour the obligation to keep the bidding alive. With a good hand, the double allows the defenders to take over the offensive or to remain defenders if the opening bidder is caught in a situation where he may be punished.

(19) ♠ K 9 5   ♡ 8   ◇ A Q 10 9 4   ♣ J 5 4 2
1S   No Bid   No Bid   ?

Bid *2D.* With a response of 2H reasonably to be expected opposite a double, the overcall is the sounder action. The bid of 2D warns partner that the overcaller may not be able to stand a heart declaration.

Particularly at duplicate bridge, the opener should rarely be permitted to steal a hand at his initial declaration of one in a suit. If you hold a weak hand, in fourth seat, it is likely that your partner has trap-passed with a fine one, and he will count on you to protect him. But do not trick him into an unsound penalty action:

(20) ♠ J 5   ♥ Q 10 8 5 4   ♦ 9 3 2   ♣ A 10 5
     1D   No Bid   No Bid   ?

Bid *1H*. Your simple overcall warns partner that you cannot contribute more than a few high cards to an offensive undertaking.

The reader has perhaps noted that the protective double, though primarily intended as informatory, may often be converted into a penalty double by partner's pass. Whenever the prospective doubler is short in the opener's suit, he must anticipate this contingency and reject the double if it may result in an unattractive penalty situation:

(21) ♠ Q J 10 9 5 4   ♥ 2   ♦ Q J 5 3   ♣ A 6
     1H   No Bid   No Bid   ?

Bid *2S*. Although you have a good hand offensively, you must foresee that a double may induce a penalty pass from partner and you will find yourself defending a contract against which you have very little to contribute. The bid of 1S would reflect a weak hand and little hope of game.

THE IMMEDIATE DOUBLE OF 1NT

The double of an opening bid of 1NT, though generally classified under informatory doubles, is often converted into a penalty action by partner's pass. When the opening no-trump is announced as 16—18 points (or its equivalent) the doubler shows comparable strength, and the fate of the opening bidder hangs on the location of the remaining few outstanding high cards. Against a 16—18 point no-trump, a part-score will ordinarily be the limit of the offensive capabilities of the doubler and his partner. With the advantage of the opening lead and with about a 22 to 18 edge in high cards, however, the opener may be badly mauled by the defenders:

(22) ♠ A Q 5   ♥ K 10 4 2   ♦ A 7   ♣ K J 3 2
     1NT

Double. The double of 1NT indicates a hand of well-balanced strength with point count at least equivalent to the opener's. With 6 or more points, doubler's partner is urged to pass.

(23) ♠ K Q J 10 5 4   ♥ A 10 9 2   ♦ Q 8   ♣ 5
     1NT   ?

Double. With sure sanctuary in a 2S contract, the double permits the exploration of the heart suit also. Observe that the doubler has little reason to fear a business pass. His hand will yield six defensive tricks without any assistance.

THE FOURTH HAND DOUBLE OF RESPONDER'S 1NT

A double of a *response* of 1NT as in the sequence one in a suit, no bid, 1NT resembles very closely the immediate double of an opening suit bid of one. Strength in all unbid suits is suggested, or the doubler is prepared to provide a suit that will stand siege without important help from partner. Since the response will necessarily be at the two level, the double must be strong enough to withstand severe punishment if partner contributes only a King and a Queen with a poor four-card suit.

(24) ♠ K 10 9 5   ♥ 8 3   ♦ A J 10 5   ♣ K Q 3
     1H   No Bid   1NT   *Double*

Since most players show a fairly good hand when they respond 1NT to an opening bid of 1C, the double of 1NT is inadvisable in that sequence unless it is backed up by a fine hand:

(25) ♠ K 10 5   ♥ 7 2   ♦ K Q 8 3   ♣ A J 5 2
     1C   No Bid   1NT   ?

No Bid. You are much better off as a defender. Any action other than a pass may be very costly. At best, your offensive potential is a small part-score.

THE STAYMAN 2C OVERCALL AS AN INFORMATORY DOUBLE OF 1NT

When an adverse opening bid of 1NT has been made, the overcall of 2C is an informatory double and indicates the strength and distribution heretofore stated for the immediate and two-suit take-out double. By assigning this function to the overcall of 2C, we remove ambiguity from the double of 1NT which is primarily intended as a penalty action. In the following sequences, the 2C bid asks partner to bid his best of the unbid suits or, with a weak hand with clubs his longest suit, to pass in rare cases.

(a) 1NT   2C

(b) INT   No Bid   No Bid   2C

The overcall of 2C when made against an opening bid of 1NT suggests a hand of great distributional strength rather than the 16—18 hand with which the immediate double is made. The 2C overcall may be used for the purpose of exploring the possibilities of sacrificing in the event the opponents reach game:

(26) ♠ K 10 3   ♡ A J 7   ◊ Q J 4 3   ♣ A Q 6
                1NT   *Double*

(27) ♠ K J 8 5   ♡ Q 10 9 6   ◊ 7   ♣ A Q 8 4
                  1NT   2C

(28) ♠ K Q 8 3   ♡ Q J 10 9 7 3   ◊ 7   ♣ A 4
        No Bid   No Bid   1NT   2C

This hand is somewhat too good for a simple overcall of 2H, yet it is a poor hand for a double. The 2C bid, followed by a minimum bid in hearts if partner should show a minor, will be very descriptive.

THE DOUBLE AS A REBID BY THE OPENER

When the opening bid has received no suit response, contention by one or both opponents may present the opener with a choice of actions on his rebid. When his hand is so distributed as to warrant urging his partner to offer a suit of his own, a double is superior to a suit rebid:

(29) ♠ A Q J 5 4   ♡ K J 10   ◊ 9 5   ♣ A Q 10
        1S   2D   No Bid   No Bid
        ?

Double. Your double will enable him to bid a heart suit on something like this:

(30) ♠ 9   ♡ Q 9 8 6 3   ◊ K Q 6   ♣ J 8 3 2

in which case a game in hearts would be difficult to beat.

In the face of partner's inability to take free action opposite his opening bid, the opener should not employ the double as a rebid in the absence of a count of 17 or a very fine suit to fall back on.

The double as a rebid, when made against two adverse suit overcalls, indicates a good hand with fine support in the fourth suit:

(31) ♠ A K Q 4 2   ♡ 9 5   ◊ A Q J 10   ♣ 3 2
        1S   2C   No Bid   2H
        Double

The double is the only action that provides for a safe return to 2S and yet makes provision for the possibility that partner has a singleton or void spade suit and long diamonds, in which event a contract of 3D may be reached.

If opener's partner has made a suit response, the double of an overcall is for penalties.

The secondary double by the opener may also be made informatorily against an overcall that has been raised, as in the sequence:

1H   1S   No Bid   2S
Double

Since partner is forced to respond at the three level, the opener implies a very strong hand.

THE REPETITIVE DOUBLE

When an informatory double is repeated in a sequence that has introduced no additional suits, the second double is also informatory. As—

1D   Double   2D   No Bid
No Bid Double

But since partner has not been ably to respond freely to the first double, the doubler should refrain from further action except with a fine hand.

THE RESPONSIVE DOUBLE

Not infrequently, the doubler's partner is confronted with a pre-emptive action by his right-hand opponent, and there are times when he has two or more suits and would like to have the doubler select the declaration. He may communicate his purpose by doubling the raised suit. By giving up the penalty function of this double, little is lost, because it is rare that doubler's partner will care to try for penalties against a supported suit.

1D   Double   2D   *Double*

Responder may have such a hand as—

(32) ♠ K Q 5 4   ♡ A 10 7 6   ◇ 5 2   ♣ Q 8 3

The responsive double may also be made after two suits have been bid:

1C   No Bid   1H   Double
2H   Double

in which case doubler's partner shows good support for spades and diamonds and puts the selection up to the original doubler, as with the following hand:

(33) ♠ K J 9 5   ♡ 5 3 2   ◇ A J 9 5 4   ♣ 8

THE PRE-EMPTIVE DOUBLE

The double of an opponent's bid at the three or four level, before partner has bid, may be informatory, business or optional depending on the suit bid and the bidding level. The double of a minor-suit three bid is clearly informatory; the double of an opening 4H or 4S bid is clearly for penalties. The double of 3H, 3S, 4C and 4D may at partner's option be passed for penalties or may be treated by him as a request for him to bid his best suit.

To a great extent, all pre-emptive doubles are co-operative in the sense that partner may disregard the primary motivation behind the doubler's action and do what he believes will give his pair the best result on the deal. The intention of the doubler is as stated below:

Opening bid

3C, 3D	Double	Bid your best suit.
3H, 3S	Double	If your hand is quite aggressive, particularly in the other major, bid your suit. If you are better suited for defence, pass.
4C, 4D	Double	If your hand is quite aggressive, particularly in a major, bid your suit. If you are better suited for defence, pass.
4H, 4S	Double	Do not rescue me unless you have overwhelming reasons.

The state of vulnerability is always an important factor influencing the conduct of the doubler's partner; the various considerations of the doubler's partner are examined later in this chapter.

There are two unusual informatory actions over the opening pre-emptive bids of 4H or 4S, and they have good utility. The bid of 4NT over 4H is a take-out double that requests partner to bid his better *minor* suit. The bid of 4NT over 4S demands that partner bid his best suit, major or minor.

(34) ♠ 5   ♡ 6   ◇ A Q J 9 5   ♣ A K 8 5 4 2
       1H   No Bid   4S   ?

Bid *4NT*. An example of the informatory double used to induce a minor-suit response.

THE DOUBLE OF THE WEAK TWO BID

The adverse double of 2D, 2H and 2S has much the same meaning as when made to an opening major-suit three bid. Doubler's partner has the option of passing for penalties or bidding. With aggressive distribution, especially when his side is vulnerable and the bidder's is not, the offensive course will generally yield a better result than the business pass. With 4-3-3-3 and 4-4-3-2 patterns and scattered high card strength, the penalty pass will usually render superior results.

(35) ♠ 9 5   ♡ K Q 8 2   ◇ A Q 5   ♣ A K 7 6
      2S   *Double*

(36) ♠ A Q 8 3 2   ♡ A K 7 6 5   ◇ 9 4   ♣ 3
      2D   ?

Bid 2S. Do not double with two five-card suits. If your partner has some high card strength, he will probably bid and give you the opportunity of showing your second suit. Before you double, consider the possibilities of your partner passing for penalties. Do not trap him into an action that makes an involuntary defender out of you.

THE PENALTY DOUBLE

A penalty double may generally be identified as such if it is

(*a*) Made after partner has bid (a pass is not a bid)
(*b*) Made at doubler's first opportunity
(*c*) Of 2NT or of a game contract.

The penalty double may be made in three different situations:

(1) The double of a part-score that does not yield a game.
(2) The double of a part-score that, if fulfilled, permits the opponents to score game.
(3) The double of game or slam contract.

THE PART-SCORE DOUBLE WHEN NO GAME RESULTS

A player will almost never hold a hand with which he can say with absolute certainty that the opponents cannot make their part-score contract. Nevertheless, to wait for such sure things before doubling for penalties would be to offer immunity to the adversaries who would fill the bidding space with overcalls knowing they were safe from punishment. The double of a partial is sound if it is *almost certain* that the opponents will be defeated and if the penalty reasonably to be anticipated will be greater than the doubler can, at the point of his action, expect to make offensively.

The penalty double, never used purely on suspicion, may be made by the stronger pair when an opponent continues to offer contention after they have reached what they feel is the limit of their offensive capabilities; or it may be made earlier as when the intervention of an adverse bid presents what seems to be an excellent opportunity to capture a sizable number of points.

The low-level double is not a dogmatic assertion of sure punishment;

it is a prediction—and if it is to succeed, partner's co-operation is indispensable. For example;

(37)   *Vulnerable* versus *Non-vulnerable*

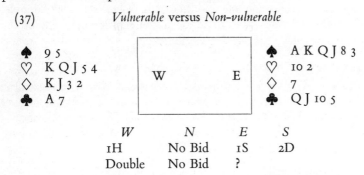

```
♠  9 5                                    ♠  A K Q J 8 3
♡  K Q J 5 4        W        E            ♡  10 2
◇  K J 3 2                                 ◇  7
♣  A 7                                    ♣  Q J 10 5
```

W	N	E	S
1H	No Bid	1S	2D
Double	No Bid	?	

East looks at a hand that will almost certainly produce a spade game worth,
with honours, 720 points. To pass the penalty double would be absurd.
If, however, we give East a different hand (say, ♠ A 10 8 2; ♡ 6;
◇ Q 8 4; ♣ K 9 8 3 2) he ratifies and confirms North's prediction of
trouble for North and South by passing the double.

The part-score double gives the doubler's partner great liberty of action.
For example:

(38)

```
            ♠  9 5
            ♡  K Q J 5 4
            ◇  K J 3 2
            ♣  A 7
```

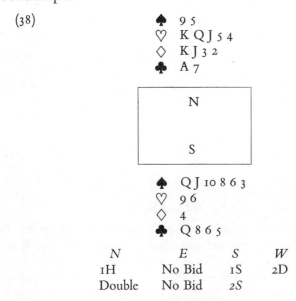

```
            ♠  Q J 10 8 6 3
            ♡  9 6
            ◇  4
            ♣  Q 8 6 5
```

N	E	S	W
1H	No Bid	1S	2D
Double	No Bid	2S	

With a hand that would play the role of spectator on defence, doubler's
partner cries out a warning of defensive poverty:

The unsuccessful double of 2C or 2D cannot be calamitous if you could have produced a part-score only; but if 2H or 2S is doubled and makes, the swing may be large enough to lose a match. The latter type of double, therefore, should always be based on a conservative appraisal of the prospective doubler's trick-taking capabilities.

EVERY PENALTY DOUBLE WILL NOT SUCCEED

If yours do, you are not doubling often enough. Learn to regard the doubles that go wrong as loss-leaders: articles of merchandise that are sold below cost to get the customers into the store. If your double department shows a good profit over the course of time, you can afford to look bad once in a while.

THE GAME DOUBLE

Many bridge players—the reader will surely know a few of them—consider that their honour has been assailed if the opponents reach a game contract against an adverse opening bid; and they show their anger at the adversaries' presumption by doubling. If we assume that you are playing against opponents who have a degree of competency at the game. your penalty double will be made only when—

(1) The deal owes you a plus-score.
(2) It calls for a lead that substantially increases your chances of defeating a close contract.
(3) The trumps break badly for the opponents and defeat seems imminent. When your opponents have arrived at a game contract, they will have reached their final declaration either after spirited competition or without challenge.

	N	E	S	W
(a)	1S	No Bid	3S	No Bid
	4S			
(b)	1S	2H	2S	No Bid
	No Bid	3H	No Bid	No Bid
	3S	No Bid	No Bid	4H

In example (a) North and South were not driven into the contract. A double made under such circumstances should be practically airtight, for North and South will almost certainly redouble. North and South have not been crowded into inexact bidding as may possibly be the case in example (b); they are at 4S because their own science has indicated that ten or more tricks will be developed in the play of the hand, but that is not to say that North and South will *always* be right.

A sound rule of practice: *Do not Double an Uncontested Game Contract unless Your Trump Holding is Abnormally Long.* There will be exceptions, of course. It would be difficult to resist a double with a hand like the following:

(39) ♠ K Q J   ♡ A 2   ◇ 10 9 5 4 3   ♣ A 6 5
         1S   No Bid   3S   No Bid
         4S   *Double*

but generally let your trump length be your guide.

In a contested auction, the considerations are quite the reverse. To begin with, you may be entitled to a plus-score on the deal and you must not permit the opponents to outbid you and escape punishment. If you think that you and your partner hold the preponderance of high cards, you should double, *regardless of your trump holding*, when you have reached the bidding limits of your cards.

In a tightly contested auction, there is little danger of a costly redouble, and so, if the double turns out badly the loss is a few hundred points at most. With the following hand, a penalty double is a must:

(40) ♠ Q 10 5 4   ♡ 7 6   ◇ A 10 5 2   ♣ Q 7 5
         1S   2H   2S   No Bid
         No Bid   3H   No Bid   No Bid
         3S   No Bid   No Bid   4H
         No Bid   No Bid   *Double*

You have a count of 8 and partner has 13 or 14 at least. You cannot bid more without penalty. With the major share of the high cards, the deal owes you a profit and you must get your full measure by doubling. Of course there will be times when the adversaries make 4H on bidding like the above. But no way has yet been devised to inform you when distributional quirks will give you a bad result. In the meantime, let the laws of averages work for you.

If, in accordance with your playing conventions, a desired opening lead will be induced by a double, especially where the lead will otherwise almost certainly not be made, the double is sound. One convention about which there is practically no difference of authority relates to the double of a 3NT contract. When the defenders have done no bidding, the double calls for the lead of the first suit bid by dummy.

RESPONSES TO DOUBLES

Let us assume that your partner has doubled an opponent's bid. Your right-hand opponent has passed. What do you do? Before you can even start to answer that question you must decide whether his double was informatory or for penalties. If he has doubled for penalties, you will naturally pass unless you have reason to believe that there are elements of your hand, *undisclosed to your partner*, which make some other action more desirable.

(41) ♠ K Q J 9 8 5 2   ♡ 5   ◇ 9 7 4   ♣ 3 2
      3S   4H   Double   No Bid
      ?

No Bid. There is nothing about your hand that has been concealed from partner. You have already told him that you hold a long spade suit and that you are very weak defensively. Nevertheless, your partner says that he can beat 4H. You must believe him.

(42) ♠ K 10 8 6 4 2   ♡ Q J 5 2   ◇ 9   ♣ A 7
      1H   No Bid   1S   2D
      Double   No Bid   ?

You have an almost certain heart game. Your partner cannot possibly visualize your fine heart support, singleton diamond and 10 points in high cards. Bid *4H.* You can hardly expect to beat 2D to the extent that will make a penalty worthwhile.

(43) ♠ Q J 10 8 6 2   ♡ 9   ◇ 10 8 4   ♣ Q 8 6
      1C   No Bid   1S   2H
      Double   No Bid   ?

Bid *2S.* You dare not rely on your partner to beat the opponents single-handed. Your hand will not help him in the slightest way. He probably counts on you for some assistance.

    If your partner has made an informatory double, you must respond unless there has been an intervening bid, or you feel that a better result will be achieved by passing and thus converting partner's action into a penalty double. There are times, of course, when your hand is ideally constructed for defence and it is clear that a business pass will be more profitable than a bid:

(44) ♠ Q J 10 9 5   ♡ 2   ◇ A 9 7 6   ♣ Q 4 3
      1S   Double   No Bid   ?

No Bid. You should be able to beat 1S badly. Offensively, the prospects of game are slight. Partner is probably champing at the bit to bid hearts and if you bid, a bad contract is probably in store for you. *The business pass of a doubled suit bid of one calls for a trump lead.* The declarer must not be permitted to make his small trumps by ruffing, for if he is allowed to do so, the penalty can never be worthwhile. A business pass should never be made with a weak five-card trump suit for there will be no way of extracting declarer's small trumps. Thus:

(45)   ♠ 5   ♡ J 9 5 4 3   ◇ Q 8 4 2   ♣ K 7 6
         1H   Double   No Bid   2D

You have no reason to expect to beat 1H.

Having identified partner's double as take-out and having determined not to convert the double into a penalty action, the player must select a response. There are certain rules governing the doubler's partner.

Rule: Holding a weak hand, one counting less than 6 points, his first responsibility is to bid his longest suit.

Rule: Holding a poor hand with two suits of equal length, both minors or both majors, the response should be made in the lower ranking of the two suits.

(46)   ♠ J 6 5   ♡ 8 3   ◇ K 9 5 4   ♣ 8 7 6 2
         1S   Double   No Bid   2C

Rule: With a count of 8—10 points and two four-card minors or two four-card majors, the doubler's partner may bid both suits, if the bidding sequence permits, and his first response should be in the higher-ranking suit.

(47)   ♠ K Q 9 5   ♡ A 10 3 2   ◇ 6 4   ♣ 9 8 3
         1D   Double   No Bid   1S

Rule: With a poor hand, one counting less than 6 points, and a choice between a four-card minor and a four-card major, make the more economical bid.

Rule: With a fair hand, 6—7 points, containing a four-card major and a four-card minor, the major should be bid first because the doubler's primary interest is in the major suits.

Rule: With suits of unequal length, both majors or both minors, the longer suit should be announced first particularly with hands warranting only one action.

Rule: With a fair hand, 6—7 points and two suits of unequal length, one a major and the other a minor, the major should be preferred even if it is the shorter suit, but . . .

Rule: With 8—10 points, the longer suit should be bid first and a second bid made later to reveal the other suit.

Rule: Holding no four-card or greater length other than in the oppo-nents' suit, doubler partner must bid the next-ranking three-card suit:

(48) ♠ 9 8 5   ♡ 3 2   ◊ J 8 6 5 4   ♣ K 7
            1D   Double   No Bid   1S

You may not bid 1NT. Remember the response of 1NT is a sign of strength and may not be employed merely in default of a biddable suit.

THE RESPONSE OVER INTERVENTION

When the doubler's partner holds 6 points or less, the intervention of a bid at his right gives him an excellent opportunity to keep his side out of trouble by passing. With 7—10 points, the doubler's partner should enter the bidding notwithstanding the intervening bid. But his action, when it is at a level higher than that anticipated by the doubler, should be sup-ported by 9—10 points:

(49) ♠ Q 10 8 6 4 2   ♡ 9 5   ◊ 8 4 2   ♣ J 7
            1D   Double   1H   ?

Bid *1S*. But when the doubler anticipates a response at the one level, his partner should have some high card strength to support an entry into the two level:

(50) ♠ 9 5   ♡ Q 10 8 6 4 2   ◊ 8 4 2   ♣ 8 7
            1C   Double   1S   No Bid

At duplicate bridge, where the part-score is as important as a slam, the requirements for "free" action may be shaded when an intervening pre-emptive action seeks to make communication difficult:

(51) ♠ 9 5   ♡ Q 10 8 6 4 2   ◊ 8 4 2   ♣ 8 7
            1C   Double   2C   ?

Bid *2H*. The doubler knows that you are acting under restraint, and he will make allowances for a possible overbid.

THE RESPONSE WITH STRONG HANDS

When the doubler's partner has 12 points or more, he should make a response that either invites game or forces to it. He may take aggressive action with (*a*) a jump response, (*b*) a no-trump response or (*c*) a bid of the opponent's suit.

(52) ♠ K 5 4   ♡ A Q 10   ◊ J 4 2   ♣ Q J 7 6
            1H   Double   No Bid   ?

Bid *2NT*. The jump response in no-trumps shows 12—14 points.

With a hand strong enough to warrant forcing to game opposite a double of minimum strength, the opponent's suit is bid for slow exploration.

(53) ♠ K J 5 4 ♥ A Q 7 6 ♦ K 10 5 ♣ 9 2
    1C   Double   No Bid   2C

Doubler's partner is sure that there is a play for game somewhere, but he is not sure whether it is in hearts, spades or diamonds. The bid of 2C forces to game and provides the partnership with ample time to investigate every possibility.

THE STRENGTH RESPONSE TO A PRE-EMPTIVE DOUBLE

When a player doubles a pre-emptive opening bid informatorily, he generally acts without quite as much strength as he would like to have, considering the level and the attendant risks. Yet, with a good hand, he must take action lest a game or slam may be missed. When the double is at the three level, it is incumbent on partner to take the pressure off the doubler by bidding game immediately if he has a good suit and some high card strength:

(54) ♠ K J 9 8 6 3 ♥ 8 6 5 ♣ K 2 ♣ Q 3
    3H   Double   No Bid   ?

Bid 4S. Partner has acted already under great handicap. If you bid 3S, he will not be able to read your hand as containing a fine six-card suit. With a tremendous hand opposite an informatory double, a bid in the opponent's suit sets the stage for a possible slam.

THE DOUBLER'S REBID

Opposite a strength-showing response, the doubler should not take action if his double is based on minimum values. With less than four cards in partner's suit, a raise is dangerous with hands only slightly better than minimum. If the doubler raises, particularly where there has been no intervening contention, he shows four-card trump support and 12 or more points:

(55) ♠ K Q 5 4 ♥ 5 ♦ A 10 6 5 ♣ Q 5 3 2
    1H   Double   No Bid   2S
    No Bid   ?

Bid 3S. With 13 points, doubler urges game.

Opposite a minimum response, the doubler may raise with 15 and may strongly invite game with 18.

When the doubler has a long, strong suit of his own, he may reveal it in his rebid, and the strength of his hand may be indicated by the level at which he uncovers his suit:

(56) ♠ A K Q 5 4 3   ♡ K Q 7   ◇ A 5 2   ♣ 6
       1H   Double   No Bid   2C
       No Bid   ?

Bid 3S. A take-out double followed by a jump to the three level indicates that doubler can win nine tricks on his cards and requires but a single winner from partner to produce game.

THE REDOUBLE AND KINDRED ACTIONS

Before leaving the subject of doubles, we devote a few paragraphs to the partner of the opening bidder and his particular problems when there is an intervening double. When does he pass, bid, redouble? And what is the significance of each form of action?

THE PASS

With no elements of strength or distribution, the responder naturally takes no part in the bidding. The "rescue" should rarely be made on a suit of less than six cards, but responder may disclose a long suit of his own in lieu of a pass when he is fearful that a pass from him will be followed by a penalty pass:

(57) ♠ Q J 10 8 5 4   ♡ 6   ◇ 8 4 2   ♣ 9 5 4
       1H   Double   1S

With a hand of intermediate strength, 9—11 points, the responder may pass with the intention of making a deferred response, thus showing a hand that could afford delay:

(58) ♠ 9 5   ♡ A J 10 8 6   ◇ 8 4 3   ♣ K J 10
       1S   Double   *No Bid*

THE SIMPLE RESPONSE

With moderate strength, it may be necessary for the responder to bid at once lest his pass be construed as a sign of weakness:

(59) ♠ 8 6   ♡ A K 8 5 3   ◇ 9 5 4   ♣ 6 3 2
       1D   Double   *1H*

If responder does not bid 1H at once, he will probably never be able to show his suit; delay will merely result in continued silence, because he does not have sufficient strength to enter the two level.

THE SINGLE RAISE

The responder should overlook no opportunity to raise an obstacle between the doubler and his partner, and a single raise should be given with the most shaded values, particularly when not vulnerable against vulnerable opponents.

THE DOUBLE RAISE

Holding four cards of partner's suit and about the strength of a full single raise, the double raise should be made when vulnerability conditions remove the risk of severe penalty:

(60)　♠　Q 8 6 4　　♡　9　　◇　K J 8 6 2　　♣　10 8 4
　　　　　　　　1S　　Double　　3S

Vulnerable, against non-vulnerable opponents, the double raise represents a hand of limited strength with a top limit of 12 points. The bid is not forcing to game. It is a sound move to prevent the opponents from discovering a suit that will offer them a cheap sacrifice against a vulnerable game.

THE REDOUBLE

When the responder holds 12 points or more, particularly when it appears that he may be able to punish severely any suit bid by the opponents, he redoubles. By this means, he beseeches partner to pass command of the auction to him. The redouble does not promise trump support; in fact it suggests that the responder is short in partner's suit and that more points will probably be made if the adversaries are allowed to struggle at their contract.

(61)　♠　8　　♡　A J 10 7　　◇　K J 6 3　　♣　K 10 9 7
　　　　　　　1S　　Double　　*Redouble*

The responder makes certain that the opener will not rebid spades and thus take the opponents out of disaster towards which they seem to be moving inexorably.

(62)　♠　K J 4　　♡　A 7 3　　◇　K Q 8 5　　♣　8 6 2
　　　　　　　1H　　Double　　*Redouble*

The redouble preserves a freedom of choice to the responder who may double for penalties or go on to a game contract at hearts or no-trumps, depending on the course of the bidding.

HAND EVALUATION BY THE DOUBLER AND HIS PARTNER

Before leaving this chapter, we remind the reader that the position of Kings and Queens in relation to other high cards held in the same suit by the opponents has a bearing on the value given to them when a player counts his hand. If an honour card is held behind the bidder of the suit in which the card is held, it is in a position of greater safety than one held under the guns. To reflect this positional advantage or jeopardy, as the case may be, a King or Queen is increased one point in value when it is to the left of the bidder, and is decreased one point when held to the bidder's right. This positional adjustment applies to all players at the table: defenders and the offensive pair.

Because the player who makes an informatory double induces his partner to bid on the basis that the doubler's distribution offers fine support in any suit partner selects, the possession of two or more cards in the suit doubled reduces, to a certain extent, the distributional richness of the doubler's hand. To compensate for this weakness, he must reduce the count of his hand 1 point if he holds a doubleton and 2 points if he holds three cards of the adverse suit. For purposes of doubling, the following hand counts 14.

    (63) ♠ K 5   ♡ A Q 8 2   ◇ K 10 8   ♣ Q 10 9 4
                1S   *Double*

Because the King of spades lies behind the spade bidder, its value increases to 4 points, but the possession of two spades by the doubler diminishes the value of his hand by a point.

17

THE OPENING GAME FORCE

UPON OCCASION a player will hold a hand so powerful that he wishes to contract for game regardless of his partner's holding. Such hands are rare, but when they do occur they bulk large on the score-sheet, and a system, if it is to be complete, must be able to cope with them.

It is not sufficient to recommend merely that a player who holds such a hand contract immediately for game. Obviously he will not always know with assurance the proper contract:

(1) ♠ A K Q 9 5   ♡ A K Q 8 3   ◇ A 7   ♣ 9

Opposite such a hand, partner may have no high cards; yet his distribution may determine whether the better final contract is 4H or 4S.

Even more important is the fact that such hands are the stuff of which slams are made, and the player who holds one will always be anxious to explore the contents of his partner's hand. A system must permit such exploration by providing some convention by which both partners may be certain that the bidding, at whatever level it begins, will not stop short of game.

All systems, therefore, include an opening bid that commits the partnership to continue the bidding until game is reached (although most systems, including our own, include a few refinements that make it possible in rare instances to stop short at 2NT or three of a major suit).

But to concede that we need such a game-forcing opening bid is to meet only part of the problem. We must still decide what bid or bids are to be arrogated to this end, and what the lower limits of these bids should be (they need, of course, no upper limit).

There have been two major solutions to the first of these problems:

(1) The use of all suit bids at the two level for the forcing bid—an original bid of 2C, 2D, 2H or 2S being forcing to game.
(2) The use of 2C for the forcing bid, the other two-bids being reserved for other uses.

The more popular of these has always been the first, but in recent years it has tended to fall steadily in esteem. Its prime disadvantage is that it monopolizes an entire bidding level to initiate a sequence that is rare at best. Even if it were more precise than other methods—a claim we are certainly prepared to dispute—it sprawls over a disproportionate area of action.

The forcing bid we adopt, therefore, is the 2C bid. The 2C bid so used does not, of course, denote a club suit.

Having selected the method, we must now fix upon the lower limits for the game-force. We have sought to set the limit at hands so strong that a responder who would not bid over an opening bid of one might still possess enough trivial strength to help bring in game. In certain instances, where the opener does not hold game in hand, we have provided clearly defined bidding sequences that permit responder to quit the auction before game is reached when he lacks even trivial strength.

One of these the reader will recall from an earlier chapter; an opening 2C bid followed at once by a rebid of 2NT shows a balanced hand and a count of 23—24. Responder may pass the 2NT rebid with a hand devoid of assets. Another such sequence is discussed later.

With this in mind, we set our lower limit at 23 for an opening 2C bid. Not all hands counting 23 will be opened with a 2C bid. The count of 23 is indispensable but not always sufficient.

In counting the hand for an opening 2C bid, several minor modifications are imposed by common sense. These are additional to the adjustments normally used in hand valuation:

(1) No values are given to the following: K, Q or J singleton; Q J, Q x, J x or J x x.

(2) One point is deducted whenever a King is held doubleton, or a Queen tripleton.

These modifications reflect the fact that the whole concept of the forcing two-bid is based on the assumption that partner can provide little promotional aid.

The following hands qualify for opening 2C bids:

(2) ♠ A Q 3   ♡ A K 5   ◇ K Q J 3   ♣ A 9 7

(3) ♠ Q 5 2   ♡ A K   ◇ A K Q J 3   ♣ A Q 6

(4) ♠ A Q J 6 5 3   ♡ K 6   ◇ A Q J 3 2   ♣ Void

(5) ♠ A   ♡ A K Q J 7 5 3   ◇ Q 6   ♣ K 9 4

(6) ♠ K Q   ♡ A K J   ◇ A K Q 3 2   ♣ A K Q

(7) ♠ A 2   ♡ A K Q J 10 5   ◇ K Q J   ♣ A 5

Notice that these hands vary in two ways. Hands (2), (3) and (6), for example, are balanced and suitable for play at no-trumps. Hand (4) is extremely unbalanced. Hands (2) and (5) will need help from responder if game is to be made; hand (6) contains a certain game at no-trumps. Our bidding system must provide for handling all these types of hands competently.

RESPONSES TO THE OPENING BID OF 2C

The responder to an opening bid of 2C must choose at the outset between a positive response or a negative one. This initial decision is a simple one, for the requirements for a positive response are unequivocal; the hand must contain at least

(1) an Ace and a King; or
(2) a King-Queen in one suit and a King in another: or
(3) any three Kings; or
(4) a five-card or longer suit headed by a count of 5 or more (K Q x x x; A J x x x).

Lacking all these, the responder *must* bid 2D. There are no exceptions to this.

Having decided to respond positively, the responder has a choice among three bids. A simple raise is not one of them: since the 2C bid does not announce a club suit, the responder has no suit to raise. He may, however, bid a suit of his own (2H, 2S, 3C, or 3D); he may bid 2NT and he may bid 3NT. In all these cases, he must have the high-card requirements for a positive bid, as listed above.

The suit response shows a four-card suit headed at least by the Ace or King; or any longer suit.

(8)   ♠ K 5   ♡ K 7 4   ◇ K 9 4 3   ♣ 8 6 4 2
           2C   ?

Bid *3D*. The jump is necessary to distinguish it from the 2D negative response.

(9)   ♠ 6 3   ♡ A Q J 10 7 2   ◇ A 8   ♣ 7 4 2
           2C   ?

Bid *2H*. This hand is overwhelmingly powerful opposite a 2C bid, but there is no need to get excited about it at this point.

The *2NT* response shows a hand that contains a count of 7 or 8, no biddable suit, and the *specific high cards* required for a positive response:

(10) ♠ 10 5 3 2   ♡ K Q 4   ◇ K 6 3   ♣ 6 4 3
           2C   2NT

The *3NT* response is a limited response showing a hand that contains a count of 9 or 10 and in addition the basic requirements for positive action.

(11) ♠ K 5 3   ♡ A 5 3   ◇ J 5 3   ♣ Q 6 4 2
           2C   3NT

THE TACTICAL SUIT BID

Hands that lack a biddable suit in response but are too strong for 3NT call for the tactical bid of a suit that does not meet the requirements of biddability

(12) ♠ 5 3 2   ♡ A J 4   ◇ A 6 3   ♣ Q 6 4 2
           2C   ?

Bid *3C.* The hand counts 11, and is too strong for 3NT. The club suit, strictly speaking, is not biddable, but since you can support partner's suit, whatever it may be, the risk is negligible.

(13) ♠ 9 6 4 2   ♡ K Q 5   ◇ K 5 2   ♣ A 5 2
           2C   ?

Bid *3C.* Tactical bids in major suits are too dangerous to trifle with.

The negative response of 2D is made with any hand that lacks the requirements for positive action. At times the negative response may be made with a fairly strong hand:

(14) ♠ K J 4   ♡ K 6 3   ◇ Q 7 5   ♣ Q J 5 2
           2C   2D

The hand counts 12 and will almost certainly bring in a slam opposite anything but the most unusual 2C bid. Nevertheless it lacks the specific high cards necessary for a positive response, and responder should bid 2D. The second response will be a strong one and will depend on opener's rebid.

RESPONDING OVER INTERFERENCE

Alert opponents will frequently attempt to disturb the bidding sequence by inserting an interference bid over the opening of 2C. In such cases, one recourse is the penalty double, which responder may make regardless of his high-card holding. Otherwise, responder passes with a hand that does not qualify for positive action, or makes his positive response at the necessary level. Responder would not bid no-trumps, however, without a stopper in opponent's suit.

(15) ♠ Q 10 5 3 2   ♡   5 2   ◊   6 5 3   ♣   8 5 2
            2C   2S   ?

Double. This indicates only that you hope to beat 2S, and suspect that this course will be most profitable for your partnership.

(16) ♠ 8 5   ♡   K 6 2   ◊   Q 6 4 3   ♣   J 6 3 2
            2C   2S   ?

No Bid. The intervening bid has made it unnecessary for you to keep the bidding open.

(17) ♠ K Q 3   ♡   K 6 3   ◊   6 4 3 2   ♣   9 5 3
            2C   2S   ?

Bid *2NT.* You have spades stopped and the necessary high cards. Game, and possibly slam, is likely to be worth more than the penalty, particularly if you are vulnerable and the opponents are not.

REBIDS BY OPENING BIDDER

Over a negative response the opening bidder's action is determined by the pattern of his hand. With an unbalanced hand, he immediately shows his suit; if the hand contains two biddable suits he bids the higher ranking if they are equal in length, and the longer of the two if they are not, with certain exceptions to be noted later.

(18) ♠ A Q J 3 2   ♡   A   ◊   6   ♣   A K J 6 5 3
            2C   2D
            3C

Your opening 2C bid did not show a club suit, and you must show it now. You will bid spades on the next round.

BALANCED HANDS

A balanced hand, by definition, contains no more than one suit of five cards, and no six-card suit. With 23—26, the rebid will generally be the appropriate number of no-trumps discussed in Chapter 12.

(19) ♠ K Q J 2   ♡   A K 7   ◊   A J 10 3   ♣   A Q
            2C   2D
            2NT

No problem arises with hands counting 27—28, since they will have been opened with 3NT.

(20) ♠ A K Q 5 ♥ A K J ♦ K Q J ♣ A K Q

   2C   2D

   2S

But hands such as these, or stronger, begin to enter the category of freaks, with which a system can hardly hope to cope specifically. They require skill and experience, rather than partnership co-operation in the bidding. Hand (20) is too strong for a rebid of 3NT.

There will be some balanced hands with which declarer will bid a suit rather than no-trumps on his rebid. These will include hands with a count in excess of 26:

(21) ♠ A K Q 6 3 ♥ A Q J ♦ A 5 ♣ K J 5

   2C   2D

   ?

Rebid *2S*. A major suit is the highroad to game and should not be concealed.

THE RESPONDER'S SECOND BID

When an opening 2C bid is followed by a positive response—any response other than 2D—the subsequent bidding falls outside the scope of this chapter. Certain important elements will be found in the chapter on slam bidding. Beyond those elements, the stage has been reached where the twenty-six cards in the combined hands refuse to fall into categories, and each situation must be met and handled on its own merits.

When the responder has made the negative 2D response, however, the partnership is still left with exploratory work to do. With the 2D bid, the responder has said only that he lacks the specific high cards required for all other bids.

The simplest case arises when responder holds a balanced hand and the sequence begins:

	S	N
	2C	2D
2NT (or 3NT)		?

North's problem is simply one of addition, since South has limited his hand and described its distribution. He may pass if South's rebid has put the partnership in the proper contract; or advance within the limits of safety.

When the opener rebids in a suit, responder with an otherwise featureless hand, will support that suit if in it he holds three cards headed by the Queen or better, or four small cards, or more. In those cases where the

Trump fit brings his count to 6 or more, he may respond with a jump raise:

(22) ♠ 9 7 4 2   ♡ 3   ◇ K 10 6 4 2   ♣ Q 5 4
          2C   2D
          2S   ?

Bid *4S*. Your hand has very strong support for spades.

In all cases, responder seeks to describe the salient features of his hand. With one exception, he will bid any five-card suit:

(23) ♠ J 6   ♡ Q 5 2   ◇ 7 5 3   ♣ 9 7 5 3 2
          2C   2D
          3D   ?

Bid *3NT*. An entry into the four level is obviously unjustified.

Responder will bid a four-card suit in those cases where whatever high-card values he may have are concentrated in that suit:

(24) ♠ 6 5 3   ♡ A 8 4 2   ◇ Q 3 2   ♣ 8 4 2
          2C   2D
          2S   3H

But the entry into the four level should be avoided:

(25) ♠ 6 4 2   ♡ 8 5 3   ◇ 9 5 3   ♣ K Q 7 5
          2C   2D
          3D   3NT

Finally, responder will bid the minimum number of no-trumps on hands that do not permit any of the bids above.

(26) ♠ 6 4 3 2   ♡ Q 6 5   ◇ 9 7 5   ♣ K 7 3

(27) ♠ 7 5 3 2   ♡ 7 5 3   ◇ 7 4 2   ♣ 8 5 3

Unless the opening bidder's first rebid is in spades, responder's second bid will be the minimum number of no-trumps on (26) and (27). In later bidding, he will be able to distinguish between the strength of hand (26) and the barrenness of hand (27).

Frequently, responder will bid 2NT with a delayed raise in view:

(28) ♠ 9 5 2   ♡ 3 2   ◇ Q 4 3 2   ♣ J 8 5 3
          2C   2D
          2S   ?

Responder will bid *2NT*, planning to support spades on his next call. If opener, however, raises the 2NT to 3NT, responder will pass, since the sequence indicates that the opening bidder is not interested in a sub-par spade fit.

FURTHER ACTION BY THE OPENING BIDDER

For the most part, when both opener and responder have made two bids, the opener's third bid is made with substantial awareness of the rough outlines of his partner's hand, and he may adopt various methods to fill in details.

With a one-suit hand that is close to the lower limits for the forcing bid, he may offer responder the opportunity of dropping the contract short of game:

(29) ♠ A   ♡ A K Q J 7 5 3   ◇ Q 6   ♣ K 9 4

2C	2D
2H	2NT
3H	?

With a barren hand, responder may now pass. With a count of 3 or more, he is expected to bid.

This refusal to proceed to game may come about only when the opening bidder has bid and rebid the *same major suit*. If the opening bidder shows any second suit, the responder must bid again.

The opening bid of 2C shows nothing concerning distribution. Opener's rebid, if in a suit, denotes the longest suit in his hand. His next bid, if in a new suit, is presumed to denote another biddable suit, and asks that it be raised if responder has normal support for it.

Here we must insert a point of departure from the general rule governing the opening 2C bid:

(30) ♠ A Q J 3   ♡ A 9 5   ◇ A K Q J 5   ♣ A

The sequence, opposite a weak hand, might be expected to begin 2C— 2D—3D—3NT. But now, if declarer bids 4S, he passes beyond the 3NT level into unknown territory.

On such hands, we recommend a departure from the general rule. The opening bidder, holding a biddable four-card major suit and a biddable five-card minor suit, will bid the major suit first and thus be enabled to show the minor suit at an economical level, *whenever responder has made the negative response to 2C bid.*

Finally, the opening bidder at this level engages frequently in tactical bids. They cannot all be shown here—bidding at this level is frequently an art, and the bidder moulds his bids as a potter moulds clay.

(31) ♠ A K Q 5 3   ♡ K Q   ◇ A K 3   ♣ K Q 5

The bidding has begun 2C—2D—2S—2NT. Declarer wishes to play the hand at 4S if partner has a delayed spade raise, or at 3NT if he has not. But if opening bidder now bids simply 3S, he invites his partner to pass. The 3C bid permits the delayed spade raise, if it is present, without ruling out 3NT.

This tactical use of the 3C (or 3D) bid imposes certain restraint on the responder. He must be wary about raising the 3C bid to 4C.

(32) ♠ 5 3   ♡ 10 8 6 3   ◇ K 6 4   ♣ J 7 3 2

2C	2D
2S	2NT
3C	?

Responder should now bid 3NT, since his strength is in the unbid suits.

(33) ♠ 5 3 2   ♡ K 5   ◇ 8 6 4 2   ♣ 8 6 4 3

On the same sequence, responder should now give the delayed spade raise. If the clubs are vital, he will be given another chance to show them.

(34) ♠ 5 3 2   ♡ 8 4   ◇ K 7 5 3   ♣ 7 5 3 2

On the same sequence, responder should bid 3D. Partner may need nothing more to venture into a 3NT contract. The delayed spade raise can safely be deferred one more round.

It should be realized that having bid negatively twice, with 2D and then with 2NT, the responder has gained a certain freedom of action. To bid a suit cannot deceive the opening bidder about its length or strength— his first two responses have limited his holdings within a narrow range. Responder must still choose his bids wisely, but for the first time he may have a choice.

At this point, we must leave the opening 2C bid. We leave the sequence in mid-course, but the subsequent bidding escapes exact formulation. The two bidders, at this stage, are in substantial command of most of the knowledge that can be elicited by formal bidding sequences, and science gives way to art. Certain phases of the subsequent bidding are treated in the chapter on slam bidding, others depend on the subtle skills of the bidders.

18

SLAM BIDDING

THE READER has surely noticed that many of the game contracts that were reached in the illustrative bidding sequences were not lay-down hands but required some skill or luck, or a combination of both for their production. This was not unintentional on our part. We have already stated many times that there is an adequate play for game when the combined hands count 26 points. You will make game about half the time with that count. With 28, play is generally fairly routine although, even then, you will not always have enough margin to be careless in the play of the hand.

In slam bidding (as in game bidding), the expert must be able to reach every slam for which the possible gain outweighs the risk. A small slam is a fair gamble if it will make half the time. A grand slam is worth bidding if it will succeed better than two-thirds of the time. And the fine player must be able to avoid slams when the odds against making them are prohibitive.

When both of the partnership hands contain balanced distribution and no long suits, a count of 33 should provide an adequate play for a small slam at no-trumps and 37 a good play for a grand slam. In the former case, the maximum off the hand in high cards will be an Ace and a King; in the latter, a King.

When one or both partnership hands contain unbalanced distribution, a suit slam should be sought, particularly when specific high cards and suit shortages are found where they will be most efficient. With unbalanced hands, the expert attempts to project bidding sequences that will permit him to discover not only the "what" and "how much" of his partner's strength, but the "where", as well.

The no-trump slam will generally be found desirable in two situations: (1) when the declarant pair owns no dominant trump suit, and (2) when it possesses two long suits either one of which will, if it runs without loss, contribute enough tricks to ensure the making of the contract. The following is illustrative of the second type:

(1) ♠ A K 2   ♠ Q 9 5 4 3
    ♥ K 7 6 5 4   ♥ A Q 3
    ♦ Q 2   ♦ K 7
    ♣ K 5 4   ♣ A Q 3

If either the spade suit or the heart suit runs without loss, 6NT will make; there are two strings to the declarer's bow. If a trump were named, success would hinge entirely on the distribution of the five outstanding cards of one suit, and the chances of making slam would be cut in half.

RECOGNIZING SLAM POSSIBILITIES

Before a slam can be bid, there must be a decision by one partner or the other to make a move beyond game. As the bidding develops, there will be a stage where a player may determine—

(1) that no slam is possible
(2) that a slam is possible
(3) that a slam is likely
(4) that a slam is quite certain.

This knowledge may come early or late in the sequence. Where a slam will depend on sheer power, a simple arithmetical calculation made early in the bidding will enable the partnership to seek or reject slam. On the other hand, where a slam depends on distributional factors as well as on high cards, the awareness of slam possibilities may come as late as the third round of bidding by the disclosure of some hitherto unknown distributional factor.

(2) ♠ A Q 5   ♥ K 4 2   ♦ J 10 7 6   ♣ A Q J (17)
                1NT (16—18)   ?

Hand (2) is an example of a deal where the responder's awareness of slam arrives with his partner's opening bid. Simple arithmetic dictates that the no-trump slam be bid.

(3) ♠ K J 2   ♥ A 7 4   ♦ 9 5   ♣ A Q 8 4 2 (15)
                1D   No Bid   2C   No Bid
                2D   No Bid   ?

With a balanced hand and no dominant trump suit uncovered, responder knows that the winning of tricks will depend almost entirely on the possession of high cards. He counts 15 points; 33 are needed for slam. Has partner the necessary 18? Impossible! Opener's rebid of 2D is a minimum and marks him with 16 at most. Since the partnership total is no more than 31 at best, responder merely proceeds to game.

SLAMS FOLLOWING THE OPENING BID OF 1NT

Of the no-trump slams that are bid, it will be found that many of them are reached after an opening bid of 1NT. When the responder has a 4-3-3-3 pattern, his course is simple. With 10 points, he will make certain that game is reached in no-trumps; with 17, he will take steps to ensure a declaration of 6NT. When the responder holds 15 or 16 points, a small slam should be bid if opener has 17 or 18 points; and when responder holds 19 or 20, a grand slam may well be within the capabilities of the partnership. The Stayman System provides a simple schedule of responses whereby the responder may show his precise count and thus place the opener in a position to select the best final no-trump contract:

POWER-BIDDING TABLE

Opening Bid	Response	Point Count
1NT	4NT	15
	2C, then 4NT	16
	5NT	17—18
	2C, then 5NT	19
	6NT	20
	2C, then 6NT	21
	7NT	22

You need not memorize the table. Just remember that the bid of 4NT indicates that a slam is just possible. Opener will have to have the best hand, 18, for his partner will contribute only 15.

(4) ♠ K 9 4   ♡ A Q 3   ◇ K 5 2   ♣ Q J 5 4   (15)
          1NT   4NT (not Blackwood)

If opener has 18, he will accept your slam invitation; otherwise he will pass and you should have no trouble with producing ten tricks.

When the responder has a long suit in a balanced hand, that suit must be discovered so that the partnership may engage for a suit slam and so gain the advantages that a trump gives in creating tricks and in nullifying outstanding high cards. The Stayman conventional 2C response may be used to great advantage with hands that are balanced but that contain some distributional factors that may make suit play desirable.

SEQUENCE 5

Opener	Responder	Opener	Responder
♠ K Q 8	♠ A 9 5	1NT	2C
♡ A Q 5	♡ K 9 7 2	2D	3D
◇ Q J 7	◇ K 9 5 4	3NT	4NT
♣ A 10 6 3	♣ K Q	6NT	

Responder's second bid of 3D is forcing and is designed to set the stage for a possible diamond slam if it develops that opener has a maximum and four diamonds. Opener's 3NT rebid does not necessarily discourage slam, but merely states that opener does not have *both* a maximum and four-card diamond support. Responder's bid of 4NT tells opener that there is a slam at no-trumps if he holds 18. Opener bids it.

SEQUENCE 6

Opener	Responder	Opener	Responder
♠ K 7 5	♠ A 9 6 3	1NT	2C
♡ A K 6	♡ J 5	2D	3D
◇ K Q 10 2	◇ A 8 5 3	3H	3S
♣ K 9 5	♣ A Q 10	4D	6D

This hand, played in an important team championship, found one team going down at 6NT while the other made a far superior contract of 6D. Responder as in Sequence 5, bids 3D to elicit information about opener's diamond length. When opener rebids 3H, a cue-bid obviously (since he denied a four-card major when he first rebid 2D), responder knows that opener has *both* a maximum and four diamonds. Thereafter reaching 6D is merely going through the motions.

When the responder holds a five-card suit, less than 33 points in high cards may produce a slam if a good trump fit can be found. Particularly when a four-four trump is available, a side suit becomes a source of great strength. With 5-4-2-2 distribution, responder probes very carefully for a slam, even when he knows that only 32 high-card points are in the possession of the partnership.

UNBALANCED HANDS. THE SUIT SLAM

As distributional patterns move out of balance, hands gain strength through long cards and increased playing control, and this added power has the effect of reducing the high-card point requirements for slam. Since the opening no-trump indicates top cards in three or four suits, short suits in the responder's hand will often be duplicated by cards that stand sentinel in the same area, and accordingly, the responder does not give too much weight to singletons and doubletons. Still, the unbalanced hand is tremendously powerful, especially when the opener's count consists chiefly of first- and second-round controls that are all useful. Because control cards do play so important a part in the bidding of unbalanced hands, the responder must be careful to prepare a bidding sequence that will induce their disclosure.

The methods by which a responder elicits the specific information he needs are impossible to systematize. Here a player becomes a virtuoso, improvising a bidding theme as his own art conceives it. But there are certain techniques common to most of the fine players, and a few simple suggestions may prove helpful to the reader.

Opposite 1NT, a strong unbalanced hand will almost certainly play at responder's suit, so it is well to put the opener's mind at ease as to the denomination at once. With the assurance that there is no further need for trump exploration, opener will be happy to provide collateral data upon which the making of slam will be contingent.

SEQUENCE 7

Opener	Responder	Opener	Responder
♠ K 9 5	♠ A Q 10 8 4 3	1NT	3S
♡ Q J 7 3	♡ 9 2	4S	5C
♢ A Q 5	♢ K J 7 6	5D	5S
♣ K Q 2	♣ A	No Bid	

Although responder is manifestly interested in slam, he cannot move beyond 5S while the heart situation is still in doubt. Since opener does not have first- or second-round control of hearts, he properly passes 5S, confident that responder himself cannot control the hearts.

SEQUENCE 8

♠ A Q 5	♠ K 7 6	1NT	3D
♡ A 10 3 2	♡ 9	3S	4C
♢ A 10 7	♢ K Q J 5 4	4H	4S
♣ K J 6	♣ A 10 3 2	5C	6D

When the opening bidder has adequate trump support and a maximum no-trump, he cue-bids over a jump response and immediately sets a slam sequence in motion. If the responder has game interest only, he returns to game, but if his jump response was based on a hand that warrants slam optimism, he also cue-bids and the partners exchange information about key control cards.

There are two techniques generally employed in slam bidding, the "direct" or "conventional" and the "indirect" or "cue-bidding". Ordinarily, cue-bidding is initiated after agreement has been reached as to the suit in which the contract will be played. Agreement may be expressed, as in Sequence 7, where the responder's spade suit is supported before cue-bidding begins; or it may be implied, as in Sequence 8 where opener's cue-bid confirms trump support.

The first cue-bid states that the bidder has possession of an Ace or void in the suit bid and that a slam is worth investigating.

The conventional method of showing controls is employed only when the making of a slam depends upon the partnership's possession of Aces and Kings. The Gerber and Blackwood conventions are designed to extract information about the *number* of controls held by partner.

(9) ♠ K Q J 9 5   ♡ K Q   ◊ K 2   ♣ K Q J 10
               1S   3S
               4NT

INDIRECT SLAM BIDDING FOLLOWING A JUMP RESPONSE

When the opening bid receives a double raise, as in the sequence 1S—3S, game is a certainty even if opener has a minimum hand. Over a double raise, only two bids are available to disclaim slam interest: 3NT and game in the suit agreed upon.

If, opposite a double raise in a major, the opener has 17 points or more, he is warranted in making a slam move. He expresses slam interest by bidding a side suit in which he holds first-round control.

(10)

♠	A Q 8 5 4	♠	K J 6 3
♡	A J 10	♡	K Q
◊	9 5	◊	A 8 6 3
♣	Q 3 2	♣	J 10 4
	1S	3S	
	4S	No Bid	

With a bare minimum, opener states that there is no more than game in the hand and the responder respects his decision by passing.

SEQUENCE 11

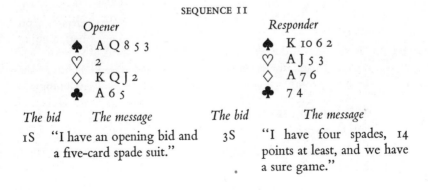

Opener		Responder	
♠	A Q 8 5 3	♠	K 10 6 2
♡	2	♡	A J 5 3
◊	K Q J 2	◊	A 7 6
♣	A 6 5	♣	7 4

The bid	The message	The bid	The message
1S	"I have an opening bid and a five-card spade suit."	3S	"I have four spades, 14 points at least, and we have a sure game."

The bid	The message	The bid	The message
4C	"My hand is much better than a minimum, and there may be a slam. I have first-round control of clubs. If you are interested, show me your controls."	4D	"I accept your slam try. I hold the Ace of Diamonds."
5D	"Good. I am quite optimistic. Have you anything further to tell me about?"	5H	"I also have the Ace of Hearts."
6S	"In that case, there should be an excellent play for slam. We have 33 points at least and all suits are adequately controlled."		

SEQUENCE 12

Opener	Responder
♠ A Q 9 5 4	♠ K J 6 2
♡ A 10 5	♡ K Q 6
◇ A 10 4	◇ K Q J 2
♣ Q 6	♣ 7 4

The bid	The message	The bid	The message
1S	"I have an opening bid and a five-card spade suit."	3S	"Even if you hold a minimum, there is a spade game for us."
4D	"My hand is much better than a minimum and I am interested in slam. I have first-round control of Diamonds."	5D	"I am willing to go along. I have no Aces, however, but am rich in Kings, one of which is the King of Diamonds."
5H	"I also have the Ace of Hearts. I am not entirely discouraged by your lack of Aces. I have at least three of them. What is the club situation?"	5S	"No good. I have no second-round control in clubs, so I am returning to our suit."
No bid	"In that case, we shall have to stop here."		

Observe that the responder denies the possession of a first-round control by bidding a suit of which first-round control has already been indicated by partner. The raise of a control-showing bid shows second-round control and inferentially denies the ability to take the first trick in any side suit. Over opener's bid of 5H, a second cue-bid, responder would have bid six spades with a singleton Club. With the King, responder could bid 6C, for it might be important to opener to know whether the second-round club control is the King or a singleton.

INDIRECT SLAM BIDDING AFTER A SIMPLE RESPONSE

Not infrequently, the awareness of slam possibilities will come after one or two rounds of bidding. The following bidding sequence and translations illustrate the manner in which, by indirect methods, side suit controls are checked when the trump suit is agreed upon:

SEQUENCE 13

Opener	Responder
♠ A K 8 7 6	♠ 9
♡ A Q 3 2	♡ K J 5 4
◇ K 9 5	◇ A Q 8 6 2
♣ 4	♣ A 7 5

The bid	The message	The bid	The message
1S		2D	"I have at least 12 points and biddable diamonds. I will bid again."
2H	"I also have a biddable heart suit."	3C	"There is a game in this hand and perhaps a slam. Make your next bid as informative as possible."
3D	"I hold an important card in diamonds."	3H	"My optimism is due to the fact that you have found me with an excellent trump fit in hearts."
4C	"I also have second-round control of clubs; slam is a sure thing."	7H	"You must have five spades, four hearts, three diamonds and a singleton club. I can count thirteen tricks."

The responder summarizes the information he has received: "The opener has cheerfully co-operated with every slam move I have made; his hand has been described as 5-4-3-1. He must hold both controls in spades and the Ace and Queen of hearts, otherwise he would have slowed me up by bidding 3NT over my heart bid. His willingness to show me a singleton club can only be based on a hand extremely rich in controls. It is conceivable that he holds only the Ace and Queen of spades, but still the grand slam will be a sound contract."

SEQUENCE 14

Opener	Responder
♠ K Q 6 2	♠ A J 5 4 3
♡ 5	♡ 8 4 2
◇ A K 10 9 4 3	◇ 8 6
♣ 6 3	♣ A 7 5

The bid	The message	The bid	The message
1D		1S	
4S	"Even if you have a bare 6 points, I am strong enough to visualize game."	5C	"I have a good hand; a fine spade suit and the Ace of clubs. Is there a slam?"
6S	"Indeed there is. Don't worry about the heart suit. I have second-round control."		

Note that opener's jump to game is not a sign-off. It is one of the strongest bids he can make, for it evidences a willingness to be in game opposite what may be a very weak hand containing only four spades and 6 points in high cards.

SEQUENCE 15

Opener	Responder
♠ K Q 6 2	♠ A J 5 4 3
♡ 5 3	♡ 8 4 2
◇ A K Q 9 4 3	◇ 8 6
♣ 3	♣ A 7 5

The bid	The message	The bid	The message
1D		1S	
4S		5C	

The bid	The message	The bid	The message
5D	"I have excellent diamonds, yet I cannot control the heart suit. You will have to take care of that department yourself."	5S	"Sorry. I can't handle the situation."
No bid	"This the end of the line."		

CONVENTIONAL SLAM BIDDING

The simple Ace and King showing conventions are Gerber and Blackwood. In the former, 4C is used to elicit disclosure of Aces, and if followed by 5C, partner is asked to state how many Kings he holds. In the latter, 4NT and 5NT are used for the same purposes. The cheapest response denies Aces (or Kings) and the response is then graduated one denomination for each Ace (or King) held. Thus

Bid					Response
4C (Gerber)	.	.	.	.	4D = no Aces
4NT (Blackwood)	.	.	.	.	5C = no Aces
4C (Gerber)	.	.	.	.	4S = two Aces
4NT (Blackwood)	.	.	.	.	5H = two Aces
5C (Gerber)	.	.	.	.	5H = one King
5NT (Blackwood)	.	.	.	.	6H = two Kings

Needless to say, neither convention should be employed when the response, if disappointing, will carry the partnership beyond the contract that can be made.

In the Stayman System, Gerber and Blackwood both are used but never in the same types of sequences. *Gerber is used only when the opening bid is 1NT or 2NT or 2C followed by 2NT; Blackwood only when the trump suit is agreed upon and the 4NT bid unambiguously asks for Aces.*
For example:

(a)	1NT	2C		(d)	2NT	4C
	2H	4C				
(b)	1NT	4C		(e)	2NT	3C
					3S	4C
(c)	1NT	3S		(f)	2NT	3H
	4C				4C	
	(g)	2C	2H			
		2NT	4C			

The foregoing are all sequences in which the bid of 4C calls for partner to disclose the number of Aces held by him. In the following sequences the bid of 4NT is Blackwood because the trump suit has been clearly agreed upon and there is no doubt that information about Aces is being sought:

(a)	1S	3S		(c)	1S	2D
	4NT				3S	4S
(b)	1D	1H			4NT	
	4H	4NT				

We do not recommend the use of either convention except where the problem facing the bidder can be solved simply by ascertaining the number of Aces and Kings. The disclosure of key cards in a series of cue-bids, is, in our opinion, a much more satisfactory method of top-card delineation and leads to finer and more exact bidding sequences.

It is our suggestion, whether the reader use Gerber or Blackwood, that when a trump suit has been agreed upon, the King of that suit be treated as a fifth first-round control. This will prevent a partnership from reaching small slam when the opponents hold the Ace and King of trumps; or a grand slam when the adversaries hold the King of the agreed suit. Using the convention in this way, a player may discover immediately when two vital controls are in the opponents' hands.

Since the conventional slam methods will not disclose singletons or voids, it is an error to impose mechanical responses on partner and thus make it impossible to communicate information of that kind when short suits will be as valuable as high-card controls. Only when Aces and Kings only will serve his purpose should a player limit communication in this way.

Blackwood or Gerber is properly employed in the following example, where opener will be able to select the best contract when he learns how many Aces responder holds:

SEQUENCE 16

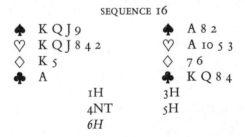

But in the following deal, singletons and voids will also be important, and their revealment will be impeded by conventional methods.

SEQUENCE 17

♠ K Q J 8 5 4	♠ A 10 6 3
♡ A K 7 6	♡ 9
◇ 9	◇ A J 8 4
♣ A 2	♣ K 7 6 5

1S	3S
4C	4D
4H	5C
5D	5H
7S	

In succession, the partners show:

The bid				The meaning
4C	.	.	.	The club Ace
4D	.	.	.	The diamond Ace
4H	.	.	.	The heart Ace
5C	.	.	.	The King (or singleton) of clubs
5D	.	.	.	The King (or singleton) of diamonds
5H	.	.	.	The singleton heart

And all tricks are in sight of the opener.

In the preceding pages we have given the reader some very difficult reading. Yet we do so without a feeling of self-reproach. Slam bidding is a delightful adventure and there is never quite so thrilling an experience in bridge as when a well-conceived bidding sequence explores the hidden retreats of every suit and guides the partnership into a slam that has been visualized almost perfectly before the exposure of dummy's cards. The language of slam bidding is the language of inference, of subtle implication, of deduction, and of creative thinking; and the facility that is gained through study is well worth every moment invested in it.